W9-BJC-557

THE
BUSINESSPERSON'S
LEGAL ADVISOR

To my wife, an invaluable assistant in
preparing the manuscript—Mariam Daniels Roberson.

THE
BUSINESSPERSON'S
LEGAL ADVISOR

CLIFF ROBERSON

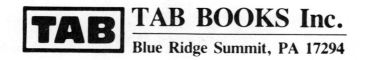
TAB BOOKS Inc.
Blue Ridge Summit, PA 17294

FIRST EDITION

SECOND PRINTING

Printed in the United States of America

Reproduction or publication of the content in any manner, without express permission of the publisher, is prohibited. No liability is assumed with respect to the use of the information herein.

Copyright © 1986 by TAB BOOKS Inc.

Library of Congress Cataloging in Publication Data

Roberson, Cliff, 1937-
The businessperson's legal advisor.

Includes index.
1. Business law—United States.   2. Commercial law—
United States.   I. Title.
KF889.3.R57   1986   346.73'07   85-27668
ISBN 0-8306-0424-3 (pbk.) 347.3067

Questions regarding the content of this book
should be addressed to:

Reader Inquiry Branch
Editorial Department
TAB BOOKS Inc.
Blue Ridge Summit, PA 17294

Contents

Introduction

This guide is designed to help the businessperson in the complex and hectic nature of today's business world. While management personnel in large corporations may find it a useful guide, it is primarily directed to the small- and medium-size business owner, manager, or supervisor who doesn't have the luxury of an in-house counsel.

The text is written to help the experienced AND the novice in business. Both should keep it available as a handy reference tool.

I am guilty of using the male pronoun "he." This isn't because I'm sexist, but it's easier for me to use than the cumbersome phrase "he or she." In addition, I've used the term "owner" in many situations where owner, manager, or supervisor could also be used. The term "owner," unless otherwise stated, also refers to managers and supervisors.

Like doctors and most other professionals, attorneys tend to get lost in their own language. One of my primary purposes in writing this book is to translate their complex, legal jargon into simple, everyday language so that the average businessperson will have something to refer to and use.

In most situations, I have placed the reader in the position of owner of a small and growing company. While this may not be ideal for your particular situation, it will give you the correct perspective of the problems discussed.

Many people are hesitant about starting their own business. Another purpose of this book is to help eliminate any hesitancy legal considerations might cause, and to provide you with a blueprint for either going into business on your own or continuing in your present one.

One of the problems with this kind of book is that not all of its readers will be interested in every chapter. For that reason, this book is divided by topics, and each chapter is on a specific subject. Readers who aren't as interested in any one chapter may quickly pass to the next. I would recommend that the reader briefly review all the chapters on his first time through the book.

This book should help you decide whether it's best for you to do business as a sole proprietorship, corporation, or partnership. It should help you avoid the common legal problems many business owners get involved in. It should also help you protect your business investment, and tell you how to get the best legal advice for the least amount of money.

A famous jurist once said that the law is a jealous mistress who keeps her secrets dear. This isn't necessarily so. The average businessperson who understands some legal terms can and should use the law as an aid, not as a hindrance to successfully doing business.

A businessperson should be alert for possible legal problems. He shouldn't take unnecessary legal risks. He should have an adequate amount of insurance. Above all else, he shouldn't get involved in costly court fights. Included in the appendices of this book are sample agreements and forms commonly used in business. These are provided as a guide and if used should be modified to fit your particular situation.

Chapter 1

Sources of American Law

Complicating our understanding of the U.S. judiciary is the realization that it consists of both federal and state branches. Each branch has separate jurisdictions, and each has a separate court system. Sources of federal law are the U.S. Constitution, federal statutes, and regulations by administrative agencies such as the National Labor Relations Board, the Federal Trade Commission, and the Securities and Exchange Commission.

The Constitution is the fundamental law in the United States. It gives Congress the power to regulate commerce between the states, with other nations, and within individual states. It also gives the federal government the exclusive right to regulate bankruptcy.

Most U.S. statutes regulating business are based on the commerce clause and the federal government's ability to regulate commerce between the states. The U.S. Supreme Court defines *commerce* as any commercial activity affecting people outside the state in which it occurs.

In one famous court case, an individual was determined to be involved in interstate commerce because he sold fried chicken to tourists who detoured six blocks off the interstate highway for his product. Likewise, most businesses today are involved in interstate commerce, over which the federal government has regulatory power.

State statutes also concern the businessperson. Most of our basic statutes—those involving contracts, the sale of goods, warranties, etc.—are governed by state law. This means that when you deal with customers or suppliers in other states, a problem arises as to what state's statute applies to the transaction. With the adoption of uniform codes such as the Uniform Commercial Code (UCC), a degree of uniformity exists among the states.

THE UNIFORM COMMERCIAL CODE

Uniform codes are model statutes drafted by the American Law Institute of the American Bar Association. Institute researchers and attorneys write what they consider to be model codes and recommend that they be adopted as state statutes. The Uniform Commercial Code is an example of this. Every state and the District of Columbia adopted the Uniform Commercial Code because their legislators saw the need for uniform standards. A similar situation exists with the Uniform Partnership Act which all but a few states have adopted.

Business owners also have to be concerned with local ordinances, those rules and regulations passed by counties, cities, and townships.

Administrative agencies are an ever-increasing source of regulation for the average businessperson. The first administrative agency was the Interstate Commerce Commission, created in the 1890s to regulate the railroads. Since then, numerous state and federal administrative agencies have been created to regulate various portions of our commercial activities. The two most important to the business owner today are the Federal Trade Commission and the National Labor Relations Board.

Unlike other governmental units, administrative agencies exercise all three functions of governmental power—executive, legislative, and judicial. For example, administrative agencies are delegated the authority to make and enforce rules in certain specific cases. As a result, much present-day business regulation is handled through administrative agencies, and the sanctions they impose resemble those a court may impose.

Another area in which there has been a limited degree of regulation for the businessperson is in executive orders. Executive orders are rules or orders issued by a president or a governor. While they are basically only guidelines and do not impose penal sanctions for noncompliance, they are used many times to interpret whether or not an individual is qualified for a specific governmental program.

Lastly, court cases are a vital part of our system of common law. Our system of court cases fills the gaps left by legislators in answering questions statutes don't cover, and to explain and interpret the statutes. The courts also have the power of judicial review to determine whether statutes and ordinances violate state or federal constitutions.

THE AMERICAN COURT SYSTEM

Courts are grouped in several categories according to the kinds of cases over which they have jurisdiction. A court's jurisdiction is the power it has over the parties involved in the lawsuit (personal jurisdiction). It also has the power to decide the subject matter involved in the case (subject jurisdiction).

Court Procedures

To ensure an orderly system of administration, courts have procedural rules governing the manner in which cases are brought before them. Procedural law ensures that all parties before the court have equal rights and thus are afforded procedural due process. Whereas procedural law concerns the mechanics of trying a case, substantive law refers to the rights and duties of a person. For example, substantive law gives us the right to protect our property, whereas procedural law provides us with the rules and methods for doing so.

Civil procedure deals with the conduct of lawsuits between parties to a civil lawsuit. Criminal procedure establishes the rules and methods by which defendants are tried in criminal court. Many of our constitutional rights in the Bill of Rights are criminal procedural safeguards. An example is the right to the assistance of an attorney in criminal trials.

Cases are usually started by filing a pleading in the proper court. The pleading should state the jurisdiction of the court, the issues involved in the dispute, why the defendants should be held responsible, and the damages or corrective action requested from the court. A copy of the pleading and a summons is then "served" on each defendant.

The defendant has a certain number of days after he has been served to file a response. If a response isn't filed in the required time—normally 20 to 30 days—then the plaintiff (party who initiates the lawsuit) may request the court to issue a default judgment. If the defendant files a response within the alloted time, then the case is placed on a calendar and scheduled for trial. In the defendant's response, he must deny all matters in the pleading he doesn't agree with. Failure to deny a statement of fact contained in a pleading normally means that the court will accept that fact as true.

The defendant may file a counterclaim and request that he be awarded damages, or that the court take corrective action on his behalf. A defendant may also file a cross-complaint. A counterclaim arises out of the same transaction or contract at issue in the original pleadings. A cross-complaint is a different transaction or contract involving the same parties and used to offset any awards to the plaintiff.

Federal Court System

The Constitution provides that the judicial power of the United States shall be vested in one Supreme Court and in such inferior courts as Congress may from time to time create. The Constitution also provides that the judicial power of the federal courts shall extend to all cases arising under the Constitution—federal law, treaties, cases affecting ambassadors, all admiralty and maritime cases, controversies to which the United States is a party, cases between a state and a citizen of another state, and cases between citizens of different states. The last two subject areas are commonly referred to as the court's "diversity of citizenship" jurisdiction. The Constitution also grants Congress the power to prescribe the rules of procedure governing the trial of cases in federal courts.

The major trial court in the federal system is the district court. Most federal cases start in district courts, which have exclusive jurisdiction in cases involving serious federal crimes, immigration matters, postal regulations, patents, copyrights, and bankruptcy. Most cases involving diversity of citizenship issues (controversies between citizens of different states) are also tried in district court.

Each state has at least one district court. In states with more than one, the courts are divided by geographic regions, e.g., the U.S. District Court for the Southern District of New York. Most district courts have more than one judge, each of whom sit alone as "the district court." In the U.S. District Court for the Southern District of New York there are more than 100 judges, and each presides as "the district court."

Stafford County Courthouse, Stafford, Virginia. Any involvement in legal proceedings, even in a friendly place like Stafford, Virginia, is expensive and time consuming.

4

COURTS OF APPEAL

Federal district court cases are appealed to the U.S. Courts of Appeal. At present, there are 11 courts of appeal. The courts of appeal decide cases based on the record of trial from the lower courts and briefs submitted by the counsel for each party. The courts of appeal only have appellate jurisdiction, and the cases are usually decided by a panel of three judges.

If a case is tried in a district court, any party unhappy with the court's decision can appeal to the court of appeals. A party unhappy with a court of appeal's decision has a right to request that the case be decided by the U.S. Supreme Court. The Supreme Court, however, can accept only a fraction of the cases that it is requested to decide each year. Therefore, it accepts only those of paramount concern to the nation as a whole. Each year thousands of unhappy persons submit appeals to the Supreme Court. The court accepts less than 200 a year. Thus, for most parties involved in lawsuit in federal court, the court of appeals decision is the final word.

There are several specialized federal courts among which are the Court of Claims and the U.S. Tax Court. Decisions of these courts are usually appealed to the Court of Appeals for the District of Columbia. As noted earlier, district courts handle bankruptcy, and have separate divisions to handle bankruptcy matters. These divisions are commonly referred to as bankruptcy courts rather than as divisions of district courts.

The federal magistrate is the lowest federal court. This court functions mostly in pretrial criminal matters and is equivalent to a justice of the peace court in the state systems.

State Court Systems

Similar to the federal system, state court systems were created by state constitutions and state statutes. Every state has a Supreme Court, and intermediate courts of appeal that function as appellate courts only. Superior or district courts are the major trial courts. They have jurisdiction over criminal violations and civil lawsuits that exceed certain monetary limits. Inferior trail courts and municipal, city, or justice of peace courts handle a large volume of cases involving minor criminal offenses and civil suits involving small monetary amounts.

In cases tried in a state district or superior court, any party unhappy with the court's decision can appeal to a court of appeal. For civil cases tried in the inferior courts, such as a municipal or city court, the unhappy party can appeal to the major trial court in most states. In cases appealed from the inferior courts, most states provide for a trial *de novo* in the district or superior court. A trial de novo is a new hearing on the same facts with the same witnesses and evidence presented in the original hearing.

Because small claims courts are used quite frequently by business owners to collect debts and bad checks, a separate discussion is presented on these courts in Chapter 10. The Appendices include a summary of the individual state rules on small claims courts.

Chapter 2

Legal Aspects
of Business Planning

T he legal aspects of planning, capitalization, and financing new and existing businesses are discussed in this chapter. The aspects of buying a franchise are also covered. According to the U.S. Chamber of Commerce, most businesses fail because they lack financial resources. Accordingly, any business plan, whether it's for buying an existing business or starting a new one, should be thoroughly planned financially. Finances necessary to start or buy the business and operating expenses needed until the business is producing revenue should also be considered. In this chapter conventional and unconventional methods of financing are discussed. A secondary aspect in developing a business capitalization plan is how taxes will affect it. How the government will treat the investment expenditures for tax purposes should also be considered.

LOANS

The traditional approaches to financing a business are with a business loan from either a bank or from a commercial finance company. Bank loans are usually more difficult to obtain and require a greater degree of credit worthiness. On the other hand, bank loans usually carry a cheaper interest rate than finance company loans.

This distinction between banks and finance companies is not as clear as it once was. More and more banks are adopting "asset-based lending programs" to compete with finance companies. And more finance companies are lowering their interest rates, eliminating the distinction that once existed between them and banks. The net result to the average businessperson is that business loans are generally easier to get, but finance charges or interest rates will be somewhat higher than in the past.

The County Clerk's Office in Placerville, California. One of the first places you should visit before starting your business is the clerk's office for information regarding local licenses.

SBA Guaranteed Loans

The federal government's Small Business Administration (SBA) guarantees bank loans to qualified small businesses. The SBA was empowered to provide financing because it had traditionally been very difficult to obtain loans for small businesses. If you qualify, it could be advantageous to take out an SBA loan rather than another type of financing. SBA loans are for a fairly lengthy period of time—six to 10 years—and are at a relatively low interest rate, usually about 2 percent points below the going bank rate. In many circumstances, they will provide financing for a person who otherwise would not qualify for a loan.

The disadvantages of applying for an SBA loan are that the application process usually takes several months, collateral and personal guarantees are sometimes required and, because of restrictions imposed by SBA, additional financing may be difficult to obtain. If you feel you qualify for a Small Business Administration loan, check with your local SBA office. There is an office in most major cities. For more information on the Small Business Administration, see Chapter 16, which deals with government assistance for businesspersons.

Equipment Leasing

Another way to partially finance a business is to use a security lease. The individual signs a long-term lease rather than buying the needed business equipment. At the end of the lease the equipment belongs to the business owner. This arrangement permits you to structure your financing over a much longer useful life of the equipment than what you usually would be allowed on a loan or chattel mortgage on the equipment.

In many cases, the lease is structured so that the cash flow the equipment generates is tied into the amount of lease payments due. Another possible advantage in using the lease method of equipment financing is the fact that the lessor may allow you to finance a greater percentage of the equipment's cost than what would be available in the usual loan situation.

Some of the problems you should look at before deciding to take the lease financing method include the allocation of tax benefits, depreciation, investment tax credit, the risk of obsolescence of equipment, the residual value of the equipment at the end of the lease, and the allocation of risk of any loss regarding the equipment itself.

Factoring

Factoring is another unconventional method many businesspersons use to obtain additional financing. Generally speaking, factoring isn't an appropriate method to finance a new business, but it can be used to provide added cash for an existing one. Basically, factoring is the selling of accounts receivable. If a business has a large volume of accounts receivable, it can turn them into ready cash by factoring or selling them to a third person or a bank. A hybrid type of factoring is one in which the bank lends a percentage of the value of the accounts receivable to the business, and in turn, takes a security interest in the accounts receivable.

Letters of Credit

A letter of credit is one in which a bank or other financial institution issues a letter of credit to a supplier or other individual creditor you are dealing with stating that the bank will advance credit on presentation of an invoice from the supplier that a payment is due. Therefore instead of C.O.D. purchases, the supplier delivers supplies to you and invoices the bank. The bank pays the supplier direct. And at the time the bank makes the payment, this becomes a loan from you to the bank. Letters of credit were once used almost exclusively in trade between foreign countries. They are becoming more common in domestic commercial arrangements.

Revolving Credit Accounts

With a revolving credit account, the bank approves a certain credit limit, and then allows you to draw, repay, and redraw funds again throughout the term of the loan according to your specific needs. You pay interest on the outstanding balance, but not on any of the unused credit. The advantage to a revolving credit account is that you aren't required to borrow money until you need it. This is a critical advantage since one of the most common mistakes new business owners make is failing to have an adequate cash reserve. Another big advantage to the revolving credit is that as you repay your loan, you automatically rebuild the amount of credit you may use in the future.

Limited Partnerships

A limited partnership arrangement is another financing method that permits a business owner to obtain needed funds. This arrangement offers investors the advantages of current tax deductions and potential capital gains. Yet, limited partners don't have a voice in the management of the partnership. A limited partnership is sometimes used in the takeover of an existing business. The new business owner forms a limited partnership with the previous business owner. Once the new business owner gains financial strength from the business he buys out the previous business owner. The old business owner's share in the business diminishes with each payment until eventually the investment he retains in the business is purchased by the new owner.

Presenting Your Loan Request

In presenting your loan request, always keep in mind that you are selling your ability to repay the loan to the bank or the finance company. Therefore, make sure you have thoroughly documented the company's financial position and your plans for using and repaying the money. It may help to hire an accountant to prepare the necessary documents and participate in the meetings with the bank or commercial finance company. Above all, remember that you are selling yourself as a person with whom it will be profitable for the bank or the finance company to do business.

The Loan Agreement

Most banks and finance companies have their own loan agreements or letters of understanding that contain their financial arrangements. Before you sign them read all of the agreements carefully. Make sure you understand them, and that you have no questions about them. Some of the essential terms you should know and which should be clearly set forth in the agreements are:

1. When will the loan proceeds be available?
2. When is the interest payable?
3. When is the principal payable?
4. How is the interest rate calculated?
5. Is there a penalty if you repay the loan earlier?
6. Are there provisions to extend the term of the loan, to renew the loan, or to convert the loan to a different type?
7. What are the reporting requirements?
8. What are the restrictions on the use of the loan proceeds?
9. What are the restrictions on incurring other debts, selling major assets, or changing business lines?
10. When can the bank or finance company declare the loan in default and demand immediate payment?
11. What events trigger a default?
12. What are the insurance provisions?
13. Who is required to insure any collateral?
14. What are the restrictions on the use of any property used as collateral?

And above all else,

15. What is the total cost of the loan?
16. Are there other loan fees, commitment fees, placement fees, points, etc., that will be charged in addition to the interest rate?

EVALUATING A BUSINESS

Probably the most difficult step in buying or selling a business is determining what it is worth as a going concern. Two basic methods are used to determine the value of the business. The first is based on an expectation of future profits and the return on investment (ROI). This method is preferred by most accountants and attorneys. It forces the buyer and the seller to give at least minimal attention to factors such as trends in sales and profit, the capitalized value of the business, and the expectations of return on investment.

The second evaluation method is based on the appraised value of the business's assets at the time of the negotiation, assuming that these assets will continue to be used in the business. This method gives little consideration to the future of the business, and it determines the value only as it relates to the present. It is more common not because it's more reliable than the first, but because it's easier to understand.

Whatever method you use to determine the value of the business, first prepare a statement projecting the income, profits, or losses for at least the next five years. To do this, prepare a sales estimate for this period along with a matching estimate of the cost of goods sold and operating expenses. The seller should be able to provide you with the historical cost data of the business. At this point you may want to ask an independent accountant to analyze the actual profits or losses of the business for the last five years. You can then use that analysis to make future projections with some degree of certainty. A study of the general and local economic changes that may affect the future of the business should be a part of the analysis. Any possible competition that may not have been present in the past but may be present in the future should also be included.

Evaluating a Business by Looking at Future Profits

Let's assume that you've made a five-year projection of the annual profits of the business, and that the profits are estimated to average $40,000 a year for the next five years. How much should you be willing to invest in this business? First, consider the return on investment. If you were to take the money you were going to invest in this business and instead put it into a safe investment such as a bank certificate of deposit that earns eight percent annual interest, your proposed business should be able to return a profit in excess of that eight percent. Keep in mind that a high percentage of businesses, almost 50 percent, have financial problems within their first three years of existence or after a change of ownership. Therefore, insure that any return of investment is sufficiently high enough to justify the financial risk involved. Unless the business will pay you a 20 to 25 percent return on capital, you should be very leary about investing in it unless it has a low risk factor. Another factor to consider before you invest in a going business, especially a small business, is the trend of profits. If all other factors are equal, a company whose profits are declining is worth much less than one whose profits are increasing.

Evaluating the Business Based on an Assets Appraisal

As noted earlier, in most cases involving the buying and selling of a business, the price is based on a value established by its assets. The assets most commonly purchased in small business buy and sell transactions are its inventory, sales, office supplies, fixtures, equipment, and goodwill. Evaluating the tangible assets, such as inventory, sales, office supplies, fixtures and equipment, won't be too difficult. However, evaluating the goodwill of an existing business is difficult. Goodwill is that asset that involves its good name, its high financial standing, if any, and its reputation for superior products or customer service, if any. An economist would define goodwill as the ability of a business to realize above normal profit as a result of its reputation. Don't put too much value in the goodwill of most small businesses. Historically few small businesses for sale produce excess profits.

In determining the merchandise inventory, the buyer should make sure that its value isn't overpriced, and that the costing method used to cost out the inventory items accurately reflects their value.

NEGOTIATING THE CONTRACT

One of the major steps in buying a going business is negotiating the purchase contract. The contract should contain details of the price, terms of payment, price allocation, type of transaction, liabilities, and warranties. In this regard, the buyer should be aware that his and the seller's interest may conflict. For example, the seller is interested in getting the best price for his business, getting his money and getting a favorable tax treatment of the gains from the sale. He also wants to eliminate any liability. Whereas the buyer is interested in getting the lowest sale price, a favorable tax treatment, and warranty protection against inaccurate financial data and undisclosed or potential liabilities.

Care should be taken that all essential terms of a purchase contract are in writing. The agreement should include as a minimum a description of the business, all the liabilities and encumbrances on the business, the right to use the trade name of the business, and the purchase price. The purchase price should be broken down into lease or real property involved, fixtures, equipment, inventory, supplies, and goodwill. The method of payment should be set out in detail so that both sides understand their obligations. Provisions should be made for adjustments at the time of the closing in the inventory, insurance premiums, rent, deposit, payroll taxes, etc. The buyer should have a clear understanding of any liabilities he is assuming. The buyer should also make sure the seller warrants that he owns the business and has good and marketable title to its assets. The buyer should also make sure that the assets are free from all debts unless specified, that all business liabilities are stated, and that the seller has no knowledge of any development or threatened developments that would be materially adverse to the business.

The buyer should insure that the contract obligates the seller to conduct the business as usual up to the date of closing, and that it requires the seller to use his influence to keep available to the buyer the services of the present employees, and the goodwill of the seller's suppliers, customers, and other persons having a business relationship with the business. It should be clearly understood who assumes the risk of any loss or obstruction or damage due to fire or other casualties up to the date of closing. In most situations the loss would be on the seller, but this should be clearly stated in the contract.

The contract should also contain a covenant not to compete. In the covenant the seller promises the buyer and his successors that for a certain period of time after the sale he will not engage in similar or competitive business within a reasonable distance. A convenant not to compete should be for a period of five years and prescribe a radius up to 100 miles.

There should be a clear statement in the contract that the seller will reimburse the buyer on demand for any payments the buyer makes toward liabilities or obligations of the seller not expressly assumed by the buyer. It should also state that the seller will reimburse the buyer for any damages or deficiencies resulting from misrepresentation, breach of warranty, or nonfulfillment of the terms of the agreement.

There should also be an agreement to arbitrate any disputes arising from the contract, and that the arbitrators selected should be neutral. The arbitration panel is usually composed of one member selected by the seller, another member selected by the buyer, and a third member chosen by the other two arbitrators. It is always advisable to have an attorney review the final contract before both parties execute it. Both parties should always sign the contract. Appendix A contains a sample buy and sell agreement that can be modified to fit your specific situation.

FRANCHISES

Most states regulate the sale of franchises under the Uniform Franchise Investment Law. This law defines a franchise as a type of security. Under this law, persons who engage in the business of selling franchises must register with the state just as any securities or broker dealer.

A franchise is defined as a contract or agreement allowing the franchisee (the businessperson) to engage in business under a marketing system substantially prescribed by the franchisor (seller). The business is substantially associated with the franchisor's trademark or other commercial symbol, and the new business owner is required to pay a franchise fee.

In most states, it is unlawful to offer for sale or to sell a franchise unless it is registered with the state. The Uniform Franchise Investment Law requires that any prospective buyer be given a copy of a perspective and a copy of all proposed agreements relating to the sale of the franchise at least 48 hours prior to the execution of any binding agreement. In addition, the seller must maintain a complete set of records of sales that occurred within the state.

The Federal Trade Commission published a rule regarding the sale of franchises involved in interstate commerce. The rule requires sellers of franchises to give each prospective buyer a booklet explaining all the important aspects of the franchise in plain English. The booklet also gives the net worth and background of the franchisor. While there are many reputable companies, such as McDonald's and Midas Muffler, that sell lucrative franchises, there are also many companies that aren't as reputable. Therefore be leary when buying a franchise.

Make sure a good market study is done. Get a careful understanding of what you are getting with the franchise fee. Find out what types of assistance will be provided, and what the restrictions are. What are your requirements? A good practice is to consult other holders of the same type of franchise. Get their personal experiences on how successful they have been with that particular franchise.

One of the key items you are buying in a franchise is its trade name and the right to use it. Therefore, make sure it's worth the money it will cost you to buy and to operate it under that trade name. Another item you are buying is the expertise of the franchisor in managing your business; therefore, get a clear understanding of how a franchisor will help you in your business.

Always check with the better business bureau in your area regarding any prospective franchise before you purchase one. Have an attorney examine the franchise agreement before you sign it.

STARTING A NEW BUSINESS

Starting a new business has definite advantages. For one thing, you aren't saddled with any liabilities or other problems the previous business owner may have caused. The first criterion in starting a new business is determining the strength of the market. The strength of the market can depend upon the population itself and its income and motivation. Population and income can be statistically measured with some degree of accuracy. Motivation cannot.

In determining the population of your market area, consider the changes in the population, its future trends, and whether it is increasing or decreasing. In looking at the income of the market area, consider your potential customers. What type of business are you going to start? Who are the potential customers? Are there enough potential customers in the area to make your business profitable? Is the population and income moving in a direction favorable to your business, or are you in a declining area?

An analysis of the market area should also study your competition. How many competing businesses are there within your market area? What are their histories? How many competitive businesses similar to yours have gone out of business or moved out of your market area? What advantages would you have over present competitors? What are the chances of future competitors locating nearby? As you can see from the market analysis, one of the key things insuring that a new business succeeds is its location. In choosing the location, consider economic factors such as will the business be located in a city or a town, or will it be located in an industrial, farming, or manufacturing area? How diverse will the area be and will it be stable? Is it a seasonal type neighborhood? And, as mentioned earlier, what will the competition be?

Local restrictions and controls on business are too often overlooked. Make sure that the location you select is favorable for your business. To determine the legal climate for your business, check with the better business bureau and a local attorney.

Chapter 3

Forms of Ownership

I n this chapter the three basic forms of business ownership are discussed. The advantages, disadvantages, and tax consequences of each form are also discussed. Many times the situation will dictate the form of business ownership. Too often, however, the form is more a matter of chance than of deliberate planning. Other times, the business climate, type of business, financing available, etc., will dictate the form of business ownership. As much thought and planning should go into this decision as any other one connected with the business. There is no preferred form of ownership for every business. If possible, consider the advantages and disadvantages of each form before making this decision. This could be the most important decision you will make regarding the business.

SOLE PROPRIETORSHIP

Sole proprietorships are the most common form of ownership for small businesses. Approximately 78 percent of all U.S. businesses are of this type. A sole proprietorship is a business that is owned entirely by one person as opposed to business ownership by partnership or corporation. If any part of the business is owned by others, then it is not a sole proprietorship. For example, if you own 99 percent of the business and someone else owns the other 1 percent, you most likely have a partnership. However, it isn't a sole proprietorship. In 1984, there were more than nine million sole proprietorship businesses in the United States.

A sole proprietorship is customarily managed by the owner. Absentee ownership in sole proprietorships is very rare. The three key advantages of the sole proprietor-

Courthouse of Madera County, Madera, California. I found the people who work here to be friendly and helpful in answering my questions regarding licensing requirements.

ship making this form of ownership so popular are the ease with which the business is formed, the lessor degree of governmental control than that which applies to partnerships and corporations, and the fact that a sole proprietorship is considered but an alter ego of the owner. This last advantage gives the owner a greater degree of control over the business and its assets. In fact, the owner has the same rights of ownership and control over the business property that he has over his own personal assets.

Many businesses start out as sole proprietorships. Later, because of the need for additional financing, growth or other factors, they become either corporations or partnerships. An owner should remember that when the business is transformed from a sole proprietorship to a partnership or a corporation, he will lose a great measure of control over the business.

The main disadvantage of a sole proprietorship is the unlimited financial liability of the owner. Thus, if the business is failing, not only can creditors attach the assets of the business, but they can also attach the nonbusiness assets of the owner. Any property that a personal creditor of the owner could attach may also be attached by a creditor of the business. A person should consider this status of unlimited financial liability before opening a business under this form of ownership.

Many small businesspersons find tax advantages in the sole proprietorship form of business because some legitimate tax deductions can also be used for their personal benefit. The sole proprietor should be careful in this area because any personal expenses charged against the business for tax purposes may constitute tax evasion, which is a crime.

PARTNERSHIPS

The Uniform Partnership Act defines a partnership as two or more persons who carry on a business for profit. One law expert defines a partnership as an association based on the expressed or implied contract of two or more competent persons to unite their property, skills, and labor to carry on a lawful business as principles for joint profit.

Because partnership agreements are considered contractual in nature, they are governed by the law of contracts. And because one partner may enter into agreements that are binding on other partners, the law of agency also applies. Generally, anyone capable of entering into a binding contract may be a partner in a partnership. In most states, a corporation may enter into a partnership agreement with persons or other corporations. In a few states, corporation acts or laws prohibit corporations from being a partner in a partnership. Except in those cases where the court implied a partnership to prevent fraud, no one may become a partner in the partnership without the expressed or implied consent of all the other partners involved.

As a general rule, no formal agreement is necessary to constitute a partnership. Unless prohibited by state law, a partnership may be established solely from the actions of the parties involved without the need for an expressed contract. However, a prudent businessperson should always require an expressed written contract setting the terms and conditions of the partnership before entering into it. The partnership agreement will be discussed in greater detail later in this chapter. A sample agreement is represented in Appendix C.

Unlike a corporation a partnership is not a legal entity. It is an unincorporated association. Accordingly, in some states a partnership may not bring suit in its own name, but must instead bring suit in the names of the partners. For some purposes however, a partnership is treated as an entity. In most states, for example, title to land may be taken in the partnership name.

More than 40 states have adopted the Uniform Partnership Act. The act restates the common laws regarding partnerships and provides a certain degree of legal uniformity. Accordingly, when most states adopted the Uniform Partnership Act, no substantial changes were made in this area of the law. Since the act contains the basic legal rules on partnerships, it is included as Appendix B.

The two basic types of partnerships are the general and the limited partnership. Limited partnerships are discussed later in this chapter. Most partnerships are of the general type. General partnerships are classified as commercial or professional, with the main distinction between the two involving the implied powers of each partner.

A professional partnership is an association of professionals such as doctors or lawyers. Unlike a general partner, a partner in a professional partnership has only limited authority to bind the other partners. A joint venture is a partnership established for a single or limited enterprise.

Partnership Existence

To determine if the business is a partnership, the courts usually look at the parties' intentions when they formed the association. If there was an agreement and the partners intended the business to be a partnership, then clearly a partnership existed.

Making the determination becomes difficult when the intentions of the parties are unclear. The courts use several tests to determine if a partnership exists. Merely taking property in the joint names of several persons will not establish a partnership. As a general rule, a partnership is presumed if the parties share in the profits of a business. However, this rule doesn't apply in situations where the share of profits goes toward the payment of debt, wages, rent to a property owner, interest on a loan, or consideration for the sale of the business by a former owner.

There is no general rule that all partners must share the burden of any losses. The lack of an agreement to share any losses is, however, evidence that the parties did not intend to form a partnership.

Partnership by Estoppel

There are several situations in which the courts imply a partnership to prevent fraud, even though the parties involved did not intend to create one. For example, if a person by word or conduct represents himself as a partner or allows others to represent him as partner, the courts will hold him liable as a partner to persons who extend credit to the partnership.

In most states, two or more persons who conduct business under an apparent corporate form of ownership without completing the necessary legal requirements to incorporate are held liable by the courts as general partners.

Partnership Agreements

As noted earlier, a formal, written agreement isn't necessary to constitute a partnership. However, partnership agreements that can't be completed within a year or those in which real property is to be taken in the partnership name are exceptions to the rule. Most state statutes of fraud require that all other partnership agreements be in writing.

All partnerships should be established by written contract. The contract should include the principal duties of each partner, the division of profits or losses, the distribution of partnership property on dissolution of the partnership, any buy-out agreements, and the rights of each partner. The contract should also state whether the partners are to be paid for any work they do for the business, and how much pay they are to receive. Any other agreements or understandings between the parties should also be included.

Appendix C contains a typical partnership agreement that can be used as a guide in drafting your own agreement. Make sure all of the parties involved understand each clause in your agreement.

Limited Partnership

In a general partnership, each partner has a role in the management of the business

This businessperson is checking the property records at the Madera County Courthouse, Madera, California. Researching the property records at the county courthouse may be necessary to determine the legal status of prospective business property. If you are uncertain as to how to do this, ask the records' clerk. I've found that the vast majority of them were very helpful.

and thus is subject to the financial liability discussed earlier. In a limited partnership, the party's liability is limited to his investment in the business. He may lose his investment, but he won't be liable for debts of the partnership exceeding his investment.

There must be at least one general partner in all limited partnerships. Because a limited partnership was unknown at common law, one can be formed only under the specific authority of a statute. Most states have adopted the Limited Partnership Act which provides for limited partnerships. The act allows persons to contribute to the business and enjoy the profits (if any) without being liable as a general partner. A limited partner is really only an investor in the business and not one of the managers. The limited Partnership Act is included as Appendix D.

A limited partner may not take part in the management of the business; if he does, he becomes a general partner and thus subject to the financial liability. The limited partner investment in the business must be in cash or property, but not in personal services. In addition, a limited partner's last name may not be used in the partnership name. In most states a limited partnership must indicate in its name that it is a limited partnership, i.e., Ltd.

Powers of Partners

In carrying on the business of the partnership, each general partner is an agent of the other partners. Each partner has the same rights and duties regarding the partnership business as a general agent. If a general agent of the business could bind the partnership in a particular situation, a general partner may do the same. Each general partner is authorized to carry on the whole business of the partnership. For a definition of a general partner, refer to the discussion on the liability of partners.

Under agency law, partners are not bound by the unauthorized acts of their other partners in situations outside the apparent scope of the business. This may be modified by placing specific provisions in the partnership agreement. If the partner's acts are within the apparent scope of the business but are prohibited by the partnership agreement, the other partners are still bound by his acts, especially if blameless third persons may be defrauded. In this situation the other partners may sue the wrong-dealing partner for any losses they suffer as a result of his acts.

If a partner commits an act beyond the scope of his authority, the other partners may ratify the act to take advantage of its benefits. In this case, the partnership will be bound on the unauthorized act.

Secret provisions do not bind persons dealing with the partnership unless they know about them.

A partner is authorized to pay the debts of the partnership and to enter into contracts in the name of the partnership. However, a partner has no apparent authority to dispose of the capital assets of the business or to sell the business.

Rights of Partners

The Uniform Partnership Act sets forth in detail some of the rights and duties of general partners. They include: the right to share equally in the profits of the business, the right to receive a repayment of his contribution, the right to receive payment for any personal funds he used to pay partnership debts, the right to share in the management and conduct of the business, the right of access to the partnership's records and books, and the right to a formal accounting of the partnership's affairs.

Duties of Partners

The Uniform Partnership Act imposes duties on partners to contribute toward any losses suffered by the partnership, to work for the partnership without compensation except for a share of the profits (unless otherwise agreed to by all the partners), to abide by a majority vote when differences occur in the conduct of the business, to account to the other partners for any profit derived from the partnership, and to share with other partners any essential information regarding the partnership business.

Liabilities of Partners

To consider the extent of a partner's financial liability, first determine if the partner is a general partner. A general partner is any partner who takes an active role in the management of the business. In most states, limited partners are liable only to the extent of their investment in the business. Limited partners may be held liable as general partners if they hold themselves out as other than limited partners to creditors, or if they take an active role in the management of the business. Generally, limited partners are only considered as investors in the partnership. To be protected the business must hold itself out as a limited partnership, i.e., The Arrow Company, A Limited Partnership, or The Arrow Company, Ltd.

General partners are liable for contracts made by the business and for any contracts expressly authorized by its parties. Each general partner is personally liable for debts arising from the partnership entity. If legal proceedings or threats of legal proceedings force a partner to pay the debts of the partnership out of his personal funds, the partner has a right to require the other general partners to contribute their pro rata shares of the debt if the firm can not pay the debt.

General partners are also liable for torts committed by any partner or employee of the business in the course of the partnership's business. Tort is a legal term that refers to a civil wrong for which a person may be sued. For example, a situation in which the reckless operation of a company truck results in the injury of a person, is a tort.

A partner usually is not liable for any criminal act committed by other partners or employees unless he either knew of the criminal act or should have known it was going to be committed. Those cases involving the conduct of a business without a license or the violation of pure food and drug acts are exceptions.

Dissolution of the Partnership

The lack of flexibility in the ownership of the business is one disadvantage of a partnership. Any change in the makeup of the partners, such as the death of one partner or the selling of a partner's share to a third person, in effect dissolves the partnership. This doesn't mean the business ends. It means that a new legal relationship for it has to be established. If the business continues after a change in ownership, then a new partnership is considered to be in existence.

Former partners are still liable for the outstanding debts of the partnership when a dissolution occurs. In addition, there is a question of liability when third persons, without knowledge of the change in partnership, extend credit to the partnership. A former partner may be liable if the third party didn't know he withdrew from the partnership. When a partner withdraws, he should notify third persons who have extended credit to the partnership that he is no longer associated with it, and that he will not be responsible for any additional credit the partnership receives.

Partnership Tax Considerations

Partnerships are considered entitles by the federal tax code and are therefore required to submit an annual tax return. A partnership, however, doesn't pay federal income taxes. The partnership's tax return is for information purposes only, and each partner must include in his individual tax return his share of the partnership profits. If the partnership loses money, however, the net operating loss usually can't be deducted on an individual partner's tax return until the partnership is dissolved. Then the loss can be deducted as a capital loss on investment.

Any distribution of property or cash made to individual partners is considered taxable income if the distribution represents profits made by the partnership. If distribution of the assets is part of the partnership capital, the distributions are then considered a return of capital and not taxable until the distributed assets exceed the partner's adjusted basis (investment less write-offs). Usually the partners are required to include their share of the partnership's profits in their personal income tax returns even though the profits are retained and re-invested by the business.

CORPORATIONS

The corporate form of business ownership is the second most popular form of business ownership in the United States. Approximately 14 percent of all businesses fall under this category. While large corporations predominate in terms of dollar volumes and gross annual sales, most businesses operating under the corporate form are small, closely held corporations.

In every state, corporations are recognized as separate legal entities having the authority to enter into contracts, to sue, and to own land. For practical purposes, a corporation is treated as an artificial person completely separate from its stockholders. A court may disregard this fiction to protect innocent persons who dealt with the corporation from fraud or injustice.

Corporations are formed as either profit or nonprofit organizations. However, nonprofit corporations will not be discussed in this book. A public corporation, also classified as a general corporation, is publicly traded in the New York Stock Exchange. A general corporation that isn't publicly traded is classified as a close corporation. Most small- and medium-sized business corporations are close corporations.

In a close corporation, the ownership of stock is restricted by the articles of incorporation to a small group of people. The stock can't be sold to the public without approval of the other shareholders.

A corporation must be organized under the laws of the state in which it was formed. A corporate name is required, and all acts on behalf of the corporation must be in the corporate name. The businesses' name must indicate that it is operated under a corporate form of business, e.g., The Blue Company, Inc.

Advantages and Disadvantages of the Corporate Form

The best-known advantage of the corporate form of business ownership is the limited personal liability of its stockholders. Stockholders usually are not personally liable except for the loss of their investments, and for the debts or other obligations of the corporation. A second advantage of this form of ownership is that the shares of stock can be freely transferred or traded to others unless restricted by provisions in the corporate charter. Another advantage is that a corporation has perpetual life. Unlike a partnership or sole proprietorship, the corporation continues when a principle investor dies. In addition, a corporation has a regular form of management, and its profits, when distributed to its stockholders, are taxed as dividends, not as ordinary income.

The disadvantages of the corporate form of ownership include more elaborate and expensive formalities of organization and management, and the fact that a corporation is a tax-paying entity, which may result in double taxation of its profits. This double taxation occurs because the corporation is required to pay taxes on its profits. When the stockholder receives dividends, they may be taxable as income.

Depending on the circumstances the tax aspects may be advantageous to individual shareholders. Unlike a partnership, the profits of a corporation are not taxable until the individual taxpayer receives dividends. If the profits are re-invested in the corporation, the stockholder is not required to pay the individual taxes. In addition, the tax rate a corporation pays is usually lower than personal income tax rates.

Foreign Corporations

States use the term "foreign corporation" to describe any corporation not organized under their laws. Thus, a corporation chartered in Delaware is a foreign corporation in New York. In an 1869 supreme court decision, Paul v. Virginia, the court ruled that a state has unlimited power to regulate foreign corporations because they aren't protected by the privileges and immunities clause in the Constitution. Under this authority, most states require foreign corporations to register with either the secretary of state or the commissioner of corporations before regularly doing business within the state.

Regularly doing business within the state means engaging in transactions within the state on a recurring basis. Infrequent sales to residents in the state from outside the state is not considered as doing business within the state.

Foreign corporations that are required to register with a state must also appoint an agent who resides within the state. He has the authority to accept the service of court or other legal papers on behalf of the corporation. The foreign corporation must also file a certified copy of its articles on incorporation with the secretary of state's office. Foreign corporations may be taxed only on business its carried on within the state. In the case of real estate taxes, only the portion of corporate property located within the state is taxable.

Rules, regulations, and tax rates affecting corporations vary among the states. Because of this, states with favorable corporate laws, such as Delaware, become known as corporate havens. Businesses are incorporated within those states with the intention of operating in different states. These advantages help large, well-financed corporations. But they usually aren't cost effective for small close-held corporations because a resident agent and registration are required.

Ownership and Control of a Corporation

The business affairs of a corporation are managed by the board of directors. In small, close corporations they are managed by a chief executive officer. Because shareholders own the corporation's stock, they elect the board of directors or the chief executive officer. However, they do not manage the corporation. Not all stockholders have the right to vote, but there must be at least one class of stockholders with voting rights.

The board of directors or chief executive officer of the corporation establish its general policies. They aren't required to be stockholders, but in most cases they hold substantial portions of the voting stock. The board of directors or chief executive officer appoint the officers of the corporation, who are considered agents of the board or the executive officer. They are obligated to enforce the policies of the board or executive officer.

Stockholders' meetings must be held at least once a year in most states. All states require that the minutes of stockholders' meetings be kept as part of the corporation's records. Other meetings may be called as provided for in the corporation's articles of incorporation. Advance notice must be given to all shareholders prior to any special meetings. How special meetings are to be called and the notification requirements should be specified in the articles. Unless required by the articles, the stockholders' meetings need not be held in the state where the corporation was formed or is doing business. An unusual number of annual shareholders' meeting are held in resort areas such as Las Vegas.

Usually a shareholder has one vote for each share of voting stock that he possesses. Shares may be voted in person or by proxy. Proxy is the written authority shareholders give to another person to vote on their behalf.

Management of the Corporation

As noted earlier, the directors or chief executive officer are responsible for the daily management of the corporation. While stockholders own the corporation and are responsible for electing the board of directors or chief executive officer, they don't manage or directly control the corporation. They have no voice in the day-to-day management of the business. If the shareholders are unhappy with the director's management of the company, a majority of them can replace the directors or chief executive officer at a regular scheduled meeting.

The directors and chief executive officer are obligated to manage the corporation using their best business judgment. Any shareholder may bring a stockholder's suit to enforce a corporate right or to protect corporate property that officers of the corporation have failed to protect. A stockholder's suit may also hold the directors and officers personally liable for any losses that result from unauthorized or illegal acts they commit. Before bringing suit, however, the shareholder must first demand that the directors take corrective action. Courts will not interfere with the actions of the directors or chief executive officer unless the shareholder can establish the presence of bad faith, gross negligence, or illegal conduct. If the shareholder wins his suit, in most states the corporation must pay his legal expenses. If the shareholder loses, however, he may be required to pay the corporation's legal costs.

Because directors are in a position of trust, they owe a duty of loyalty to the corporation and are not permitted to make a profit at the company's expense. They are obligated to exercise "due care and prudence" in the management of the corporate business.

Dividends

The directors have the authority to declare dividends that may be payable in cash, property, or corporate stock. The stockholders can't force the directors to declare dividends unless they can establish that the directors are acting in bad faith. If at least one-third of the stockholders request it in most states the board must provide written justification for not declaring dividends. Usually, dividends can be paid only from the profits of the corporation. If cash or property dividends are paid in excess of the profits, the directors who declared the dividends may be personally liable for the excessive dividends when innocent third persons suffer damage.

The Corporation's Basic Documents

The corporation's structure and organization are set forth in its articles of incorporation. They contain a general statement of the corporation's purposes. The articles are drafted by the founders of the corporation (incorporators) and are approved by the secretary of state or the commissioner of corporations of the state where the corporation was created. Any modifications to the articles must be approved by the state.

The second basic document of the corporation is its bylaws which contain the basic operating procedures of the corporation. Bylaws cannot conflict with the articles of incorporation. The articles of incorporation should provide procedures for self-amendment and stipulate any restrictions on the directors' ability to amendment the bylaws. If the articles do not include the restrictions, the directors or the chief executive officer may revise the bylaws without shareholder approval. The state will not approve a corporate charter until the articles of incorporation have been approved. By state law, certain provisions must be included in the articles.

Formation of the Corporation

Incorporators of a business may be individuals, partnerships, or other corporations. Incorporators don't have to live in the state where the corporation is formed. If they don't live in the state, then the incorporators authorize a resident of the state with the authority to accept the service of notices, court orders, etc., on behalf of the corporation. This requirement gives the state a certain degree of control over the corporation.

The incorporators must file proposed articles of incorporation with the appropriate state office and pay the required fees. When the state accepts the articles and issues a charter the corporation is born. The original corporation officers must be listed in the articles of incorporation. While one person may hold more than one office, most states require that at least two individuals serve as corporate officers. In many states, corporate secretary and the treasurer positions must be held by different individuals.

Self-Incorporation

The easiest and most convenient way to incorporate your business is to hire an attorney to do it for you. This isn't the most economical method because attorneys aren't cheap. The average businessperson can form his own corporation without consulting an attorney.

If you decide to take this route, first get a copy of the state's regulations on incorporating from the commissioner of corporations' office or secretary of state's office in the state where you wish to incorporate. Make sure you request the regulations for a profit-type corporation, not a nonprofit one. If they don't give you enough help, buy a "how to do it" book. If you follow this approach, find a book about incorporating in your state, because each state differs. Appendix E contains sample articles of incorporation. If you use them as a guide, modify them to meet your state requirements.

In many states private individuals establish close corporations that have broad general powers. The individuals then sell all of the corporation's stock to business owners who transfer their business to the corporation. They then have a corporate form of business ownership. When you use this method make sure the articles of incorporation fit your particular needs.

Dissolution of Corporation

A corporation may be ended voluntarily by its shareholders, or involuntarily by the state in which it was chartered. If a corporation fails to pay taxes or violates the statutes under which it was created, the secretary of state can take legal action to either suspend its operations or dissolve it. Involuntary bankruptcy can also be grounds for dissolution. A corporation cannot carry on any activities except those leading to dissolution while it is suspended.

Shareholders can voluntarily dissolve the corporation by filing articles of dissolution with the state and winding up the corporation's affairs. When voluntary dissolution occurs, the state corporation office will issue a certificate of dissolution once the state approves the shareholder's articles of dissolution.

If the state or the shareholders take no formal action, the corporation becomes dormant, but it isn't formally dissolved. Dormant corporations can be reactivated by the payment of back taxes, fees, or assessments.

Prior to the state's approving its voluntary dissolution, a corporation must send notices of intent to dissolve to all of its creditors, and authorize an agent to collect its assets, pay all of its debts, and distribute its remaining assets.

Piercing the Corporate Veil

In some circumstances, the courts will disregard corporate status and hold the shareholders and directors liable to prevent fraud from occurring or to achieve equity. There are three situations in which the courts disregard corporate statues (known as piercing the corporate veil): 1) When corporate goals and formalities are ignored; when the shareholders treat the corporation's assets as their own property; and then the corporation's officers fail to keep the necessary records. 2) When the corporation is undercapitalized. The general rule is that the shareholders must forward enough capital to cover any liabilities that may occur in carrying on the business. 3) When the corporation is organized for fraudulent purposes; when the corporate statues is used for fraudulent purposes, such as an individual shareholder's transferring all of his property to the corporation to avoid paying his personal debts.

If the court pierces the corporate veil, only active shareholders or those who participated in the fraud are held personally liable. Passive investors who have acted in good faith are usually not held personally liable. When shareholders are held liable under this concept, the entire amount of their investment is liable. Their personal assets are also subject to attachment and sale. Usually, only creditors or persons who have been defrauded by the corporation may pierce the corporate veil.

The concept of piercing the veil is a drastic step and usually isn't ordered by the courts except in situations where justice clearly requires it.

Professional Corporations

Professional corporations are established by doctors, lawyers, accountants, etc., for tax advantages such as pension plans and deferred income programs. (Recent changes in federal income tax laws have made professional corporations less attractive than they had been in the past.) State statutes permitting professional corporations do not change the basic relationship between the professional practitioner and the client.

Professional corporations are formed much like usual corporations except that they can be formed by only one person. Professional corporations may engage in only one category of professional service, such as law or medicine, and only individuals licensed in the particular profession can own shares in them. Unlike those of standard corporations, the shares of professional corporations cannot be transferred without the permission of the secretary of state or the commissioner of corporations. The professional shareholder is personally held liable for his malpractice, but he cannot be held liable for the malpractice of others.

Chapter 4

Starting the Business

I n this chapter obtaining business licenses, fictitious name registration requirements and sales tax permits for starting a business are discussed. This chapter also covers the buying and selling of the entire or substantial portion of the stock of a business. This latter subject is commonly known as "bulk transfers" and is covered under the Uniform Bulk Sales Act. Most city and county governments have adopted business license requirements for revenue and to regulate certain businesses. In almost every state, the issuance of business licenses is controlled by either incorporated cities or counties in the exercise of their police power. Only in highly regulated businesses, such as legal services, medical services, etc., does the state get involved in the licensing process.

BUSINESS LICENSES

A business license is the privilege or right to operate a business or to carry on a trade. Unlike the goodwill or trade name of a business, a business license is not property and cannot be transferred. When a person purchases an existing business, the license cannot be transferred to the new owner. In these cases, however, it is usually easier to get a license because the city or county has already approved the operation of that type of business at that location. Before purchasing an existing business, find out if you will have any problems getting the license in your name. Before licenses are issued to cer tain businesses police records checks are required. In some cases the city or county may require the new owners to post performance bonds.

In most states, it is a misdemeanor (minor crime) to operate a business or carry on a profession without getting the necessary licenses. It is also illegal to continue the business under a license issued to the previous owners. As defined in licensing statutes, a business engages in commerce or trade to make a profit or livelihood. Many local ordinances exempt organizations and activities whose activities are not profit motivated. In this regard, check with city or county offices to determine if your activities require a license.

In imposing licensing requirements cities or counties cannot discriminate between persons similarly situated and exercising the same privileges. However, they can classify occupations and make different rules regarding each one. Cities or counties can also make different rules regarding merchants who have a fixed place of business and those who do not. In one case, a city wasn't permitted to place a higher tax on solicitors who had been in business for less than a year, than on those who had been in business longer.

FICTITIOUS BUSINESS NAME REGISTRATION

State laws require businesses that operate under "fictitious business names" to register and maintain an up-to-date fictitious name statement. These laws provide the public access to records of businesses that are operated under names other than those of the owner or owners. Fictitious name statements are usually filed with the city or county where the business operates. Most states have standard forms for filing fictitious names. Check with your local city or county clerk for specifics.

Partnerships, corporations, and sole proprietorships must file fictitious name statements unless their owners conduct the business in the surnames of all owners. A partnership must file a fictitious business name statement unless the business name contains the surnames of all general partners. Corporations have to file a statement unless it does business under the exact corporate name stated in its articles of incorporation.

A sole proprietorship that operated under the name of W.F. FIELDS, Co. was determined by one court to have a fictitious name. The name was considered fictitious because it implied the existence of additional business owners.

Words describing the type of business are not considered fictitious names, i.e., John Brown's Meat Market, or Joe Brown's Car Repair Shop.

A business whose owners have failed to file the required statement cannot maintain any legal actions or transactions made under its fictitious name. The business owners, however, can still be sued in their own names or in the business's name. Filing a false statement is a criminal offense.

Filing is usually required 30-60 days from the time that business transactions begin. In most states, business owners must publicize the fictitious name in a local newspaper, either before filing the statement with the clerk or shortly thereafter. Owners have to refile every three to five years, or whenever changes occur in ownership or business addresses. A person who withdraws from or abandons a business is required to file a statement of withdrawal or modification of ownership.

SALES TAX PERMITS

If your product or service is subject to state, city and/or county sales tax, your business is obligated to pay the tax. This tax is considered an excise tax levied for the priv-

Check One:

C ☐ Corp.
P ☒ Partnership
S ☐ Individual

CITY OF FRESNO
BUSINESS TAX CERTIFICATE
APPLICATION

PRINT CLEARLY OR TYPE:

THIS SPACE FOR OFFICE USE

T
C
N $

Tax Year: _____ Qtr: _____
Dates:

THRU

1. BUSINESS OWNER(S):
   Joe & Jane Owner
   ENTER YOUR NAME, PARTNERS NAMES, OR CORPORATE NAME IF A CORP.

2. dba (Business Name): Joe's Small Business

3. Type of Business: retail

4. Do the business owner principals on Line 1 own the property (building/land) at the location of the business? ☒ YES ☐ NO

5. BUSINESS ADDRESS: 740 Level, Fresno, California   Zip Code: 93740

6. MAILING ADDRESS: P.O. Box 3233 , Fresno, California   Zip Code: 93740

   NOTE: FOR A BUSINESS ADDRESS OR MAILING ADDRESS CHANGE ONLY, USE INSTEAD FORM 3100.

7. Your Start Date for
   This Business in Fresno: January 1, 19XX

ISSUANCE OF A CERTIFICATE DOES NOT PERMIT OPERATING A BUSINESS IN VIOLATION OF ANY FRESNO MUNICIPAL CODE SECTIONS OR OTHER LAW. ZONING APPROVAL OF THE BUSINESS ADDRESS IS THE RESPONSIBILITY OF THE APPLICANT.

8. Signature: _____ Title: Co-Owner   Date: 12-27-XX

9. Residence Address: 540 Level Street   Res. Phone: 235-5406
   City, St. & Zip: Fresno, California, 93740   Bus. Phone: 236-7890

10. Partners / Co-Owners / Corporate Officers:

NAME	TITLE	RESIDENCE ADDRESS
Joe Owner	Co-Owner	same as # 9
Jane Owner	Co-Owner	same as # 9

11. Principal Product and/or Service to be Performed:
    retail- cleaning supplies

12. If Merchandise is to be Sold, Indicate How (✓):

5-302 ☒	Retail Store/Shop for walk-in customers	
5-331 ☐	Door-To-Door/Place-To-Place Order-taking.	
5-328 ☐	Door-To-Door/Place-To-Place Direct Selling.	
5-338 ☐	Temporary merchandise sales on lot or in building.	

    5-328 ☐ Sidewalk Peddler (roving).
    5-331 ☐ Party Plan Presentations.
    5-302 ☐ Mail Order Business.
    5-302 ☐ Manufacturing for Wholesale Wholesale supplier
    ☐ Other: _____

13. Is merchandise or equipment stored at the business location address? YES NO
    If 'NO' give address of storage place: _____

14. USE OF RESIDENCE FOR HOME OCCUPATION ONLY: I, _____, have read and
    agree to abide by Section 12-105 H of the Fresno Municipal Code.

15. (CONTRACTORS ONLY): CONTRACTOR NUMBER: _____ TYPE: _____

• • • • • • • • • • BELOW SPACES ARE FOR OFFICE USE ONLY • • • • • • • • • • • •

BUSINESS IMPR. DISTR. ZONE: _____ F M C SECT. _____ Date Billing Sent
For Initial Fee: _____

RATE: _____ COMPTR. CHG-BK (Y,N): _____

BILLING CYCLE: D A C N R   BILLING PRINT: BUSINESS TYPE   TAXES & PERMITS:

B F G H I J K Q

1 2 3 4
5 6 7 8

A C I
P R W

☐ A=Admissions Tax
☐ C=Cardroom
☐ D=Dance
☐ G=Amusement Games
☐ M=Massage
☐ R=Room Tax
☐ T=Taxicab Company

SLS. TX. CODE: _____

S.L.U.C. BUSINESS CODES: (P) _____ (S) _____

T C N: _____ By: _____ REV. 12/84 W.G.

Record of fictitious business names on file with the county clerk in Austin, Texas.

SEE REVERSE SIDE BEFORE COMPLETING

Space Below for Use of County Clerk Only

CLK 2025 00 E01 71 R01-85

FICTITIOUS BUSINESS NAME STATEMENT
[X] NEW FILING
[ ] RENEWAL
FILE NO.

INSTRUCTIONS DO NOT PUBLISH INSTRUCTIONS		THE FOLLOWING PERSON(S) IS (ARE) DOING BUSINESS AS:			
• Insert the fictitious business name(s) and the street address of the principal place of business in California. • If no place of business in California, insert the street address of the principal place of business outside of California. • NOTE: only those businesses operated at the same address may be listed on one statement.	1	FICTITIOUS BUSINESS NAME(S) (Type or Print) Joe's Small Business			
		Street Address (P.O. Box not acceptable) 740 Level Street	City Anytown	State USA	Zip Code 00000
• If an individual, insert full name and residence address. • If a partnership or other association of persons, insert full name and residence address of each general partner. • If a business trust, insert full name and residence address of each trustee. • If a corporation, insert the name of the corporation as set out in the articles of incorporation and the state of incorporation. • Attach additional pages if necessary.	2	FULL NAME OF REGISTRANT (Type or Print) Joe Owner			
		Residence Address (P.O. Box not acceptable) 540 Level Street	City Anytown	State USA	Zip Code 00000
		FULL NAME OF REGISTRANT: (Type or Print) Jane Owner			
		Residence Address (P.O. Box not acceptable) 540 Level Street	City Anytown	State USA	Zip Code 00000
		FULL NAME OF REGISTRANT (Type or Print)			
		Residence Address (P.O. Box not acceptable)	City	State	Zip Code
		FULL NAME OF REGISTRANT: (Type or Print)			
		Residence Address (P.O. Box not acceptable)	City	State	Zip Code

• Check statement which best describes the nature of the business(es). • NOTE: Check one only.	3	THIS BUSINESS IS CONDUCTED BY: [ ] An Individual [ ] An Unincorporated Association other than a Partnership [X] Husband and Wife [ ] A General Partnership [ ] Joint Venture [ ] A Limited Partnership [ ] A Business Trust [ ] Other (Specify): [ ] A Corporation [ ] Copartners
• Do not check this box unless filing as a trustee, guardian, conservator, executor, administrator, assignee or purchaser. See all special instructions on reverse side before checking this box.	4	(DO NOT PUBLISH THIS ITEM UNLESS BOX IS CHECKED.) [ ] THIS STATEMENT HAS BEEN EXECUTED PURSUANT TO SECTION 17919 OF THE BUSINESS AND PROFESSIONS CODE.
• If an individual, must be signed by individual. • If a partnership or other association of persons, must be signed by a general partner. • If a business trust, must be signed by a trustee. • If a corporation, must be signed by an officer. State Title of Officer.	5	Type or Print Signature Signed. Joe Owner TITLE (For other than individual) Co-Owner
• This item for use of the County Clerk Only. DO NOT INSERT DATE.	6	THIS STATEMENT FILED WITH THE FRESNO COUNTY CLERK ON NOTICE THIS STATEMENT EXPIRES ON GALEN LARSON, COUNTY CLERK A NEW STATEMENT MUST BE FILED PRIOR TO THE EXPIRATION DATE. NO FURTHER NOTICE OF EXPIRATION WILL BE GIVEN By

[Space Below for Use of County Clerk Only. Do Not Publish Certification.]

CERTIFICATION

I hereby certify that the foregoing is a correct copy of the original on file in my office.

GALEN LARSON, COUNTY CLERK

Dated: Fresno, California: .... By _____ Deputy

Fictitious Business Name Statement. As noted in the chapter, if your business will operate under a fictitious business name, a fictitious business name statement must be filed with the clerk's office.

ilege of selling tangible personal property. In most states, the seller may pass the tax on to the buyer, but the tax itself is actually imposed on the seller who must pay it. In most states a buyer has no direct obligation to pay the sales tax. If you fail to collect sales tax from your customers, your business becomes liable for the amount that should have been collected.

Application for Sales Tax Permit

To obtain a sales tax permit in most states, complete the appropriate application and submit it to the state comptroller or the state franchise board. In some cases you may be required to post a performance bond to ensure that all collected taxes are forwarded to the state on time. If a bond is required, find out if the state will accept a certificate of deposit from you through a local financial institution. Obtaining a bond from an authorized bonding company will cost you money. Whereas, with a certificate of deposit you are required to pay only the deposit, from which you will then draw interest.

The application must include the name under which the firm will transact business, the business location and the type of business that will be carried on. Depending on the type of business, the application must be signed by the owner, a general partner, or a corporate officer.

Gross Receipts of Sale

Sales tax is imposed on the gross receipts of the sale (sales price). The sales price is the total amount for which tangible personal property is sold, leased, or rented. If anything of value is given as full or partial payment for the sale, the market value of the item is also included in determining the sales price or the gross receipts of the sale.

In most cases, the sales price doesn't include cash discounts, any amounts charged for installing or applying the product to be sold, any tax paid on the property, and/or separately stated transportation or delivery charges. If transportation or delivery charges aren't stated separately on the sales invoice or receipt, in most states that amount is included in the taxable gross receipts.

Tangible personal property means property that may be seen, weighed, measured, felt, or touched. It usually doesn't include telephone transmission lines, stocks, bonds, or currency.

The tax is levied on the completed sale but not on the intermediate steps involved in the sales event. A sale doesn't have to occur during the regular course of business to be taxable, although some states exempt these occasional sales from the levy. The sale doesn't have to be for profit, as long as it meets all other requirements. It is sometimes presumed that the gross receipts of a sale are subject to the sales tax. The burden of proof that they aren't is on the person claiming the tax exemption.

Resale Certificates

To avoid double taxation, persons or businesses who buy taxable property for resale to retail customers can give the wholesaler a "resale certificate" instead of paying a sales tax. This certificate relieves the seller from paying sales tax if it is accepted in good faith from a person or business that sells tangible personal property at retail.

BT-400 REV. 30 (8-84)

APPLICATION FOR SELLER'S PERMIT AND
REGISTRATION AS A RETAILER
AND
EMPLOYMENT DEVELOPMENT DEPARTMENT
REGISTRATION AS AN EMPLOYER

STATE OF CALIFORNIA
BOARD OF EQUALIZATION
DEPARTMENT OF BUSINESS TAXES

1. Office	Date	2. HQ Registration Unit	Date

3. Reinstatement Fee		4. Are You Buying a Business?	5. Date of Purchase	7. Account Number		
Amount	Receipt Number	Yes ⌐ All ⌐ Part ⌐	6. Purchase Price	Office	Number	
$		No ⌐ Reorganization ⌐	$			

8. Owner(s)

9. Firm Name 2201   /N.

10. Location of Business: (if different from Mailing Address) [10]   Street & Number   City or Town [11]   State CA

11. Mailing Address [10] P.O. Box or Street & Number   City or Town [11]   State CA   Zip Code [12]

12. Type of Organization: Husband and Wife Co-ownership ⌐
Individual ⌐   Partnership ⌐   Corporation ⌐   Other ⌐

13. Corporation Officers: President   Vice-President   Secretary   Treasurer

14. Name of Former Owner   Business Name of Former Owner   Former Owner's Account Number

15. Type or Nature of Business (If Mixed, Underscore Principal Types and Product)

Check Principal Activity: Jobbing by   Performing Business, Pro-   Construction   Type of A.B.C.
Retailing ⌐   Manufacturing ⌐   Wholesaling ⌐   Repairing ⌐   fessional or Personal Services ⌐   Contractor ⌐   License

16. Part Time?	Itinerant	Is Business Located Within City Limits?	18. REGISTRATION – EMPLOYMENT DEVELOPMENT DEPARTMENT
No ⌐ Yes ⌐	No ⌐ Yes ⌐	No ⌐ Yes ⌐	A. Are you now registered as an Employer with EDD? No ⌐ Yes ⌐

Date Started This Address

A. Are you now registered as an Employer with EDD?   No ⌐ Yes ⌐
If yes, enter Employer Account Number
B. If no, will your payroll exceed $100 in any calendar quarter?   No ⌐ Yes ⌐
(If no, do not complete C through G.)
C. If yes, enter ending month and year of the first quarter in which wages will
exceed $100. Mo._____ Year_____ Number of employees _____
D. Business Name _____
E. Federal Employer Identification Number _____
F. Enter first month that personal income tax withheld exceeds/is expected to
exceed $350 _____
G. Do you have more than one establishment?   No ⌐ Yes ⌐

17. FOR DISTRICT USE ONLY
Any Delinquencies for Prior Periods?   No ⌐ Yes ⌐
If Yes for What Period? _____
Action Taken to Clear _____
New ⌐   Temporary ⌐   Issue & Cancel (Attach BT-406) ⌐
NO Reinstatement After Revocation ⌐
EDD Reinstatement After Revocation & After Close-out ⌐
COPY Reinstate. After Revocation & Interdistrict Move (Att. BT-1047) ⌐

19.	Bus. Code	Area Code		Original Starting Date		Owner Code	Account Analysis	FOR HEADQUARTERS USE ONLY					O.S. Audit Office	Transit District Code	Except. Code	Special Return Processing Code	Ext. Code
Basis		Co.	Jur.	Month	Year			Effective Date			O.S. Location						
								Month	Day	Year	State	Zip					
					01												

20. Forms Furnished Taxpayer
BT-1241-C ⌐   BT-400-Y ⌐
GA-324-A ⌐   BT-741 ⌐
BT-519 ⌐   BT-162 ⌐
BT-1009 ⌐   ⌐
BT-467 ⌐   Reg. 1700 ⌐
Regulations _____

Returns No ⌐ Yes ⌐
Periods _____

21. FILING INSTRUCTIONS: You are hereby notified that you are required to file sales and use tax returns
and pay tax on a calendar _____ basis. Returns are due on or before the last day of the
first month following the close of the reporting period.

22. CERTIFICATION: I HEREBY CERTIFY THAT I AM DULY AUTHORIZED TO SIGN THIS APPLICATION AND THAT
THE STATEMENTS CONTAINED HEREIN ARE CORRECT TO MY BEST KNOWLEDGE AND BELIEF. I FURTHER
CERTIFY THAT I AM OBTAINING THIS PERMIT TO ACTIVELY ENGAGE IN BUSINESS AS A SELLER OF TANGI-
BLE PERSONAL PROPERTY.

Signature _____ Title _____ Date _____
Residence Address _____   Driver's License Number _____
Residence Phone ( ) _____   Business Phone ( ) _____   Social Security Number _____

23. TRANSIT DISTRICT INFORMATION
You are further notified that if your location of business is in a transit district which imposes a transactions (sales) tax and use tax, or if you engage in
business in such a district (see Section 9 on the reverse of this application and Form BT-741, Your Privileges and Obligations As A Seller, attached),
you are required to report the applicable transit district tax on your State, Local and District Sales and Use Tax Return.

84 89680

An application for a Sales Tax Permit. As noted in the text, if you are involved in retail sales, you must obtain a sales tax permit. The local office of state business taxes will assist you in completing the application.

A resale certificate must be signed by and bear the name and address of the purchaser. It must also indicate the permit number the purchaser was issued and the general nature of the property being sold. Giving a resale certificate for property that isn't to be resold in order to evade paying taxes, is a crime. If an article bought for resale is instead used by the purchaser, he has the duty to report this fact and pay the required sales tax.

Exemptions from Sales Taxes

Statutes in every state exempt certain tangible personal property from sales tax. The exemptions vary state to state. Most states exempt groceries and medicine. States are also required to exempt goods being transported interstate or to a foreign country.

A recurring problem in most states is trying to determine if product containers should be taxable. Generally speaking, nonreturnable containers that are sold to persons who fill and then sell them are not taxable, because a tax will eventually be collected when the full containers are sold. In this situation, the retailer who sells the full containers must collect a sales tax on both the sale of the contents and the price of the container. Returnable containers are not taxed since the retail customer usually pays a deposit for the container.

Automobiles, aircraft, and motor fuels are usually taxed under provisions separate from those for general sales tax. In dealing with the sale of personal property, the business owner should remember that all sales are presumed to be subject to the general sales tax.

Use Taxes

A use tax is a tax on the value of tangible property used, stored, or consumed in a state. Unlike sales tax, the purchaser is responsible for paying it. If the state's sales tax was paid on the property when it was purchased, no use tax is due. The purpose of the use tax is to equalize the tax burden on property purchased outside the state, and used, stored, or consumed with the same type of property taxable by the state. The use tax, therefore, helps retailers in one state compete on equal terms with out-of-state retailers who are exempt from paying that state's sales tax. In this situation, the buyer is usually given a tax credit for any out-of-state sales tax he pays on the property. For example, if a person pays five percent sales tax in one state and brings the property back to his home state where the tax rate is 6%, he then owes a 1% use tax on the property to his home state.

Absorption of Tax By Retailer

In most states, it is unlawful for a retailer to advertise or to say to anyone that he will assume the sales or use tax, or that it won't be added to the property's selling price. There isn't a requirement to collect the tax if the retailer pays it, but the retailer cannot advertise that fact. On the sales receipt or other proof of sales, the retailer must display the amount of sales tax collected from the customer separately from the price of the product.

BULK SALES OF INVENTORY

Article 6 of the Uniform Commercial Code (UCC) covers the bulk sales of the stock or inventories of businesses. Bulk sales are commonly regulated by the Bulk Transfers or Bulk Sales Acts. While the laws in each state may vary on this subject, they all have the main purpose of preventing fraud. The two most common types of fraud are: (1) When the business owner, owing debts he is unable or unwilling to pay, sells his inventory for less than its value and still can't pay his debts. While he is still liable on the balances, the business owner has no other assets and is either bankrupt or without resources for creditors to attach. (2) The business owner, being in debt, sells his stock in trade for any price, takes the proceeds, and disappears leaving his creditors unpaid.

To prevent these types of fraud, bulk transfer statutes provide methods by which creditors may obtain advance notice of the sale of a merchant's stock. Once the creditors know of a pending sale, they can investigate the circumstances of the sale before it occurs and take steps to protect their rights. If creditors determine that fraud is present, they may take court action to either halt the sale or to impound the proceeds of the sale if necessary to protect their rights. The objections to the bulk sales acts are that they delay sales and place additional "red tape" on legitimate sales.

Bulk Transfers

A bulk transfer is any sale or change of ownership of a large portion of the inventory, materials, supplies, or merchandise of a business not ordinarily a part of the original owner's business.

It is necessary to determine whether the purchase of a business that also includes its inventory is subject to regulation by the bulk transfer act. If it is and the necessary requirements are not met, the new business owner may find himself liable for the debts of the previous owner. The liabilities of the buyer for the debts of the seller are usually limited to the value of the bulk sale items purchased.

A transfer of a substantial part of a business owner's equipment is a bulk transfer if it is made in conjunction with a bulk transfer of inventory. Bulk transfers do not include transfers of investment securities, money, accounts receivable, contract rights, negotiable instruments, or mortgages. The transfer of these items is covered under other regulations.

Bulk transfers do not include sales by executors, administrators, receivers, trustees in bankruptcy, or any public officer acting under judicial process. Excluded from the act are sales made in the course of any judicial proceeding. Not included are transfers to a person who agrees to accept liability for the seller's business debts and who remains solvent after becoming liable for the debts. Both the seller and buyer will be liable for payment of the debts. A transfer to a new business organized to take over and continue the business under a business reorganization is also excluded. In this last situation, the new business must agree to assume liabilities for the debts of its predecessor and give public notice of the reorganization.

Certain transfers are exempted from the provisions of the act. The general exclusions are: those made to give security for the performance of an obligation, general assignments for the benefit of all creditors, and those in settlement of a lien or security interest on the inventory.

Schedule of Property

In those sales subject to a bulk sales act, the new owner must obtain from the seller a schedule of property to prevent the new business owner from being liable for the debts of the previous owners. The schedule of property must include a list of existing creditors and a description of the property sufficient to identify it.

The list of creditors must be signed and sworn to by the seller or his agent and contain the names and business addresses of all the creditors of the seller, and the amounts of the debts owed to each. The seller must also list the names and business addresses of all persons who are known to assert claims against him, including those people with claims the seller disputes.

As noted earlier, the owner's failure to comply with the requirements of the act enables his creditors to ignore the sale and levy on the property for the amount of the debts. The submission of a false schedule by the seller is a criminal offense. If the buyer accepts a false schedule of property in good faith and complies with other aspects of the acts, he is usually protected from creditors' attempts to levy on his property.

Because failure to comply with the act makes the buyer liable for the debts of the seller, the noncompliance can be resolved by the buyer's paying the unpaid creditors. If the debts of the seller are paid as they mature, then no liability occurs.

Notice to Creditors

The requirement to notify creditors is another major condition of the bulk transfer act. Creditors must be notified at least 10 days before the buyer takes possession of the goods or pays for them, whichever comes first. The notice shall contain:

- A statement that a bulk transfer is about to be made.
- The names and business addresses of both the seller and the buyer, and all other business names and addresses used by the seller in the past three years.
- Whether or not all the seller's debts are to be paid in full by the buyer as they fall due as a result of the transfer. If so, the address to which creditors should send their bills must be included.
- If the debts of the seller are not to be paid in full as they fall due or if the buyer is in doubt on that point, then the notice shall further state the location and general description of the property to be transferred, the estimated total of the seller's debts, an address where the schedule of property and list of creditors may be inspected.
- Whether the transfer is to pay existing debts of the seller and if so the amount of those debts and to whom owing.
- The amount of value to be paid by the buyer and the time and place of payment.
- The place where creditors of the seller are to file claims or objections to the sale.

This notice must be in writing and delivered personally or by registered or certified mail to all persons on the list of creditors the seller furnished, and to all other persons who assert claims against the seller.

Auction Sales

A bulk sale at auction is subject to the act, but the reporting requirements are different and failure to comply subjects the auctioneer for an amount equal to the proceeds of the sale. The validity of the sale or the title of the buyer are not affected by the auctioneer's failure to comply. In a recent case, one court concluded that an auctioneer is liable only if he knows that the auction constitutes a bulk transfer. If goods are received on consignment for sale, the auctioneer may not know that a bulk transfer is involved.

Protected Creditors

All business creditors of the seller whose claims are based on transactions occurring before the bulk transfer are protected under the bulk sales or transfer act. Previous creditors with unliquidated claims (claims in which the amounts due are disputed) are also included. Creditors whose claims are based on transactions occurring after a notice to creditors is given are not included.

Limitations of Actions and Levies

Unless the bulk transfer has been concealed, court action or levies must be made within six months after the date the buyer took possession of the goods. When the transfer has been concealed, court action must be taken or levies made within six months after its discovery by the creditor.

"Levy" means not only levies of execution orders of a court judgment, but also attachment, garnishment, trustee process, receivership, or any other proceeding used by the state courts to apply a debtor's property toward payment of his debts.

If the buyer sells the goods in a situation in which the bulk sales or transfer act was not obeyed, a question arises whether the subsequent buyer takes the goods subject to the creditors' claims of the first seller. Generally, if the second buyer takes the goods without knowing the defect and pays a reasonable price for them, he takes a good title to them and is not liable to the original seller. If the second buyer either knew of the defect in sale or did not pay a reasonable price for the goods, i.e., received them as a gift, he may be liable to the original seller's creditors.

Chapter 5

Trademarks, Service Marks, and Trade Names

I n this section, trademarks, service marks and trade names are discussed. A trademark is any word, name, symbol, device, or any combination thereof adopted and used by a business to identify goods it makes or sells. A trademark also distinguishes those goods from goods made or sold by other businesses.

A service mark is used in a sale or in advertising to identify the services of one business and distinguish them from another.

A trade name is a word, name, symbol, device, or any combination thereof of a person, corporation, or partnership used to identify the business, vocation, or occupation, and to distinguish it from another business.

The term "marks" is commonly used by the courts to include both service marks and trade names. Not all marks are considered acceptable by the courts and thus, may not be registered by the owner. Listed below are the most common reasons that a mark will not be accepted for registration by a state or the federal government. Any mark that:

- Includes immoral, deceptive, or obscene language.
- Includes words, symbols, or forms that may falsely suggest a connection with persons, living or dead, institutions, beliefs, or national symbols.
- May bring institutions, beliefs, or natural symbols into contempt or disrepute.
- Includes any flag, coat of arms, or other insignia of the United States, any state, municipality, or foreign nation.
- Comprises the name, signature, or portrait of any living individual unless that individual has given his written consent to the user of the mark.

• Consists of a mark that when applied to the goods or to the services is merely descriptive or is primarily geographic.

• Consists of words or symbols so closely resembling another business trademark that it is likely to cause confusion or depict the products as belonging to the other business.

Both state governments and the federal government register and regulate the uses of service marks and trademarks. If your trademark or service mark is being used solely within the state, usually only the state's requirements must be met. But if you are involved in interstate commerce, not only must you meet the state's requirements but also those pertaining to the federal government.

TRADE NAMES

In most states and under federal rules, trade names cannot be registered. However, there is a common law property right in a trade name. The person who first adopts and uses the trade name is the original owner. A trade name may be transferred in the same manner as personal property, and it is included in the sale of the goodwill of the business. Except for the inability to register a trade name, the rules governing its use are very similar to those pertaining to trademarks and service marks. In many cases, your trade name may also be considered as a trademark or service mark, and it may be registered as such.

PERSONAL NAMES

The names of a manufacturer, seller of goods, or business owner may be used as a trademark or trade name. The adoption of that same name by someone else is an infringement on the trademark or trade name if there is a likelihood of confusing the products of one and the other. For example, an individual by the name of Jones can operate under the trade name of Jones. An individual named Smith cannot use the trade name of Jones when to do so would confuse potential customers as to the origin of the products or services being sold.

Ordinarily, personal names cannot become restricted trademarks, because persons of the same name have an equal right to use the name. For example, an individual by the name of May could start a business called the May Company even though a major retail outlet on the West Coast goes under the trademark of the May Company. The theory behind this is that each person has equal right to use his own name in his own business. The individual inherently has the right to use his name to identify his own business as long as he doesn't intentionally deceive the public or other individuals to his benefit.

Courts have consistently held that infringement of a trademark or trade name cannot be predicated on the bona fide use by one individual of his own name in his own business. In some states, an exception is that if the name has become so well known that it has a secondary meaning, an individual may be restricted from using that business name.

The general rule that personal names cannot become restricted trademarks or trade names is not limited to family names. It can also be applied to a business owner's first name or even his nickname. For example, a business owner could not be restricted from using his nickname "Mel" as the name of his diner. If, however, the name doesn't stand alone but has some other term associated with it, such as the Original Jones' Brothers Shoe company, this of itself may allow it to be a trade name.

DESCRIPTIVE WORDS AND DESIGNS

As noted earlier, terms commonly used to describe trades, occupations, or products cannot be subject to trademarks or service marks. For example, the name Idaho Potatoes cannot be registered because it merely describes potatoes from the state of Idaho. The size or shape of the carton used to market the product also cannot be registered or protected against infringement.

In one case, a company that sold canned tuna wasn't permitted to register and appropriate for its exclusive use a picture of a fish used on its can labels. The court stated that to give a company the right of exclusive use the sign or figure must be in an arbitrary form not suggestive of the nature of the article it describes. One raisin company wasn't allowed to register as a trademark language used to describe the method of curing the grapes, such as "sun cured," "sun dried," or "sun made." But the company was allowed to register the word "sun-maid" as a trade name because it isn't a correct spelling of the product.

In another case, the name "Atlanta Transfer and Storage Company" could not be protected because it related only to a description of the business and where the business was conducted. Likewise, the word "blue ribbon" cannot qualify as a trademark because blue ribbon merely describes a quality of the product. In a similar case, a seafood company wasn't allowed to register the phrase "of the sea" as a trademark because the phrase indicated where the product came from, and therefore was descriptive in nature.

If, however, the words are arbitrary and fanciful, such as "sunbeam," "bonton," "don juan," etc., they may be registered. Because the courts have commonly held that these types of words don't relate to the name, quantity, or description, they may be subject to a trademark or service mark.

STATE REGISTRATION OF A MARK

A person who wants to use a trademark or service mark should register it with the Secretary of State of each state in which the business will be conducted. Registration applications should include: the name and address of the applicant; if a corporation, the state of incorporation, and the goods or services to be associated with the mark; how the mark is to be used in connection with such goods and services; the date when the mark will first be used; and a statement that the applicant owns the mark and that no other person has the right to use such a mark in this state. In most states, the application must be signed and verified by the applicant, or in the case of a corporation, by an officer of the corporation, and include a facsimile of the mark. The fees for registering a mark with a state vary from $10 to $75.

A certificate of registration issued by the Secretary of State upon his approval of an application is considered evidence of ownership of a trademark or service mark. In most states, a mark must be re-registered every few years. In California, for example, it must be re-registered every 10 years. If it isn't re-registered, it expires and may

Stack files of trademark registrations on file with the U.S. Patent and Trademark Office, Arlington, Virginia. These files are open to the public for research on prior trademark registration.

be used by someone else one year afterward.

Each Secretary of State keeps a public record of all marks registered in his state. If you don't know whether a certain mark is registered, go to the Secretary of State's office at the state capital, and look at the public register. There are professional examiners in every state capital who will do this for you for a fee.

Any mark registered in most states can be freely transferred and assignable as part of the goodwill of the business. The same is true for the use of personal names in a business. For example, if the Jones Company, owned by Mr. Jones, was then sold to Mr. Smith, Mr. Smith could continue business under that name even though he couldn't register it as a mark because it is a common name.

CANCELLATION OF STATE REGISTRATION

As noted earlier, in most states registered marks expire after a certain period of time.

In addition, the Secretary of State may cancel any registered mark if it is determined that the mark has been abandoned, that the registrant in the application doesn't own the mark, and that the registration was granted improperly or obtained fraudulently. To cancel a state-registered mark, an individual must get a local court order cancelling the mark. The court order is then sent to the Secretary of State's office ordering him to cancel the registration of the mark.

Any person who fraudulently files an application for a mark is guilty of a misdemeanor. In addition, a person's use of a previously registered mark or any reproduction, counterfeit, copy, or imitation of a registered mark without the owner's consent makes that person liable for damages to the owner of the mark. Injunctive relief is also available to the owner of a mark. In other words, if someone is using or imitating your trade name or trademark, you can get a court order to stop that person from continuing the use of your trade name or trademark. The court could also order that you be paid for any damages you suffered as a result of the improper use or imitation of your trade name or mark.

FEDERAL REGISTRATION OF MARKS

As noted earlier, trade names cannot be registered with the federal government. Trademarks and service marks may be registered with the Commissioner of the U.S. Patent and Trademark Office, Washington, D.C. 20231 (202 557-3178). Federal registra-

If you are unsure as to the proper office to direct your questions, don't hesitate to ask the employees in the courthouse.

tion is regulated by the Trademark Act of 1946 (as amended), also cited as Title 15, U.S. Code, Section 45.

To start the registration process, file an application and the necessary fee with the U.S. Patent and Trademark Office. You can get an application by calling or writing to the office listed above. If you have any questions in completing the application, call one of the employees in the office. They have been very helpful to me.

Mail the application, the required fee and a self-addressed, stamped envelope to the above address. The fee in 1982 was only $35; by 1985 it had increased to $175. So a quick check with the office will determine the correct amount. When the Trademark Office receives your application, a duplicate copy of it will be returned to you in the self-addressed envelope. The duplicate copy will contain a stamp indicating the date the office received the application and a serial number. The copy establishes the time of filing, which is important in a contested case regarding first use of a trademark or service mark. You should use the serial number for identification purposes in all of your correspondence with the Trademark Office.

When your application is received in the Trademark Office, it is first checked by a clerk who ensures that it is completed correctly. Next it is referred to an examiner. The examiners in the office are attorneys who have the judicial authority to accept or reject your application. The examiner decides if the mark can be registered and if it is sufficiently dissimilar to other registered marks to be distinct and not confusing.

The clerk or examiner may return the application with a letter indicating any problems it has. This gives the chance to amend your application or submit a statement rebutting the examiner's conclusions. I've found the most expedient method is to amend the application rather than rebut the examiner's conclusion.

If the application qualifies for registration, then a notice of pending application is published in the *Official Gazette* of the Patent and Trademark Office. The gazette permits any person to file an objection to the application within thirty days of the publication date.

If no one objects, then under usual conditions the examiner accepts the application and issues a certificate of registration. The entire process usually takes about six months.

Any person who believes he would suffer damages by the registration of a mark can file a sworn statement with the office stating why the mark shouldn't be registered. If a statement is filed, the examiner will give you an opportunity to rebut the information it contains. The examiner will then decide whether or not to accept the application and register the mark. His decision is subject to judicial review in federal court.

FEDERAL TRADEMARK RESEARCH

Before submitting an application to the Trademark Office, make sure a trademark similar to yours hasn't already been registered. You can have a professional researcher check on this, or you can do it yourself at a major university or law school library.

If you take the latter route, first research the *Trademark Register of the United States* published by the Trademark Register, 454 Washington Building, Washington, D.C. 20005. Use only the latest annual edition of this book because only marks currently in use are included. The first few pages of the book explain how to use it.

Next, look at each monthly issue of the gazette to see if a mark has been registered or is pending registration since the annual edition of the register was published. Each month the gazette also lists the applications for registration the Trademark Office received the previous month.

If someone has registered a mark similar to the one you want to register or an application for registration is pending, you can get a copy of the registration certificate or pending application from the Trademark Office. Call the Trademark Office for specific instructions and the current fee for getting a copy of a pending application or registration certificate.

The Trademark Office publishes the *Trademark Manual of Examining Procedure* sold by the Superintendent of Documents of the Government Printing Office. This manual gives detailed guidance concerning trademark procedures. It also contains instructions for trademark and service mark research. The price of the manual in 1985 was $24.

The complete details of any registered mark is included in the copy of the *Official Gazette* for the month in which the mark was registered. Most major libraries have back issues of the *Gazette* on file.

Chapter 6

Business Insurance

I n this chapter business insurance coverage is discussed. A discussion on buying insurance, determining the amount and types of coverage, dealing with an insurance agent, and collecting on your policy when a loss occurs is also discussed.

Insurance is a contract between the insured and the insurance company. Under this contract, the insured agrees to pay premiums, and if he suffers a loss the insurance company is obligated to pay for the damages. There are so many types of insurance policies that a discussion on every conceivable type would be impossible. For a price, almost any type of risk can be insured. But only those commonly used in businesses are discussed.

Property insurance is the most common type of business insurance, and covers risks of fire, theft, wind, hail, etc. The next most common type, liability insurance, protects the business owner against third person claims for losses and damages caused by an activity of the business. A third type, business interruption insurance, protects the business owner when he can't conduct business as usual because of fire, etc.

Insurance is a highly regulated business. In every state, insurance boards, commissioners, or superintendents regulate and supervise the transaction of insurance business in the state.

DEALING WITH AN INSURANCE AGENT

Dealing with an insurance agent is in many respects similar to dealing with an attorney. Your first goal is to select the right agent. Ask businesspersons in your area to recommend a reliable agent. It pays to shop around. Find an independent agent who can get quotes from more than one insurance company. Stay clear of the agent who tries to sell you a package deal without first taking the time to analyze your business needs.

After you have chosen an agent, tell him your specific needs. Mention any unusual risks that may be present. Be frank with him because you want his advice and recommendations to be based on sound information. Remember, that he represents the insurance company, too. Review your coverage with the agent when any major changes occur or at least once each year.

INSURANCE COVERAGE

Like other businesses, insurance companies are designed to operate at a profit. Because less than 60 percent of the premiums are returned to policyholders in payments for losses, over the long run the average businessperson will pay more in premiums than he will ever recover as insurance payments for losses. In many ways, insurance coverage is a gamble. If every possible risk is covered, the insurance premiums will be a heavy burden on the business. In determining the amount and types of insurance coverage your business needs, the goal is to have just the right amount. The only problem is that you never know if you have the right amount and coverage until a loss occurs. With this in mind, the business owner should try to determine the risks of a certain type of loss and weigh the risks against the premiums charged.

One way to reduce insurance expenses is by self-coverage. Because most losses are small, a businessperson may want to self-insure for small losses and have outside insurance protection for casualties that would destroy the business. Another way to keep the cost of your insurance premiums down is to have a higher than normal deductible. The higher the deductible the lower your premiums.

In deciding what types of coverage and policy limits you need, balance the cost of the premium against the odds of the risk covered and the effects of the loss on your business. If your business can absorb the loss without too many problems, don't insure it. Be sure to insure against that single catastrophe that could destroy your business.

If you lease your building, insurance on the structure is probably covered by its owner. If the building is destroyed, the owner's insurance will pay him for his loss, but you will be without a place to do business. In this case, not only should you insure your supplies, inventory, and equipment but also the cost involved in relocating your business. Another aspect to be concerned about is the liability that can be incurred if your business operations cause the fire or other damage. The building owner's insurance company may sue you after they have paid the claim. Check your liability policy for this type of coverage.

If you own your building, you need property insurance to protect your investment. If you insure the property for more than its value or replacement cost, you will still recover only the value of the property or its replacement cost should it be totally destroyed. Therefore, you have paid extra premiums for the over-insurance. Most businesses are insured for much less than their present value or replacement cost. The average businessperson insures the building for its original cost without providing for any increases in the value of the building or increasing replacement costs. This can cause a problem with the "co-insurance" clauses discussed later in this chapter. Most insurance companies now sell property insurance whose face value increases with inflation or the increasing cost of replacement. This coverage is more expensive, but to offset this increased cost, the business owner may want to increase his deductible.

If your business has a large inventory, consider the effects on your business if this inventory were destroyed. In most cases, your business insurance would cover the loss of inventory and supplies. If your business is a personal service type with small inventory of products, etc., this insurance may not be needed. Ask your agent for his recommendations regarding your particular situation.

Liability insurance is almost a necessity for businesses. Although the chances of someone being hurt as a result of your business operations may be small, one such claim can destroy most businesses.

The dollar amount of your policy is an important factor to consider in liability coverage. If you conduct your business in California, Florida, or New York, I recommend that you get higher than usual coverage for liability insurance than in states where hugh recoveries are not as common. For example, million-dollar judgments are not unusual in those states, but are very unusual in Texas, Arizona, Oklahoma, and Virginia. The policy should cover liability to people injured on the business premises.

If your business manufacturers, sells, or distributes products, you need product liability insurance to cover any person injured by a defective or unsafe product. Company automobiles and trucks should also be covered by your liability policies. In some cases, a employee who uses his own car for business purposes could expose your business to liability if an accident occurs while he is using his car. Coverage is needed for these situations, too.

The business owner should also consider getting business interruption insurance. Key factors to consider here are: how long would the loss of your building put your company out of operation; could you easily relocate with a minimum of expense; and what impact would any business stoppage have on the earnings of the company. Most policies covering business interruption use the "gross earnings" approach. Under this approach the company's estimated gross earnings during any period of interruption are estimated. The insurance company then pays from 50 to 80 percent of the gross earnings depending on the terms of the policy. Gross earnings under these policies is defined as the profits plus all continuing expenses.

If you purchase business interruption insurance, make sure you get a clear understanding what business interruptions are covered. For example, most policies will cover interruptions caused by the destruction of the business building, but will interruptions caused by strikes,work stoppages, computer system failure, lack of raw materials, etc., be covered? If your business deals almost exclusively with a few customers, look into the cost of coverage if one of these customers suffers a disaster and can't continue to do business with you.

Another type of business interruption coverage has a "selling price" clause. Regular property coverage of your inventory covers the cost of replacement only at its cost. It is not based on your anticipated profits. If your business is highly seasonal in nature and its destruction occurs during the high season, this could be a disaster for you. It is unlikely that you could replace your inventory in time to meet the seasonal demand, therefore, you would basically lose any opportunity for profit during that season. The "selling price" clause would allow you to cover part of the anticipated profits also.

In some cases, instead of business interruption insurance, it may be more appropriate for your business to have "extra-expense" insurance. If you could continue your business in temporary quarters but at additional costs, this type of coverage may be cheaper to get. Extra expense coverage protects against the loss of future income because of the added expense of doing business at another location other than your present one. It is not protection for current income while you are out of business.

Many businesses are now being insured against employee thefts and misconduct. If your employees will be in positions of trust and can do substantial damage to your business, seriously consider this type of coverage.

It is very hard to get the right amount of coverage. Too much and the premiums will diminish your profits. Too little is playing "Russian roulette." Discuss the extent and types of coverages you need with your attorney, insurance agent, and other business associates. Get their advice, but make the decision based on your best business judgment. It is also important to constantly review your insurance needs to ascertain if your coverage is appropriate for your current needs.

CO-INSURANCE CLAUSES

Most property insurance policies have "co-insurance" clauses. If you insure the property for less than 80 percent of its value, the insurance company will consider you as a co-insurer. The percentage may vary, but the principles are the same. If you own a building valued at $100,000 and insure it for $80,000, the insurance company will pay the full amount of any loss up to the policy limit of $80,000. If, however, you insure the building for only $40,000 (40 percent), the insurance company will consider you as a co-insurer only for the amount necessary to constitute the 80 percent, i.e., 40 percent. If a loss of $20,000 occurs in this latter situation, the insurance company will pay only $10,000 because you carried only half of the 80 percent coverage required by the policy.

To determine whether or not a business is insured for 80 percent, the deductible portion of your policy is included as part of the insured coverage. For example, if the building is valued at $100,000, is insured for $80,000 but has a $5,000 deductible, you still have coverage for 80 percent of the building's value, even though you can recover a maximum of $75,000 if the building is totally destroyed. If your loss is $5,000 or less you will not recover anything on your policy. The premiums will be much less because most damages are for less than $5,000.

In most cases it would be better for the business if you were to insure the property for 80 percent or more of its value and have a higher deductible, than to insure it for less than 80 percent of its value. Not only will the premiums be cheaper, but your coverage when major damages occur will be more. For example, if you insure the building for 40 percent of its value with a $100 deductible, you become an equal co-insurer of the building. If the loss amounts to $20,000, the insurance company would pay $9,900 (50 percent of loss minus the deductible). If however, the building is insured for $80,000 with a $5,000 deductible and the loss is $20,000, you would receive $15,000, not the $9,900, and your premiums would probably be lower.

THE INSURANCE POLICY

As noted earlier, an insurance policy is a contract between the insured (policyholder) and the insurer (insurance company), and is governed by contract laws of the state in which the policy is written. The insurance industry is highly regulated, therefore, most states have prescribed clauses and provisions that must be in each policy. An insurance policy is invalid if it violates a state statute or is contrary to public policy. For example, insuring property such as illegal drugs would be against public policy. The average businessperson won't have these problems, but he could have problems with the contract language and standard clauses, such as the co-insurance clause discussed earlier.

Have your agent explain the terms and phrases in your policy that you don't understand. If there's a conflict between what he tells you and the terms of the policy, make him explain it to you in writing. Also tell him that you consider what he said to be a modification to the policy because it conflicts with its terms.

Modification, Cancellation and Termination of Coverage. Like other contracts an insurance contract can be modified by the agreement of both parties. In many cases, the insurance company reserves the right to cancel or modify the policy upon written notice, and to refund the unearned part of the premiums. The policy must clearly state this right. The insurance company usually also reserves the right to cancel the policy when premiums aren't paid on time or when a false application for insurance is discovered. Know the rights you and the insurance company have under the policy to cancel your coverage.

If you feel that the insurance company has wrongfully cancelled your policy, check with your attorney. The courts generally hold that the policyholder has three courses when an insurance company wrongfully cancels a policy: (1) He can consider the policy at an end and recover any damages he has suffered. (2) He can bring court action and request that the court order the reinstatement of the policy. (3) He can offer to pay the premiums, and when it is refused consider the policy as being in effect. Then if any losses occur, he can sue for the losses. This last remedy isn't recommended because you won't know until after a loss whether or not the policy is in force.

The insurance application can be just grounds for the company to cancel the policy, if fraud or misrepresentation are a material part of the contract. For example, saying that a company truck was red in the application when in fact it was white, was held by one court not to be a material misrepresentation. In one case, the insurance policy on an automobile was declared void for a material misrepresentation. The insured had stated that he was using his automobile only for personal use when, in fact, he was using it to deliver newspapers.

MAKING A CLAIM AGAINST THE INSURANCE POLICY

The terms of the contract determine the rights and obligations of the policyholder and the insurance company after a loss occurs. Most policies require the policyholder to provide notice and proof of the loss within a certain time. If no time limit is stated in the policy, the notice and proof of the loss must be reported within a reasonable time, preferably as soon as possible. Keep a copy of the notice in case it is disputed and request a claim form from your agent. If the loss is large, consult your attorney immediately.

The best approach to take in dealing with insurance companies is to prepare your claim as if it were to be disputed. By doing this you reduce the chances of being unable to prove your claims in court later on. Take pictures of the damaged property, make detailed notes, get statements from witnesses, and collect bills or other documents that establish the value of the destroyed or stolen goods. If the police were called, get a copy of the police report.

You will be in a better position to talk settlement with an adjuster if you have documented your losses. If there is any question of criminal misconduct, report it to the police. A standard clause in many insurance policies requires that any possible criminal misconduct be reported to the police. By reporting it to the police, you get an additional record of the loss with the police report.

Submit a claim if it is questionable that the loss is covered by your insurance policy. If you feel the loss is covered and the agent or company states that it isn't, consult your attorney. I have learned that by being aggressive, insurance companies are more likely to pay those doubtful claims. If you have a substantial amount of insurance with the company, they may pay doubtful claims to keep you as an insured.

Dealing With An Adjuster

Because of the nature of their work, most adjusters are basically conservative people, and approach most claims with the goal of denying them or making as low a settlement as possible on them. Remember, they don't get bonuses for making liberal settlements. Most adjusters are pressured by their supervisors to close cases promptly. This pressure to close quickly may work to your advantage if you have your claim well documented.

Adjusters have the authority to settle claims within certain limits. For claims above their pre-authorized limits, they have to check with their office. In the first meeting with the adjuster, his only objective is to determine the type of case, its probable range of settlement, and any other problems associated with it. If the amount of loss is clear and there is no question of liability, settlement may be made at the first meeting.

If the insurance company disputes the amount have your attorney negotiate for you. Studies have shown that adjusters will offer higher settlements when dealing with an attorney. In one insurance company studied, the average recovery of clients represented by attorneys was four to 12 times higher than those without legal representation.

If You Are Sued For More Than Policy Limits

There usually is no need for an attorney, when liability cases are involved, if the insurance company had agreed to represent you and there is no question of coverage. However, if the suit is for more than the face amount of your policy, consult an attorney to ensure that your rights are represented.

Your insurance company has a duty under the policy to protect your interests. Therefore, if the company refuses a reasonable offer to settle within the policy limits, it may be required to pay the entire judgement, even that above the policy limits. This requirement is based on the premise that the insurance company had a duty to protect you and should have done so by settling within the policy limits.

The business of insurance coverage is tricky and sometimes very technical. Therefore, see an attorney any time you are sued and there is a possibility of recovery in excess of policy limits.

Chapter 7

Product Warranties

T he normal warranties that accompany any products or merchandise your business sells are discussed in this chapter. Disclaimers of warranties and limited warranties are also discussed. Warranty is a contractual term concerning some aspect of a product, such as its title, its quality, and its fitness for a particular purpose.

There are two basic types of warranties, implied and expressed. An implied warranty is assumed in the sale of a product unless a specific disclaimer is agreed upon when the product is sold. Express warranties are those agreed upon by the parties at the time of the sale.

Words such as warrant or guarantee aren't required in a warranty to validate it. Any promises the seller makes pertaining to the product and becoming a part of the contractual bargain establish an express warranty that the product conforms to the promises.

A statement of a product's value is not considered a warranty, but only the personal opinion of the seller. The seller's claim that his product is worth $3,000 is not a guarantee of the value of the product. It will not support a breach of warranty action when the buyer learns that the item is not worth $3,000. A similar situation exists if the seller says the product will "probably" not need repair in the next six months. However, the seller's saying that the item will "not" need repair in the next six months may be considered a warranty.

In many cases, the courts have ruled that promises contained in advertisements are express warranties, especially when the advertisements imply that the products have certain qualities. A seller's description of a product has also been held to be an express warranty. One court held that the description of a product as "boned chicken" constituted a warranty that the product was indeed boned chicken.

In cases involving the use of product samples, the courts have stated that an implied warranty exists guaranteeing that the products are the same type and quality as their samples. This concept also applies to the sale of bulk products by samples. In sales by models, a warranty also exists guaranteeing that the model is an accurate representation of the actual goods.

The Uniform Commercial Code, adopted by 47 states, provides the statutory bases for most warranties involving the sale of personal property. For a warranty to exist, there first must be a sale. In one case a shopper was injured by a soft drink bottle she had that exploded in a self-service supermarket before she reached the cashier to complete the sale. The court held that a warranty did not exist because the sale had not been completed. (Note: The shopper recovered damages on other grounds.)

FRAUDULENT REPRESENTATIONS

There is a key difference between fraudulent representations and warranties. A fraudulent representation is a false statement about the present condition of the product, whereas a warranty is a guarantee as to the fitness or condition of the product. In some cases, a statement by the seller may both be a fraudulent statement and a warranty. For example, in cases involving statements about the ownership or right to sell the product, a false statement that the seller has the right to sell the item is both a warranty of title and a fraudulent representation.

If there is a breach of warranty, the person must sue for damages under the contract, and the only recoverable damage is for the monetary loss reasonably foreseeable as the result of the breach of contract. In cases involving fraudulent representation, however, the buyer may sue not only for monetary losses but also for additional money for punitive damages.

IMPLIED WARRANTY OF TITLE

Any time a product is sold, there is an implied warranty that the seller either owns the product or has the right to sell it, that the product will be free of any security interests or other liens, that the product will be delivered free of the rightful claim of any third person, and that the buyer will receive a marketable title to the product. This is considered a preferred warranty and is implied in all sales unless clearly waived by the buyer.

IMPLIED WARRANTY OF FITNESS

Unless otherwise informed, the buyer has a right to expect that the product he is buying is free from defects of materials or workmanship, and that the product is reasonably fit for its intended purpose. There is also an implied warranty that the goods are of "merchantable quality" or free from defects rendering them "unmerchantable." Other implied warranties of fitness include promises that the products are adequately contained, packaged, and labeled, and conform to the promises made on the label.

The implied warranty of fitness does not apply to products manufactured to the buyer's specifications. In these cases, the buyer takes the risk that the product will be fit for its intended purpose. The seller, however, warrants that the product will conform to the buyer's specifications.

DISCLAIMERS

Disclaimers, or waivers of warranties, are often called "as is" contracts. In this type of contract the buyer assumes all risks as to the fitness of the product and accepts the product "as is." The buyer assumes any expense in the product's repair or servicing. The buyer must accept the "as is" statement before the contract is complete, to defeat any implied warranties of fitness. Similar statements such as "as they stand" and "with all faults" are sufficient if it is clear that the buyer accepts the product in its present condition. Note: There is still an implied warranty of title.

The "as is" contract is not a favorite with courts, and they tend to find reasons to ignore the "as is" restriction. If you sell products in this manner, make sure the buyer is aware that the product is being sold "as is." In one case, a drum of insecticide was labeled "Seller makes no warranty of any kind, express or implied, concerning the use of this product. Buyer assumes all risk in use or handling, whether in accordance with directions or not." The court stated that this statement would be an effective disclaimer of any warranties only if the seller can establish the buyer was aware of the disclaimer when he purchased the insecticide.

Any disclaimers regarding the product can be printed on notices, letterheads, labels, etc., provided that their existence is conveyed to the buyer before the contract is completed. The disclaimer can be verbal, but problems of proof can occur when they are entirely verbal.

If the written contract contains statements excluding other agreements, such as "this contract constitutes the entire agreement of the parties"; the courts may not allow the buyer to establish any disclaimers that were not included. This rule is based on the concept that the entire contract is contained in the document, and to allow evidence of any other disclaimers would conflict with the written contract.

The buyer's consent is only to honest disclaimers of warranties. The courts will ignore the disclaimer to prevent fraud.

CONFLICTING WARRANTIES

Conflicts sometimes occur in the separate warranties of the products being sold. The courts will try to interpret the terms of the warranties in a manner as to carry out the parties' intentions when the contract was entered into. If this is not possible, a rule of construction is that specific descriptions or terms override general descriptions or terms.

LIMITED WARRANTIES

As noted earlier, express warranties are made by the seller regarding the fitness, etc., of the product. Express warranties are in addition to the above noted implied warranties.

If a seller wants to include only certain guarantees in the sale of his product, he should give a limited warranty. In a limited warranty, the seller expressly states that the only guarantees applying to the sale are those listed in the contract or in accompanying papers. A sale with a limited warranty also automatically includes the implied warranty of title unless otherwise stated. Limited warranties are often used.

PRIVITY

Privity of contract is the term the courts use to describe the original parties to the contract. In some jurisdictions, the courts have ruled that for a warranty to be applied, a privity of contract must exist between the seller and the person who suffered an injury or damage because of the breach of a warranty. In these jurisdictions, privity of contract between the plaintiff and the defendant is essential to recovery on a warranty.

In one famous case involving privity of contract, a Mr. McPearson was driving his new Buick when the front wheel failed and he was injured. He sued General Motors for breach of contract and claimed that GM had violated the warranty of fitness in selling him a defective auto. GM contended that the auto was sold to a dealer and not to Mr. McPearson, therefore, there was no privity of contract and the warranty did not cover Mr. McPearson. The court in rejecting this argument abolished the requirement for privity of contract in warranty cases. The court stated that because the auto was sold to the dealer who GM knew would resell the auto, the warranty extended to the ultimate purchaser. This rule (decided in 1919) has been accepted in almost every state.

The trend is clearly toward eliminating the requirement of privity in warranty cases. In most states, any warranties included in the sale of a product now extend to the buyer's family, household, and guests, and other persons expected to use the product.

UNIFORM VENDOR AND PURCHASER RISK ACT

To eliminate some of the difficult questions regarding which warranties apply to the sale of real property (buildings and land), many states have adopted the Uniform Vendor and Purchaser Risk Act. Its purpose is to establish a uniform law regarding warranties in the purchase of real estate.

The act states that any executed contract for the purchase and sale of real property shall include an agreement giving the parties the following rights and duties unless the contract expressly provides otherwise:

(a) If all or a material part of the property is destroyed before legal title and possession have been transferred (without fault of the buyer), the seller can not enforce the terms of the contract and the buyer has a right to return any portion of the purchase price he paid.

(b) If all or a material part of the property is destroyed without fault of the seller after the buyer has accepted possession or legal title to the property, the buyer is not excused from his duty to pay the agreed price.

The theory behind this act is that by establishing clear and concise rules as to who will suffer the loss in the event all or a material part of the property is destroyed, the parties can take the necessary steps to get insurance to protect themselves.

Chapter 8

Hiring and Firing an Attorney

L egal advice is like medicine in many ways. You can take it to cure problems or to prevent them. Sometimes the problems are aggravated by either failing to consult an attorney or waiting too long to seek his advice and assistance. Selecting an attorney and your relationship with him, reducing your legal fees, and firing your attorney are discussed in this chapter.

SELECTING THE ATTORNEY

It's very difficult to evaluate an attorney and his ability to give you the legal advice and assistance you need in specific situations.

The world's greatest criminal lawyer probably isn't a competent business attorney, so seek one who is competent in the field of law in which you need assistance. Many people wrongly believe that gray hair or maturity indicates an attorney's experience and ability to handle your case. This could be a grave mistake. While it is nice to have an attorney with 20 years of experience in the issues involved in your situation, it's also important to have an attorney who is abreast of the current status of the law. Many attorneys fail to keep current and may not know as much as an attorney fresh out of law school. In addition, many attorneys, have one year's experience repeated twenty times rather than have 20 years of varied experience.

Selecting an attorney is like selecting a family doctor. His ability to handle your affairs and the fees he charges may have little relationship to each other. There are many good attorneys who have very reasonable fees, and unfortunately there are some inept attorneys who charge high fees. It's difficult for the average person to tell if he is getting the best legal advice and assistance for his money. Your best guarantee of competent legal advice for a reasonable price is selecting the right attorney.

It pays to do some comparison shopping for an attorney. The promise of lower fees isn't an important factor the client should consider because an incompetent attorney is too expensive at any cost. Like other professionals, attorneys vary in their abilities and in the amount of time they need to provide the necessary services. An attorney who charges $75 an hour is more expensive than an experienced attorney who charges $100 an hour but completes the job in half the time.

The usual areas of expertise for attorneys are bankruptcy, probate and estate planning, criminal, corporate, commercial and trade. Attorneys who specialize in commercial or trade law are more appropriate for business-related problems.

In many states, attorneys can get their bar certification in selected areas and thus hold themselves out as "certified specialists." In most situations, the businessperson doesn't need to pay the extra cost of getting a "certified specialist" to handle his routine business problems.

Attorneys also specialize in certain areas or limit their practice to selected areas. This usually means that they accept cases only in those areas. They may be the best type of attorney to retain as they should be fairly competent in the needed area and usually not as expensive as a "certified specialist."

Finding the Attorney

Using common sense in hunting for an attorney is important. This isn't something that a person should rush into. As in selecting a family physician, professional referral is the best method. If you know an attorney whose opinion you value, ask him for a referral. An attorney working for the government or for a corporation may be able to recommend a competent attorney for you. A second preferred method is to ask your banker, accountant, and business associates for their recommendations.

Another approach is to check with other businesspersons in your area for the names of attorneys who have assisted them. If that is still unproductive, check with the local bar association referral services. Their numbers are in the telephone book under the bar association. Most county bar associations operate a lawyer referral service in which an individual can get a free 15 minute consultation with an attorney.

Usually, any attorney who wants to be listed by the bar referral service can do so by agreeing to give a free initial consultation to persons referred to him. Attorneys list several areas of law they want to practice. They are then referred to clients in rotating order by the referral service. Fees for services beyond the initial consultation are determined by an agreement between the lawyer and his client. During this initial consultation, the attorney should determine how complex his client's problem is and give him an estimate of the legal fees involved.

The major problem with referral services is that bar associations don't evaluate the competence of the attorneys on their lists. Any local attorney who has malpractice insurance and agrees to provide the initial free consultation is usually listed. Many people wrongly believe that the bar association, in referring them to a specific attorney, is also recommending him. A positive factor in using referral services is that most of them have procedures to informally settle conflicts between the referred attorney and the client.

Original law office of President James Monroe (now a museum). Not all lawyers have Monroe's concept of ethical duties. Therefore, take care in selecting your attorney.

Another method is to ask local public interests groups or trade and business associations for their recommendations. Using a prepaid legal plan is another way to select an attorney. Prepaid legal plans are discussed later.

A less reliable source is to ask your neighbors or relatives for recommendations. If you do this, make sure they aren't basing their recommendation on a divorce case when you need help on a commercial matter.

Attorneys Who Advertise

Attorneys have been allowed to advertise since 1976. This method of selecting an attorney isn't recommended and should be your last alternative. While many good attorneys advertise, unfortunately an unusual number of incompetent attorneys hire good public relations firms. That an attorney advertises can mean that he isn't getting enough new clients from referrals by former clients who were happy with his performance. In addition, the quality of legal services varies so greatly that there is no way to evaluate an attorney by merely looking at his ad. I would rather select an attorney from the telephone book than to select one from a newspaper or a television commercial. A competent, affordable attorney more often than not gets more referral business than he can handle without resorting to advertising.

Law Directories

To get information on attorneys, such as their experience and the schools they attended, check in a law directory at your local public library. The most popular and complete directory is the *Martindale-Hubbell Law Directory* consisting of seven volumes, each about 5 inches thick. Attorneys are listed alphabetically by cities.

Legal Clinics

Legal clinics are generally storefront-type law offices located in shopping centers and are designed to provide cheap legal services for simple legal problems. If your problem is relatively simple, it may be advantageous to use a legal clinic. If your legal problem is something more than the preparation of a simple will, beware of getting cut-rate legal advice.

Prepaid Legal Plans

Prepaid legal plans are new to the legal profession. They were first used by labor unions as a benefit to union members. Now the plans have grown in both number and types. Today many of them resemble medical plans.

INITIAL CONSULTATION WITH AN ATTORNEY

Having made an initial appointment with the attorney you have selected, continue to consider whether or not he is the right one for you. The initial appointment should be a screening process for both of you to decide if you want to continue the association.

Prepare for your appointment much like you would prepare for a job interview. Be on time. Bring all your papers with you. Above all else, don't bring your children.

How Can I Find and Hire the Right Lawyer?

Complaints Against Attorneys and Grievance Procedures

A CENTURY OF SERVICE

STATE BAR OF TEXAS
P.O. BOX 12487
AUSTIN, TEXAS 78711

May, 1982

Published in the Public Interest
By The State Bar of California

The California Bar Association provides a pamphlet on how to find the right attorney. The State Bar of Texas provides a pamphlet on how to file a complaint against your attorney. Most state bar associations publish informative pamphlets that may be obtained from their offices at no charge.

You and the attorney should be free from unnecessary distractions to concentrate on the legal problem.

At the first meeting, clearly and concisely tell what help you need. This isn't the time to gossip, because you are usually billed by the clock. Find out if he or an associate will handle your case. If he promises you the world, be wary. In most legal situations there are no clear answers to problems. If you are uneasy about the attorney, end the association before it starts. Above all, make sure you understand what his fees are and what he will do for you. Attorney fees are discussed more in detail later in this chapter.

Before you retain an attorney, get a commitment from him regarding his accessibility and willingness to handle your problems. If he is too busy, you will have accessibility problems. A busy attorney usually indicates that he is competent. But if he is too busy to handle your problems, go elsewhere.

Many attorneys tend to nitpick and get bogged down in details. Such an attorney will cause you unnecessary expense in dealing with your problems. In your initial consultation look for this fault in the attorney. Look for another attorney if you feel he is a nitpicker.

Look for personal compatibility, good judgment, legal expertise, a habit of thorough preparation, prompt response to your needs, and reasonable fees in the attorney you eventually select.

RELATIONSHIP WITH YOUR ATTORNEY

Try to maintain a professional relationship with your attorney. Never enter into an attorney-client relationship with a friend; it only causes problems. Convince the attorney that it is in his best interest to give you the best service he can. Convince him that you are important and that you can be the source of future business and references in the community.

Attorneys are generally conservative in nature in their advice. Their theme is to prevent problems before they begin. While this is usually the most prudent course of action to take, the client should be aware of this conservative trend when dealing with an attorney. If you are willing to take certain legal risks to save money, make sure your attorney is aware of the level of risk you are willing to take.

A second factor a client should be aware of is the fact that most attorneys have a very high opinion of themselves and may tend to oversell their abilities. Because of this, attorneys often try to give advice in other than legal areas. If this happens, remember that you have latitude in disregarding this advice.

In all appointments with your attorney, be on time, be prepared, be concise and don't waste his time. He may be too polite to say that you are wasting his time, but he won't be too polite to bill you for it. To accomplish the most in the shortest period of time, do your homework before you meet with your attorney. Have your papers and records complete and in a form the attorney can readily understand.

REDUCING YOUR LEGAL FEES

One famous person once said that "in law, nothing is certain but the expense." With this in mind, never, never, hire an attorney without a clear understanding of the fees he will charge, when they are due and what he will do for them. Three general methods attorneys use to set legal fees are by the hour, by a flat fee, and on a contingency fee in which he receives a percentage of any recovery the client receives. In some cases, the attorney may combine any of the above methods.

Legal fees are negotiable. If you feel the attorney's quoted fees are unacceptable, ask for a modification. Do this before your relationship is established but after your attorney has an idea of the nature and complexity of your problem. Don't give your attorney an unlimited budget to work with.

If your problem will require only a few hours of legal work, an hourly rate may be your best choice. In most cases, this is the most economical way to employ an attorney. It may be to your advantage though to use a combination of an hourly fee with a maximum fee—for example, $100 an hour but not to exceed $500.

If your attorney uses an hourly rate, find out if he has a minimum billing time for work he performs for you. For example if he has a minimum billing time of 15 minutes, plan your calls to take full advantage of the 15 minutes you will be charged for. Call him instead of visiting him; because telephone calls will inevitably take less of his time than personal visits.

In many situations the attorney may ask for a retainer fee. A retainer fee is merely an employment fee that the attorney charges to handle your case. It usually isn't a payment for any time he expends on your behalf. If you can guarantee him a minimum number of hours each month or year, he may forego the retainer fee or reduce his hourly rate.

In most states attorneys are not permitted to pay court fees or costs. Therefore, any fee an attorney quotes does not include court fees or costs. The client should make sure that at specific times the attorney will submit an itemized bill that includes a progress report in lengthy or prolonged cases.

Because the attorney's time is the standard measurement of his fee, the client should do as much as he can on the case to reduce the time the attorney needs to spend on the problem. If certain records are needed from a government office, get them for the attorney, so that he won't have to spend the time getting them. If possible, give draft contracts to your attorney for him to review rather than asking him to draft the contracts.

FIRING YOUR ATTORNEY

The attorney and the client have certain basic rights that each other should honor. The client has the right to be treated fairly, honestly, and courteously, to be charged only reasonable fees as agreed upon, to receive prompt response to inquiries regarding the case, to be informed of the status of the case, and to have his legal problems handled diligently and competently. The attorney is also under a duty to keep your confidences.

If you feel your attorney isn't handling your case properly or respecting your rights as a client, you may want to end your relationship with him. When you change attorneys it usually costs you extra time and money to establish a relationship with a new attorney. You usually lose any money you paid to the first attorney, and the new attorney will need time to get current on the case. So if possible try to settle any conflicts and retain the attorney. Many times the only problem may be a failure to communicate. If all else fails, consider firing your attorney.

A client always has the right to terminate the attorney-client relationship. However, there may be a problem with the client's right to any legal fees he has already paid. If this occurs, check with another attorney regarding your right to get these legal fees back.

If the conflict results from a serious breach of duty by the attorney, consider filing a complaint against him with the state bar association. This can be done by explaining the problem to the association in writing. The association's address is in your telephone book. I wouldn't recommend writing to the bar until your association with the attorney has ended.

Most conflicts between attorneys and clients are over time and the money billed to the client. Keep an accurate record of your relationships with your attorney. If you feel his bill is too high, talk it over with him. Ask him to explain why the bill is higher than you feel it should be.

If you are still unhappy, check with the bar association. Many state bar associations have fee arbitration panels you can refer to. Usually, the dispute is referred to an arbitration panel of one or more persons who listen to both sides and then decide the fee the attorney should have charged. In some states, such as California, the attorney has to arbitrate if the client chooses to.

Chapter 9

Accounts Receivable

T his chapter discusses establishing credit terms, debt collection restrictions, the advantages and disadvantages of using a collection agency, using small claims court to collect debts, enforcing debt judgments, and dealing with credit reporting agencies.

ESTABLISHING CREDIT TERMS

Most businesses deal in credit; therefore, credit can be the key to your business's success or failure. In a recent government study, three out of five retail shoppers used credit to make retail purchases. Therefore, the retailer who sells only for cash limits himself in the availability of customers. In addition, people are more apt to be repeat customers if they have an account with a store. Using credit also increases the ability of small, medium-sized businesses to compete with the larger stores who routinely offer their own credit systems.

There are some distinct disadvantages in using credit. First, there is the added cost associated with operating a collection system. Foremost is the added expense of financing a credit program. Bad debt losses will occur, and historically, a larger percent of credit sales results in sales returns than those made in cash. So consider all the advantages and disadvantages before establishing a credit system. In many cases, the best system for your business are the major charge card systems, such as Visa and MasterCard. The clear advantages to using these major cards are that people are more likely to possess them, and that they eliminate the need to have your own credit system. The obvious disadvantage is the approximately five percent service fee charged for their use. Your sales are automatically discounted by that amount.

Legal restrictions involved in the granting of credit usually fall into four general categories. The first is the credit application and investigative process. The second is the amount of carrying charges or late fees that you can legally charge. The third is the type of information that you must provide to all of your customers who purchase on credit. The fourth are the restrictions on the practices you can engage in when collecting debts.

A related problem involves employee misconduct in using a credit card system. Either willful misconduct or negligence by your employees could open your business to liability from cardholders. It is not unusual for employees to engage in credit card fraud.

In getting the information you need to make your credit decision, there are certain legal restrictions regarding the type of questions that you may ask. For example, on the credit application you may not ask for the race, color, sex, national origin or religious beliefs of the applicant, nor may you ask for a statement of his philosophical or political beliefs. You may ask the applicant's sex for identification purposes only, not to help you decide whether to grant or deny credit.

In deciding whether to grant or deny credit, you face additional restrictions. For example, you cannot base your credit decision on the race, color, sex, religion, or philosophical or political beliefs of the applicant, or deny him credit because he lives in a certain part of the community (commonly known as "red-lining"). A businessperson must avoid making any decisions based on discrimination.

To avoid this, most credit lending agencies have developed a numbering system to help determine an individual's credit worthiness. For example, so many points are awarded for the length of time he has lived in the neighborhood and held his present job, and for the ratio of his debts to his salary. This objective formula helps to avoid any charges of discrimination, either open or unconscious.

Finance or carrying charges a businessperson may impose on an account depend on state law. In every state, there are laws regarding the maximum amount of interest, the finance charges, etc., that a merchant can charge. State laws also determine whether or not late charges are to be considered finance charges. Check with your better business bureau or your local retail credit agency to find out what the regulations and laws are in your state.

The Federal Truth and Lending Act requires that anyone who offers consumer credit provide sufficient information regarding the credit terms to enable the customer to make a knowledgeable decision. In addition to the Federal Truth and Lending Act, discussed in detail later in this chapter, there are similar state statutes that may apply to the granting of retail credit in your state.

Certain restrictions apply to individuals who collect debts. Most of the restrictions are stated in the Federal Fair Debt Collection Practices Act of 1978 discussed later in this chapter. There are also state restrictions on debt collection.

The Equal Credit Opportunity Act (ECOA) of 1974

The federal government passed the Equal Credit Opportunity Act in 1974 to prevent and eliminate many of the abuses in granting credit that were occurring up to that time. This law forbids discrimination in any aspect of a credit decision because of a person's sex, marital status, race, national origin, age, religion, or receipt of welfare income, or because the person has sued a previous creditor in good faith. The act gives both the Federal Trade Commission and the courts authority to impose certain restrictions on debt collections, and to eliminate certain unethical practices.

Before the passage of the Equal Credit Opportunity Act, lenders routinely refused to grant credit to married women or to allow them to get credit in their own name. Before one major creditor would grant credit to a working wife, she was required to promise in writing that she would practice birth control or get an abortion if she became pregnant. These practices are now illegal under the ECOA.

Since the enactment of the ECOA, one major credit card company was successfully sued because they cancelled a woman's credit when she got married. A major oil company was required to pay a $200,000 judgment for discriminating against women because it failed to consider any income they had from alimony, child support, or separate maintenance payments. Miscellaneous provisions under the ECOA require that if you apply for a credit card or a loan, the creditor must either issue credit within 30 days or notify you that your application is denied.

The company must provide you with written notification if your application is denied. The notification must include the reason, or advise you of your right to request the reasons, for the denial of credit. One major problem in this regard is that the notice may use vague language, such as insufficient income or poor credit history, and not give specific reasons.

Other restrictions on credit decisions in the ECOA include the fact that you cannot deny a person credit because they are over a certain age. A creditor may ask your age, but if you are over the age of 18 or 21 depending upon your state law, he cannot turn you down or decrease your credit. He cannot ignore your retirement income in rating your application or close your credit account or require you to reapply when you reach a certain age limit. He also cannot refuse to grant you credit because credit life insurance is not available to persons in your age group. In this regard, however, the law does permit a creditor to consider certain information, such as how long it will be before a person retires and how long his income will continue.

Creditors may not ask about you birth control practices, or whether you plan to have children, or assume anything about your plans regarding children. They may not consider whether you have a telephone listed in your name, because this has been determined to discriminate against most married women. However, they may consider whether or not there is a telephone in your home.

The Federal Truth and Lending Law

The Federal Truth and Lending Act requires businesses to give certain basic information to credit applicants regarding the cost of buying on credit or taking out a loan. The basic theory behind the act is that credit transactions shall be an open and knowing transaction between the creditor and the debtor.

The Finance Charge and Annual Percentage Rate (APR)

Under the Truth and Lending Act, the creditor must explain the finance charge and the annual percentage rate to the debtor in writing and before the debtor signs any agreement. The finance charge is the difference between a cash price sale and the total dollar amount paid when a person uses credit. It includes interest cost, service charges, credit-related insurance, appraisals, cash discounts, etc.

The Annual Percentage Rate (APR) is the percentage cost or relative cost of credit on a yearly basis. This is the most important figure to use in comparing credit costs. It should apply regardless of the credit amount or the amount of time a person takes to repay the credit. The Federal Truth and Lending Act does not regulate interest rates or credit charges. It merely requires their disclosure so that the debtor can compare credit costs.

The Truth and Lending Act also requires a certain degree of accuracy in the advertising of any credit terms. If a business advertises important features of a credit, sale, or lease, such as a down payment or the length of time to pay, it must also state the annual percentage rate. For example, an ad saying that you can buy a new car for $99.00 down must also state the annual percentage rate.

The Fair Credit Billing Act

The Fair Credit Billing Act is another federal statute designed to protect consumers. It basically requires businesses offering credit to set up procedures for promptly correcting any billing mistakes. It also allows debtors to refuse to make credit card payments on defective goods, and requires creditors to promptly credit any payments to a debtor's account.

Under the Fair Credit Billing Act, a creditor is required to correct errors promptly and without damaging a person's credit rating. Under the law, errors are defined as charges for items you didn't purchase, as purchases made by someone who was not authorized to use your account, as charges that are not properly identified on your bill, as amounts that differed from the actual purchase price, as amounts entered on a date different from the purchase date, and as something you did not accept on delivery or that was not delivered according to your agreement. Billing errors also include errors in arithmetic, the failure to promptly reflect payment or other credit to your account, and the failure to mail your statement to you at least 15 days before the due date, provided you have notified the creditor of your appropriate address at least 20 days before the billing period.

If the debtor feels that an error was made in his billing and notifies the creditor within 60 days after the bill was mailed, he is not required to pay that part of the bill until the company conducts an inquiry into the circumstances. The creditor must acknowledge the debtor's letter within 30 days unless the bill can be corrected sooner. The bill must be corrected or the creditor must explain to the debtor why he believes the bill is correct within two billing periods or within 90 days.

The Fair Credit and Billing Act also allows the debtor to withold payment for any damaged or shoddy goods as long as an attempt is being made to solve the problem with the merchant. The right to withhold payment for defective goods or services is limited if the card was not issued by the store where the debtor made the purchase. If the card was a bank, travel or entertainment card, the sale must have been for more than $50, and must have taken place in the debtor's home state or within 100 miles of the debtor's home address.

Federal Fair Credit Reporting Act

The Federal Fair Credit Reporting Act allows debtors to examine information in their credit files, and sets up procedures to correct any errors they discover. If a lender refuses credit because the debtor's report contains unfavorable information, the debtor has a right to know the name and address of the credit reporting agency keeping the report, and the right to request the information from the credit agency either by mail or in person. While the debtor doesn't have the right to get a copy of his file, he will at least be provided with a summary of it. In addition, the credit agency must help the debtor interpret the data. If an individual was refused credit within the past 30 days, the credit agency cannot charge a fee for giving the debtor that information. However, a debtor can be charged a fee if he hasn't been denied credit, but still wants a summary of his credit report.

The act also requires that bankruptcies be removed from a debtor's credit history after 10 years, and that suits, judgments, tax liens, arrest records, and other kinds of unfavorable information be removed after seven years.

The Fair Credit Reporting Act also guarantees the right of privacy in regard to the credit information on a person. Only individuals with a legitimate business may get the credit information. In most cases the information may be given out only upon the written consent of the person involved.

Penalties under Federal Statutes

Each of the federal statutes mentioned have criminal penalties in the form of fines, and in several cases imprisonment for up to one year. In addition, a person whose rights have been violated under these statutes may bring a civil suit. If he is successful in court he can recover his damages, his court costs, and an additional penalty fee in the form of punitive damages. Check with the Federal Trade Commission for more information regarding violations of these statutes.

DEBT COLLECTION

Because debt collection has a history of abuse, there are both state and federal statutes setting forth debt collector's responsibilities and prohibiting certain acts. For example, a debt collector may not collect or attempt to collect a consumer debt by force, threat of force, or criminal means to cause harm to the debtor or his reputation or property.

In most states a debt collector can't try to collect a debt by using profane or obscene language, by placing telephone calls without disclosing his identity, by calling collect, or by causing the telephone to ring repeatedly to annoy the person being called. Nor can he telephone or see the debtor with a frequency that would constitute harassment.

Contacting the debtor's employer is also restricted. In most states, a creditor is not allowed to inform a debtor's employer about the debtor's payment of a consumer debt. An exception to this is a communication necessary to the collection of the debt if made only to verify the debtor's employment, locate the debtor, or garnish the wages of the debtor.

A debt collector may not communicate with the debtor in the name of an attorney or counselor-at-law or upon stationery bearing the name of an attorney or counselor-at-law, unless such communications are previously authorized by an attorney.

The collector may not threaten to increase the consumer debt by the addition of attorney fees, investigative fees, service or finance charges, if such fees or charges may not be legally added to an existing obligation. The collector may not falsely represent himself as being a representative of a credit reporting agency.

The Federal Fair Debt Collection Practices Act of 1978 supplements state restrictions. Basically, the act prohibits telephone calls from being made at unusual or inconvenient times, interpreted to mean usually calls before 8:00 A.M. or after 9:00 P.M. Repeated calls are prohibited even if they are made during convenient hours. If the debtor is represented by an attorney and requests the creditor communicate only with the attorney, then all future communications must be with the attorney. A creditor may contact a debtor's place of employment only to obtain the debtor's current address. The creditor may not call neighbors, relatives, or third parties of the debtor, except in a bonafide effort to locate him.

If the debtor sends a letter stating that he does not intend to pay the debt, then the collector must stop all communications with the debtor except to inform him of any legal action being taken.

The penalties for violations of this act are $1,000 plus attorney fees. In addition, the act provides for civil suits against the collector, in which the collecting agency may be held liable for $500,000 or up to 1 percent of the creditor's net worth, whichever is less.

Chapter 10

Using Small Claims Court to Collect Your Accounts

T here are small claims courts in most states. In this section, the basic procedures of the small claim courts and how to use them to collect your overdue accounts are discussed. Because there are some differences in each state, you should check with the local court clerk to determine the specific rules in your state. Appendix F contains a summary of the small claims courts' rules and regulations for each state. These courts were established to provide citizens with a convenient method to collect the amounts due without having to resort to the complicated and complex rules of procedure and evidence that prevails in regular courts.

Many states prohibit attorneys from appearing in small claims courts. In those that do, the modest jurisdictional amounts makes it uneconomical for them to appear. In some states, such as Texas, the maximum amount a person may request is only $500 plus court costs. The highest limit is in Tennessee where the maximum limit is $10,000. If your losses are above the maximum limit in your state, you may reduce the amount claimed to the maximum limit and still bring your case in small claims court. While a person may sue in small claims court for other than failure to pay a debt, most cases involve attempts to collect debts.

As a businessperson, you can use the court to collect those accounts that are too small to refer to an attorney, and to reduce the legal expenses in the marginal accounts by collecting them yourself.

VENUE

Venue refers to the location of the specific court in which you may bring suit. In all states, you may sue the defendant in the county where he resides or has a place of business. In most states, you may also sue the defendant in the county in which the damage or injury occurred or where the defendant was to perform the obligation. In some states, you may sue the defendant in the county in which the contract was entered into. Make sure you bring the suit in the proper court. Otherwise a delay will be caused by your needing to refile in the appropriate court. (See Appendix F for the venue requirements in your state.)

COST

Filing fees for small claims courts vary from $5 to $20. In some states, if the plaintiff files more than six small claims actions a year, then filing fees are higher. The only other cost involved, other than the loss of time from work to file and try the case, is the cost for service of the summons on the defendant. In most states, the defendant may be served by registered mail. Thus this expense is small. In those states that require personal service, either a professional process server or a police officer can serve the summons. The usual cost in the latter situation is about $20.

STARTING THE CASE

A small claims case is started by filing a petition with the proper court. When you file, check with the clerk's office to make sure you are bringing the case in the correct court and at the proper location. Usually filing a case consists of completing a simple form and paying the required filing fee. Most small claims courts have a person who will help you fill out the form and answer your questions. After the case is filed, the summons (notice of pending court case) must be served on the defendant either by register mail or by a process server. Ask the small claims court clerk what the normal methods of service are in your county.

When you file the case, you should also obtain a date for your hearing from the court. If the date that the clerk suggests is inconvenient, ask for a more convenient one. Remember to leave enough time to serve the defendant and permit him to have the required notice time. In most states, you are required to give the defendant at least 15 days' notice before the court date.

CHANGING A COURT DATE

If the defendant or plaintiff have problems going to court on the scheduled date and requests a different date, the court will usually allow at least one delay. After the first delay, however, any person requesting another one must provide sufficient justification to warrant it. To request a delay, ask the clerk for the proper procedure in your district or county.

If either party fails to appear at the scheduled time and that person has received proper notice, the court will usually rule in favor of the other party. If a default occurs, i.e., the defendant fails to appear, you may be required to prove that the defendant was properly served.

THE HEARING

On the scheduled hearing date, you should be on time and in the right courtroom. Check

State of California, County of Fresno.

Case No. 89-456849

I, the undersigned declare: I was, at the time of the service of the papers herein referred to, over the age of eighteen years and not a party to the within-entitled action; I served the within Claim and Order in the above-entitled action by delivering to and leaving with the person or persons personally here-in-after named, a copy thereof, at the address and on the date set forth opposite each name of said person or persons, in the County of Fresno , City of Pinedale ,
State of California, to-wit:

Name of Person Served	Street Address and City Where Served	Date of Service
Tom No-Pay	5348 Main St. Pinedale, Ca.	June 2, 19XX

Fee for service $ 20.00   Mileage $ 1.75   Total $ 21.75

(To be completed in California by process server, other than a sheriff, marshal or constable*)

[ ] Not a registered California process server (CCP 417.40).

[X] Registered: Los Angeles County.

Number: 874503-9

I declare under penalty of perjury that the foregoing is true and correct and that this declaration was executed on (insert date) June 3, 19XX at (insert place) Pinedale, , California.

(Type or print name, address, and telephone number)

Les Server
24234 Pacific Ave.
Los Angeles, California 92203
(213) 345-5683

Signature: Les Server

(To be completed in California by sheriff, marshal or constable*)

I certify that the foregoing is true and correct and that this certificate was executed on (insert date) .... at (insert place) .... , California.

(Type or print name, title, county and, when applicable, Municipal or Justice Court District)

Signature: _____

Proof of Service. If the defendant does not appear for the court hearing or submit an answer to the pleading, you must establish that the defendant was properly "served." This is the most common method of establishing service.

71

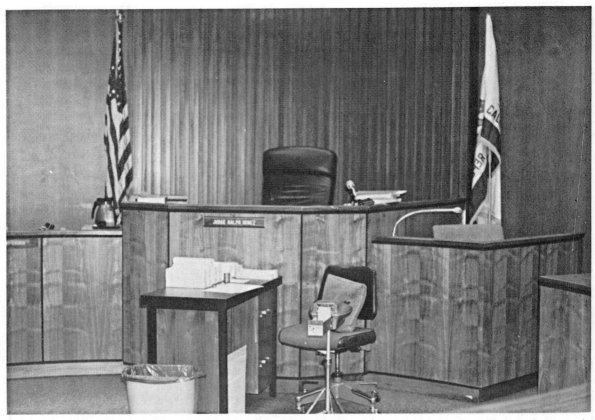

A courtroom in the Fresno County Courthouse, Fresno, California. When you are required to appear in court, come early before the case starts and get familiar with the courtroom, so that you will be more relaxed when you are called as a witness or party to a lawsuit.

this out ahead of time. Bring any documents and witnesses you need to prove your claim. The hearings are informal, without the need to comply with the strict rules of evidence present in other civil court proceedings. The judge will first allow the plaintiff to state the facts surrounding his complaint, and then allow the defendant to tell his side of the case. After listening to both sides, the judge makes a decision on the merits of the case. He will either announce his decision or tell you that you will receive his decision by mail in a few days. In most states, persons are notified by mail.

Remember to ask the judge to award you your costs in bringing the suit. In most states, the allowable costs are your filing fee, the costs to serve notice on the defendant, the witnesses' fees, and the cost of preparing documents for the case.

There are no rights to a jury trial in small claims court. The decor of the court will depend on the judge. Most judges in small claims court are relaxed and informal. Occasionally you will meet a judge who demands a certain degree of formality. Always be polite to the judge, and do not argue with him.

If you bring witnesses, discuss their testimony with them before you go into the courtroom. By this, I mean that you should be very familiar with the testimony they are going to present. Do not, however, suggest or tell the witnesses what to say in court.

FOR COURT USE ONLY

FILING FEE $ _____

SERVICE MAIL $ _____ _____

(A—Unlaw. Det.

SNEW,S_____, _____07 _____   (B—Auto Damages   PS

(C—Other

FILING DATE: _____/ _____/ _____   SO

HEARING DATE & TIME: _____/ _____/ _____ ____:_____   RECEIPT #_____

FRESNO BRANCH
1100 Van Ness
Fresno, Ca 93724
(209) 488-3450

In the Small Claims Court, Fresno Judicial District
County of Fresno, State of California
Plaintiff's Statement and Claim

State your name and mailing address, and the name and address of any other person joining with you in this action. If this claim arises from a business transaction give the name and address of your business and your name and title.

► MY NAME (Plaintiff) _____

Joe Owner

COMPLETE ADDRESS (Bus or Res) ____ 741 Level Street, Pinedale, California _____

PHONE # (209) ____435-6789_____ _____ ZIP ____93640____

(NOTE) (a) If you are suing an individual, give his full name. (b) If you are suing a business firm, give the firm name and the name of the owner. (c) If you are suing a partnership, you must name the partners. (d) If you are suing a corporation, give its full name and name a corporate officer. (e) If your suit arises out of an automobile accident, you must be the registered owner of your vehicle and you must name the driver and also the registered owner as a defendant(s) in this action.

► MY CLAIM IS AGAINST (Defendant)

NAME(s)	ADDRESS	CITY	ZIP	PHONE
Tom No-Pay	Unknown			

► AMOUNT OF CLAIM $ __213.00_____
(DO NOT INCLUDE COURT COSTS)

► MY CLAIM IS FOR (describe briefly & itemize) ____ Defendant failed to pay for merchandise purchased ___
at Plaintiff's store.

► DATE OF LAST TRANSACTION OR DATE DAMAGE OCCURRED OR OWING DATES OF RENT: _____
June 3, 19XX

► PLACE WHERE DEBT WAS INCURRED, OR WHERE DAMAGE OCCURRED, OR ADDRESS OF RENTAL: _____
Pinedale, California

► PLAINTIFF HAS DEMANDED THAT DEFENDANT PAY THIS SUM AND IT HAS NOT BEEN PAID.

► Have you sued this party before? __no_____ If yes, give case No. _____
(yes or no)
In the preceding twelve months I have filed (CHECK ONE) [X] 0-12 claims [ ] Over 12 claims

I understand that:
a. Although I may consult an attorney, I cannot be represented by an attorney at the trial in the small claims division;
b. I must appear at the time and place for trial and have with me witnesses and evidence, such as books, papers, receipts, and exhibits, to prove my claim;
c. I have no right of appeal from a judgment on my claim.

► DECLARATION OF NON-MILITARY SERVICE:
I THE UNDERSIGNED, SAY: THAT THE ABOVE NAMED DEFENDANT(S) AND EACH OF THEM, IF MORE THAN ONE IS NAMED HEREIN, IS NOT NOW A PERSON IN THE MILITARY SERVICE OF THE UNITED STATES AS DEFINED IN SECTION 101 AND SUBDIVISIONS THEREOF, OF THE SOLDIERS AND SAILORS CIVIL RELIEF ACT OF 1940, AS AMENDED, AND IS NOT ENTITLED TO THE BENEFITS OF SAID ACT AS AMENDED.

I declare under penalty of perjury that the foregoing is true and correct and that this declaration was executed on __June6, 19XX__
(insert date)

_____ at Fresno, California.   *Joe Owner*

| You have a right to a small claims advisor free of charge. | SIGNATURE OF DECLARANT |

If case is paid or settled before trial, sign below and mail this form to the above court. THIS CASE MAY BE DISMISSED WITH/WITHOUT PREJUDICE.

DATED: _____   _____

Signature of Declarant

FMC 344 (1/83)

A small claims case pleading form. The small claim court case is started by completing and filing the above form. The forms may be obtained from the clerk of the small claims court in your county or city.

DEFAULT JUDGMENT

If the defendant fails to appear on the scheduled date, the judge will require you to prove that the defendant was properly notified of the hearing. He may also ask you some of the basic facts of the case. If he is satisfied that your claim is proper, he will enter a default judgment in your favor. If you fail to prove that the defendant was given proper notice, then in most cases the judge will reschedule the case.

After a default judgment against the defendant, he has a short period of time to appear in court and explain his absence. To set aside a default judgment, not only must the defaulting party establish a sufficient excuse for failing to appear at the scheduled time, but also that he should prevail in the lawsuit. If both of these requirements are met, then a new hearing date is set.

APPEALS

In some states, including California, only the defendant can appeal a small claims judgment. This limitation is based on the concept that the plaintiff, by bringing the case in small claims court, agrees to abide by that court's decision. In most states, either party unhappy with the decision may appeal by giving notice and filing an appeal bond within a few days after the decision is announced or mailed. The time in which the appeal must be filed varies from 15 to 30 days. If an appeal is not filed within that time, the judgment is considered final.

In 15 states, the appeal from the small claims court goes to the district or superior court, and the case is tried "de novo." "De novo" means that the case is completely retried in the higher court. The judge makes a decision based only on the evidence presented before his court. In the other states, the appellate court does not hear any evidence and decides the merits of the appeal based on the record of trial and briefs submitted by the parties.

ENFORCING A JUDGMENT

After you win a case in court and the judge orders the opposing party to pay a sum of money to you, your next step is to collect the money. In most cases, threat of court intervention will cause the losing party to pay the judgment. If that isn't sufficient, you must execute the judgment to get your money. In most states a court judgment creates a lien on the property of any person who is ordered by a court to pay a sum of money (judgment debtor). The extent of the lien and the mechanics of enforcing it vary from state to state.

This judgment lien operates as a general lien on all of the debtor's property, but it isn't a specific lien on particular property. It is in reality a right to levy on the property of the judgment debtor. In most states, statutes provide for a single writ by which the person with the favorable court judgment may seize any property of the debtor and have it sold to satisfy the debt.

To obtain a writ of execution, see the clerk of the court that issued the judgment and request that he issue one. No hearing or other court proceedings are required. After the clerk issues you the writ, take it to the sheriff's office or some other authorized authority. If in doubt about this procedure, ask someone in the clerk's office. The clerk may charge a small fee to issue the writ.

ATTORNEY OR PARTY WITHOUT ATTORNEY (Name and Address)	TELEPHONE NO	FOR RECORDER'S OR SECRETARY OF STATE'S USE ONLY

Joe & Jane Owner   (209) 235-5406
740 Level Street
Fresno, Ca. 93740

ATTORNEY FOR (Name)   (without attorney) for Plantiff

NAME OF COURT	FRESNO MUNICIPAL COURT
STREET ADDRESS	1100 Van Ness Rm 200
MAILING ADDRESS	Same
CITY AND ZIP CODE	Fresno, CA 93724
BRANCH NAME	Main Branch

PLAINTIFF   Joe & Jane Owner

DEFENDANT   Tom No-pay

ACKNOWLEGMENT OF SATISFACTION OF JUDGMENT	CASE NUMBER
[X] FULL [ ] PARTIAL [ ] MATURED INSTALLMENT	86-999200 AFSOJ

FOR COURT USE ONLY

1. Satisfaction of the judgment is acknowledged as follows (see footnote* before completing).
   a. [X] Full satisfaction
      (1) [__] Judgment is satisfied in full.
      (2) [__] The judgment creditor has accepted payment or performance other than that specified in the judgment in full satisfaction of the judgment.
   b. [__] Partial satisfaction
      The amount received in partial satisfaction of the judgment is
      $
   c. [__] Matured installment
      All matured installments under the installment judgment have been satisfied as of (date)

2. Full name and address of judgment creditor.
   Joe & Jane Owner
   740 Level, Fresno, Ca. 93740

3. Full name and address of assignee of record if any:
   none

4. Full name and address of judgment debtor being fully or partially released:
   Tom No-Pay, address unknown

5. a. Judgment entered on (date): July 2, 19XX
     [X] (1) in judgment book volume no.: 1056   (2) page no.: 1346
   b. [__] Renewal entered on (date):
     [__] (1) in judgment book volume no.:   (2) page no.:

6. [__] An [__] abstract of judgment [__] certified copy of the judgment has been recorded as follows (complete all information for each county where recorded): none

COUNTY	DATE OF RECORDING	BOOK NUMBER	PAGE NUMBER

7. [__] A notice of judgment lien has been filed in the office of the Secretary of State as file number (specify)

NOTICE TO JUDGMENT DEBTOR: If this is an acknowledgment of full satisfaction of judgment, it will have to be recorded in each county shown in item 6 above, if any, in order to release the judgment lien, and will have to be filed in the office of the Secretary of State to terminate any judgment lien on personal property.

Date   ▶

_____
(SIGNATURE OF JUDGMENT CREDITOR OR ASSIGNEE OF CREDITOR OR ATTORNEY)

FMC 236 (12/83)

*The names of the judgment creditor and judgment debtor must be stated as shown in any Abstract of Judgment which was recorded and is being released by this satisfaction. A separate notary acknowledgment must be attached for each signature

Form Approved by the
Judicial Council of California
(1100) Rev. July 1, 1984

ACKNOWLEDGMENT OF SATISFACTION OF JUDGMENT   CCP 724.060 724.120
724.250

Acknowledgment of Satisfaction of Judgment. When you have received payment of your judgment from the defendant, one of the above forms should be filed.

The writ is directed to the sheriff and orders him to levy on the property of the judgment debtor and after due notice, to sell such property at a public sale. The writ will have a "return date" on it. The sheriff is ordered by the court to return the writ to the court by that date with an endorsement stating that the property listed in the writ was sold or that it was impossible to find leviable assets.

If no property that belongs to the judgment debtor can be found, then in most states the debtor may be called to court and examined under oath by the other party regarding his property (a debtor's examination). False statements regarding the status of the debtor's property are criminal offenses in all states.

Execution Sales

After obtaining a writ of execution and having it levied on the property of the debtor, the next step is the sale of the property and the distribution of its proceeds. Most states require that an appraisal of the property be made before the sale. If the sale brings less than a stated percentage of the appraised value, then either the sale must be cancelled or the required percentage must be credited against the debt.

The proceeds of the sale are first applied to the fees and expenses of the sale, then to the judgment debt. If any money remains, it goes to the judgment debtor.

At an execution sale, unlike a judicial sale, no specific property is designated and the court gives no directions regarding the sale. At the sale, however, the buyer buys only those interests that the judgment debtor has in the property. There are no implied warranties on anyone's part. It is a sale "as is." If there are pre-existing liens or mortgages on the property, they remain a charge against the property. Another problem with an execution sale is that if the purchaser loses the property because either it did not belong to the debtor or there was a superior claim to it, the buyer is not entitled to a return of his purchase money.

Right of Redemption

In most states, the judgment debtor has a right of redemption of any real property sold at an execution sale. This means that within a stated period of time, the judgment debtor may reclaim the real property by refunding to the buyer the amount that he originally paid. In some states, the debtor may also redeem personal property by repaying the purchase price. The usual period of redemption for real property is four to six years and from six months to one year in those states that allow redemption of personal property.

GARNISHMENT

Garnishing a judgment debtor's property that is possessed by a third person is another method that may be used to collect a judgment debt. The most common use is to garnish the wages of an employee by serving an order of garnishment on his employer. Unlike a writ of execution which is issued by the clerk, a garnishment order requires a court order and in most states a court hearing. In most states, if an employee's wages are being garnished, there are limits and restrictions on the percentages of his wages that are subject to garnishment.

EXEMPT PROPERTY

In all states, certain properties of a judgment debtor may not be attached and sold at an execution sale. The most common exempt property is the homestead of the debtor. In some states, the debtor must have registered or recorded the property as his homestead to protect it from the judgment creditor. Other property commonly exempted includes the family automobile, personal clothes, tools of trade and items such as the family bible. Because the list of exempt property varies among the states, check with your court clerk's office for a list of exempt property in your state.

Chapter 11

Checks and Other Negotiable Instruments

I n this chapter the rules and regulations regarding checks, bonds and other negotiable instruments are discussed. In today's modern, hectic, and complex business
world, it is impossible not to get involved with negotiable instruments. Therefore, it
is essential that a business owner, manager, or supervisor understand the rules and
regulations regarding them. The failure to comply with the requirements in negotiable
instruments law could result in severe financial hardship to the business owner.

Unlike most business issues the average businessperson is involved in, there is a
high degree of uniformity among the states and the District of Columbia where checks,
bonds, and other negotiable instruments are concerned. All states, including the District
of Columbia, have adopted Article III of the Uniform Commercial Code (UCC). The
Uniform Commercial Code is one of the most comprehensive statutes enacted in U.S.
history. It replaced several previous, popularly accepted uniform laws, including the
one dealing with commercial instruments, the Uniform Negotiable Instruments Law.
The rules and regulations discussed in this chapter are taken from Article III of the
UCC. There are some variances among the states but differences are minor compared
to the other areas of the law.

The two types of negotiable instruments that Article III of the Uniform Commercial Code regulates are notes and drafts. A note is a simple promise by one person
(maker) to pay money to the order of another person or the bearer of the note (payee).
A draft is an order by one person (drawer) to a second person (drawee) ordering the
second person to pay money to yet a third person (payee). The most common form
of draft is a check. Basically, a check is an order by the drawer (the person who writes

the check) to the bank (the drawee) directing the bank to pay money to a third person (the payee).

The most common types of notes are promissory notes and certificates of deposit. A note is usually considered a time instrument in that it is due at a future time fixed in the instrument. It isn't payable until that date. Whereas a draft, i.e., a check, is an instrument payable on demand and is basically subject to be paid from the day it is issued.

NEGOTIABILITY

The concept of negotiability allows the instrument to be traded among persons. It allows you to take a check, and by endorsement, transfer full rights and ownership of it to another person.

Negotiability refers to the form of an instrument. If an instrument is not negotiable, then the rules stated in Article III of the Uniform Commercial Code do not apply, and the instrument is merely a contract. To determine whether it is negotiable, the UCC requires that:

- It must be signed by the maker or drawer.
- It must contain an unconditional promise or order to pay a certain sum of money.
- It must be payable either on demand or at a definite time.
- It must be payable to the order of a certain person or to the bearer.

If the instrument doesn't meet all of these requirements, it is not negotiable; therefore, it cannot be a check or a bond or a certificate of deposit. It could be at the most a formal contract between the parties involved. And, of course, a formal contract would be governed not by Article III of the Uniform Commercial Code, but by the law of contracts in each state. Therefore, variances would exist as to the rules, rights, obligations, and privileges affecting the maker of the contract, and the holder or the person to whom the obligation under the contract is due.

As noted earlier, the negotiable instrument must be in a written form. The UCC, however, is liberal as to what constitutes a writing. For example, printing, typing, or any other intentional reduction to a tangible form is considered writing. There are several cases pending that are trying to determine whether or not a video tape can constitute a writing under this section of the code.

The second requirement is that it must be signed by the maker or drawer. The Uniform Code is liberal as to what constitutes a signature. A signature may be made by the use of any name, trade or assumed, or any mark that is intended to be a signature. It is acceptable to use a stamp. The signature doesn't have to be at the bottom of the instrument. Signing the instrument with a trade name or assumed name is sufficient. In each of the above examples, however, the maker or drawer must intend that the mark, etc., be his signature on the instrument. If the requisite intent was there along with the mark, the signature, the stamp, etc., it fulfills the requirements that the note or check be signed by the maker or drawer.

An unauthorized signature, forgery, etc., does not bind a person who did not sign the instruments. In other words, if someone stole one of your checks and signed it, you would not be liable for it unless you ratified or approved the signature. However, the unauthorized signor (the person who forged your name) is liable on the check or instrument as if he had signed his own name.

The promise or order to pay must be unconditional. An instrument is not negotiable if it states that its promise is subject to or governed by the terms of another agreement, no matter what the substance of the other agreement is.

The promise or order must also be free of any expressed conditions. Including the phrase, "this promise to pay or this order to pay is conditioned upon a presidential election being held every four years", would make this promise conditional; therefore, it is not a negotiable instrument document.

The full credit of the maker or drawer behind the document is necessary for it to be an unconditional promise. For example, a draft with the statement that the obligation incurred under this document is to be taken out of a certain fund and no other funds, would make it a conditional promise. While a check is an order to the bank to pay out of only one fund, the full credit of the maker or drawer is behind that check. If there are insufficient funds in that account to pay the check, the maker or the drawer is obligated to make good the check.

An exception to the requirement that the full credit of the maker or the drawer must be behind the check is in those cases where a person executes a check on behalf of a partnership, corporation, trust, etc. In this case, the full credit of the partnership, association, trust, etc., must be behind the instrument to make it negotiable.

As noted earlier, there must be either a promise or an order to pay. A promise is an affirmative undertaking to pay. Merely acknowledging the existence of a debt is not sufficient. You must actually promise to pay a certain amount. For example, "I owe you $150" is not negotiable; whereas, "I promise to pay you $150," if it meets the other requirements, is negotiable.

The UCC defines an "order" as a direction to someone to pay to the order of a person or to the bearer of the document. It does more than authorize you to pay. For example, "I hereby authorize you to pay A," is insufficient. It must be in words telling the individual with reasonable certainty that a payment should be made. The words mostly commonly used are, "I order you to pay" or "pay to the order of."

A fixed amount or a certain sum of money must be contained on the instrument. It is sufficient if you can look at the instrument and ascertain the exact amount of money due. For example, an instrument that says, "I will pay the amount I owe you within 60 days," is not a certain sum. Therefore, it is not negotiable. A note that says, "I will pay $5,000 plus 10 percent" is negotiable because you can determine the amount due by looking at the instrument.

If there is any interest included in the transaction, the interest rate must be stated on the note to make the amount certain. In one recent case, the court held that a note with the statement "payable with interest at prime rate" was not negotiable because the rate of interest could not be determined from the note. This rendered the amount due uncertain.

An additional requirement of negotiability is that the instrument must be payable on demand or at a certain time. An instrument is considered payable on demand if it contains the words "payable on demand," "payable a sight," or "payable on presentation." If the instrument states something such as "payable 60 days after the first snowfall," the instrument is not payable at a definite time and is therefore not negotiable.

80

A further requirement of negotiability is that it must be payable to "the order of" or "to the bearer." An instrument is considered payable to the order of when it states "pay to the order of Jerry Smith," "pay to Jerry Smith on order," or "pay to Jerry Smith or assigns." If the instrument simply says "pay to John Smith" without the phrases noted above, it is not negotiable. The concept of negotiability means that it should be transferable. Therefore, an instrument that provides "pay to Jerry Smith," doesn't on the face of it give Jerry Smith the authority to transfer the document.

An instrument may also be made payable to "the bearer." This means that it is payable to whoever possesses the instrument. An instrument is considered payable to the bearer if it is written payable to "the bearer," "payable to whoever has possession," "whoever possesses this note," "payable to John Smith or bearer," "payable to cash," or payable to a fictitious person. If the instrument says "pay to the order of" and that order is blank after these words the instrument is considered a bearer instrument and whoever possesses it may fill in his own name. It is then payable to him.

NEGOTIATION

Under Article III of the Uniform Commercial Code, negotiation is the physical transfer of a commercial paper with the rights of ownership to another person. It is the process by which the instrument is transferred to another party who qualifies as a holder. A "holder" has a technical meaning under the Uniform Commercial Code. He is a person who possesses the instrument and has a good title to it. In order for a person to be a holder, he must have received it by proper endorsement and without notice of any fraud.

Bearer instruments can be negotiated or transferred merely by passing them from one person to the next. Order instruments, i.e., instruments made payable to Jerry Smith or Order, require an endorsement in addition to a physical transfer of the document. For the holder of the document to possess the basic rights, the payee's signature must be valid. For example, if you pick up a check made payable to the order of Jerry Smith and fraudulently endorse Jerry Smith's name to the back, then this is an invalid transfer of the document.

ENDORSEMENT

To affect an endorsement of a negotiable paper, it is not necessary that the endorsement be written on the reverse side of the instrument. It may be placed anywhere on the instrument as long as it is firmly affixed to or written on the instrument and becomes a part of it. A signature anywhere on the document that is not the maker or the payee is considered by law as an endorsement.

Words of negotiability such as pay to the order of, etc., are not required in an endorsement. A blank endorsement is one where the payee merely signs his name to the document. A blank endorsement changes an order paper into a bearer paper. Then, it may be transferred by delivery alone. A typical blank endorsement would be one in which a check is made payable to the order of Jerry Smith. Then Jerry Smith endorses the check with only his name "Jerry Smith." This is a blank endorsement, and the instrument has now become a bearer instrument transferable by mere delivery alone. If Jerry Smith had written on the instrument, "pay to the order of Paul Smith," this would be a special endorsement. Unlike a case involving a blank endorsement, Paul Smith must endorse it to transfer ownership of it. Note that there is no requirement to include the term "pay to order of," because it is assumed that Paul Smith would have the right to transfer it.

Any blank or special endorsement includes the implied warranty that the instrument will be paid upon demand or when due, that the instrument is valid, and that there are no forgeries involved on it.

If the check or instrument is not paid, the individual who holds it may collect the amount due from any of the endorsees. He cannot collect the amount when the endorser adds the words "without recourse." This type of endorsement is considered a qualified endorsement. The words "without recourse" mean that the endorser does not guarantee payment of the document. The implied warranty of title, however, is still present.

HOLDERS IN DUE COURSE

"Holders in due course" is a technical term used by the courts to describe persons who in good faith possess a check or other negotiable instrument which is free and clear of any forgery of those names necessary in the chain of title. According to the UCC, a holder in due course is one who in good faith takes the instrument for value without notice that it is overdue or has been dishonored, or has any defense against it or claim on the part of any person.

Value merely refers to the fact that the note or the check was received, not as a gift, but for something of value that was given in exchange for a promise of goods or other consideration.

Good faith means honesty in fact, the test of which is subjective. It also means what the individual actually believes. It doesn't have to be reasonably good faith, only good faith. Thus, as long as the individual honestly believes something, regardless of the reasonableness of his belief, it would qualify as a good faith belief.

The third requirement is that the check or instrument be taken without notice that it is overdue or has been dishonored. If a check is presented within a reasonable time after it is made, and there is no indication that it has been refused payment by the bank, then it is not considered overdue. If, however, it is a note with a payment date and the date has passed, then the note is considered overdue.

DEFENSES

In order to promote the negotiability of checks, bonds, etc., and therefore, the transferability of negotiable instruments, the courts have established two types of defenses when the legality of negotiable paper is challenged, personal defenses and real defenses. Personal defenses cannot be used to defeat the claim of a holder in due course. Personal defenses are effective only between the maker and the original payee. If the check or negotiable instrument has been transferred to a holder in due course, a personal defense may not be used to prevent him from collecting the note. Only a real defense may be set up.

The only real defenses are:

- Infancy (that the individuals who made the check or negotiable instrument were not old enough to enter into a contract).
- Incompetency to contract, in that the individual has been declared judicially incompetent.
- Illegality in the underlying transaction which renders the entire obligation void.
- Duress, in that the check or negotiable instrument occurred in a situation where one party acted involuntarily because of duress.
- Forgery of the signature of a necessary party to the document or a material alteration in the terms of the document. If any name not necessary to the chain of title is forged, it is immaterial. However, to be a holder in due course, an individual must take good title. Therefore, the names of the persons required to transfer the title cannot be forged.

A material alteration of a document is when its terms have been changed without the maker's approval. If the document is materially altered, a holder in due course may enforce the document in its original terms, but not in its materially altered forms. For example, if a check was written for $100 and was altered illegally by someone to read $1,000, a holder in good course could still enforce the instrument for $100 but not for $1,000. All other defenses that may be set up to prevent payment of a negotiable instrument are personal defenses and cannot be used against holders in good course to justify nonpayment.

COLLECTING ON A NEGOTIABLE INSTRUMENT

The Uniform Commercial Code specifies certain procedures that will operate in the trial of cases involving the collection of, or in attempts to collect, negotiable instruments. Production of an instrument by a holder entitles him to a directed verdict or a verdict in his favor unless the defense establishes a defense. Under the UCC a holder isn't required to prove that he is a holder in due course unless that defense is raised. Unless the defendant specifically denies the validity of any signatures in the pleadings, the signatures are considered genuine. If the defendant denies the validity of his signature, the signature is nevertheless presumed valid and the defendant must establish that it is not his.

LIABILITY

No one is liable on a negotiable instrument unless his signature clearly appears on it, or unless his signature is placed on it by an agent he has authorized to sign for him. By signing an instrument in the proper form, its maker agrees to pay it according to its tenure when it is due. If the check is dishonored (not paid when presented), he then has guaranteed that he will pay the amount due.

If an authorized agent signs the principal's name without putting his own name on an instrument, only the principal will be liable. If the agent was not authorized to sign the principal's name and does, he will be held personally liable just as if he had signed it with his own name. If an authorized agent signs his and his principal's name and discloses the agency relationship, only the principal will be liable. If an agent signs only his own name and doesn't disclose the fact of the agency or the principal's name, he will be liable on the instrument whether he was authorized to sign it or not.

An endorser is one who usually signs on the back of the instrument. However a signature anywhere on the document that cannot be accounted for otherwise is considered an endorsement. Under usual circumstances, an endorsement transfers all the rights of the transferor to the recipient. An endorser is liable if the check is returned for insufficient funds or if it is otherwise dishonored.

To hold the endorser liable, he must be notified within a certain period of time that the check was dishonored. Signing a negotiable instrument with a general endorsement in effect guarantees that it will be paid. If you endorse the note or check "without recourse," the only things you are guaranteeing are that the title is genuine and that there are no forgeries. You are not guaranteeing payment of the instrument at the time it is presented for payment.

Chapter 12

Protecting Your Invention

T he laws governing patents are discussed in this chapter. The U.S. Constitution gives Congress the power to enact laws relating to patents in Article 1, Section 8. Under this power, Congress from time to time has enacted various laws relating to patents. The first patent law was enacted in 1790, and the current law is a general revision that was enacted in July 1952 and became effective in January 1953. That statue established the Patent and Trademark Office as a part of the U.S. Department of Commerce. The Patent and Trademark Office is responsible for administering the law that relates to the granting of patents, and to other provisions relating to patents.

WHAT CAN BE PATENTED

Patent law determines the general field of subject matter that can be patented, and the conditions under which a patent may be obtained. According to the statute, any person who invents or discovers any new or useful process, machine, manufacture, or composition of matter, or makes any new or useful improvements thereto, may get a patent subject to the conditions and the requirements of the patent statutes and regulations prescribed by the Patent and Trademark Office.

In order for the item or process to be patented, the patent law requires that it be useful. The term useful has been interpreted as referring to the condition that a subject matter have a useful purpose. If a machine under patent consideration doesn't perform its intended purpose, then a patent will be refused. For example, at the turn of the century the U.S. Patent Office refused to patent an airplane because it determined that machines couldn't fly. Recently, inventions of alleged perpetual motion machines have been refused patents based on the Patents Office's conclusion that they do not operate as intended to.

The courts have added certain limits as to what can or can not be patented. For example, a method of doing business cannot be patented. The Atomic Energy Act of 1954 excludes the patenting of inventions used solely in the utilization of special nuclear material or atomic energy for atomic weapons. A patent cannot be granted on mixtures of ingredients, such as medicines, unless there is more to the mixture than the affect of its components. For this reason, so-called patented medicines are ordinarily not patented. A patent is granted upon a new machine, a manufacture, a process, etc., and not on the mere idea or suggestion behind them. To be patentable, a complete description of the actual machine or process or subject matter must be submitted with the patent application.

For an invention or a process to be patentable, it must be new as defined in the patent law. It isn't considered new if it was known, sold, or used by others or patented or described in a publication in this country or a foreign country before its development by the applicant for the patent. Thus, a patentable item must be sufficiently different from anything used or described in the past that it is unobvious to a person having ordinary skill in the technology relating to the invention. For example, substituting one type of material for another or changing the size of an object are not sufficiently different changes to allow the patenting of the item.

THE PATENT OFFICE

The original Patent Office was established in 1802 and fell under the auspices of the Department of State. In the reorganization of 1836, a Commissioner of Patents was appointed. In 1849, the office was transferred to the Department of Interior. It was later transferred to the Department of Commerce where it is today.

The primary responsibilities of the Patent Office are to administer the patent laws as they relate to the granting of letters of patents for inventions, and to perform other duties relating to patents. The office examines patent applications to ascertain if the applicants are legally entitled to patents. It grants patents when it determines that they are patentable. It maintains a search room for the public to use to examine patents and records, and supplies copies of records and other papers. The Patent Office has no jurisdiction over the questions of infringement and enforcement of patents over matters relating to the promotion or use of patents or inventions.

Examining patent applications is the largest and probably the most important function of the Patent Office. The work is divided among a number of examining groups, each group having jurisdiction over certain assigned fields of technology. Each group is headed by a group director and staffed by examiners. In 1985, the Patent and Trademark Office had approximately 3,100 employees, about one-half of whom were examiners. The others had technical or legal training.

When a patent application is received, an examiner reviews the application to determine whether a patent can be granted. If he determines that a patent should not be granted, the applicant has a right of appeal to the Board of Appeals within the Patent Office.

Patent applications are received at the rate of 100,000 a year. In 1984, the office received more than 5,000,000 pieces of correspondence.

Files of approved patent applications, located in the searchroom of the U.S. Patent and Trademark Office. The files are open to the public. Prior to submitting an application for a patent, visit the searchroom and look at previous applications for form and content. Note, the files are very similar to those pertaining to trademarks noted in Chapter 5.

PUBLICATIONS OF THE PATENT OFFICE

Printed copies of any patent identified by a patent number may be purchased from the Patent Office for $1 each plus postage. Plant patents in color are $8 each (prices as of 1985).

The Patent Office also publishes the *Official Gazette*. It is published in two parts each Tuesday. One part pertains to patents and the other to trademarks. For a discussion on trademarks, see an earlier chapter regarding trademarks. The *Official Gazette* is sold by subscription and by single copies from the Superintendent of Documents, U.S. Government Printing Office, Washington, D.C. 20402.

Since July 1952, the illustrations and claims of patents have been arranged in the *Official Gazette* according to the Patent Office's classification of subject matter. This permits ready reference to patents in any particular field. A geographical index of the residences of inventors has been included in the gazette since 1965. Copies of the *Of-*

ficial Gazette may be found in public libraries in larger cities and in most major universities.

INDEX OF PATENTS

A two-volume annual index to the *Official Gazette* is published each year. One volume is an index of patent applications by the inventors or patentees name, and the other is an index by subject matter of the patents. In addition, the Patent Office also publishes a loose-leaf book listing all of the classes and subclasses of inventions in the Patent and Trademark Office classification system. There is also a subject matter index and other information relating to the classification. This book is revised from time-to-time. An additional area regarding regulations is contained in Title 7 of the Code of Federal Regulations (CFR). All of these publications are available from the Superintendent of Documents.

GENERAL INFORMATION ON PATENTS

Any requests for information on patents should be addressed to the Commissioner of Patents, Washington, D.C. 20231. The Patent Office is located at Crystal Plaza #3, 2021 Jefferson Davis Highway, Arlington, Virginia. Because patents are subdivided by subject areas, individuals should write a separate letter of inquiry regarding each patent. Any letters concerning a patent should state the name of the patentee, the invention, the patent number, and the date.

The Patent Office will not respond to inquiries concerning the novelty or patentability of an invention in advance of filing an application. It also will not give advice as to the possible infringement of a patent, or advise of the propriety of filing an application, or to say whether or not or by whom the alleged invention has been patented. However, the office will give general information. Call or write to the office at the above address.

PATENT SEARCHES

The scientific library of the Patent Office is also in Arlington. It has available to the public more than 120,000 volumes of scientific and technical books in various languages, 90,000 bound volumes of periodicals devoted to science and technology, the official journals of 77 foreign patent organizations and more than 12 million foreign patents. A search room is provided for the public, and it is open Monday through Friday. Patents are arranged according to the Patent and Trademark classification system of more than 300 classes and 112,000 subclasses. By searching in this classification system, it is easy to determine whether or not a previous application has been patented on the same subject matter before actually filing an application. The search room also contains a set of U.S. patents arranged in numerical order, and a complete set of the *Official Gazette*. It is open from 8:00 A.M. to 8:00 P.M. Monday through Friday, except on legal holidays. Clerks are available to tell you how to search for patents. They will not search a specific case for you.

In addition to the search library in Arlington, the Patent Office has 32 branch offices throughout the United States listed as Patent Depository Libraries. The depository libraries receive current issues of U.S. patents and maintain collections of earlier issued patents. They should contain enough information for you to search out any patent question. For the location of the depository library nearest you, contact the Patent Office in Washington, D.C. Officials there can give you the address and operating hours of the one nearest to you.

APPLYING FOR A PATENT

According to the patent laws, generally only the inventor may apply for the patent. There are exceptions, but if an individual is not the inventor, but applies for a patent, in most cases, the patent would be invalid even if it were obtained. It is a criminal offense to state that you invented a patented product when you did not. If two or more persons jointly develop an invention, they apply for a patent as joint inventors. A person who only makes a financial contribution toward the development of an invention is not considered a joint inventor. Any officers or employees of the Patent Office are prohibited by law from applying for a patent or directly or indirectly acquiring any patent right or interest in any patent, except by inheritance or bequest.

Application For Patent

An application for a patent is made to the Commissioner of Patents and Trademarks. As a minimum it should include a written document that comprises the specification (description and claims of invention), an oath regarding the truth of the information contained in the document, the drawings in cases where drawings are possible, and the filing fee. The oath or declaration must be legibly written and printed in permanent ink on one side of the paper.

A patent application is not forwarded to an examiner until all of its required parts are received. If the papers are incomplete or so defective that they cannot be accepted, the applicant will be notified of the deficiencies and given a time period in which to remedy them. An additional surcharge may be required for correcting an incomplete application. The applications are numbered consecutively when they are received. The applicant is informed by a filing receipt of the serial number and filing date of the application.

The applicant's oath is required by law. The inventor must swear that he believes himself to be the original and first inventor of the subject matter of the application. The inventor must swear the oath before a notary public or other officers authorized to administer oaths. If the individual does not believe in taking an oath, a declaration may be used instead.

The application and oath must be signed by the inventor or by a person legally entitled to make application on the inventor's behalf. The inventor's first or full middle name, or his first or middle initial, are required on the application and oath. The inventor's post office address is also required. The Patent Office does not furnish a blank form for filing a patent, however, but it will provide specimen forms that may be retyped with the appropriate spaces completed.

Filing Fees

The total filing fees for an application, except in design and plant cases, consist of basic and additional fees. The basic fee in 1985 was $300. A discount is given if the inventor is a "small entity," i.e., an individual inventor, a small business, or a nonprofit institution. In this case, the filing fee is $150.

DESCRIPTIONS AND CLAIMS OF PATENTS

The application must include a written description of the invention and the manner and process of making and using it. The description must be written in full, clear, and exact terms to enable anyone skilled in the technological area to which the invention pertains to make and use the same invention.

The specifications must describe the precise invention in such a manner as to distinguish it from other inventions. It must completely describe the process, the machine, the manufacture, and the composition of matter or improvements invented, and it must explain the mode of operation or the principle, whichever is applicable.

In the case of improvements, the specifications must particularly point out the part(s) of the process, the machine, the manufacture, or the composition of matter to which the improvement relates. The description should be confined to the specific improvement and to the parts necessary for a complete understanding of the improvement.

The title of the invention should be as short and specific as possible. It should head the first page of the specification. If it doesn't, then it should appear at the beginning of the application. A brief abstract of the technical disclosure in the specification must be stated on a separate page immediately following the claims in a paragraph entitled abstract of disclosure. A summary of the invention should precede the detailed description.

A brief description of several views of any drawings should be included. The detailed description of the invention should relate to the different views through the use of reference numerals.

The following order is required in the specification:

- The title of the invention and a preamble stating the name, citizenship, and residence of the applicant.
- Cross references to any related applications, if any.
- A brief summary of the invention.
- A brief description of several views of the drawings, if any.
- A detailed description.
- Claim or claims.
- An abstract of the disclosure.

Models were once required to be submitted with all patent applications. They are no longer required because the description, the specifications, and the drawings of the invention must be clear-enough to disclose the invention without the aid of a model. Models should not be submitted unless the examiner specifically requests them. This doesn't happen very often, but models have been required lately in applications for alleged perpetual motion devices. When an invention relates to a composition of matter, the applicant may be required to furnish specimens of the composition or its ingredients for inspection or testing. If the invention is microbiological, a deposit of the micro-organism involved is required.

EXAMINATION OF APPLICATIONS

When the applications are accepted, they are assigned to an examining group in charge of the technology related to the application. The groups examine the applications in the order in which they have been filed or, in certain cases, in an order established by the commissioner. Applications will not be advanced out of turn for examination except on the order of the commissioner or by a federal court order.

The applicant or his attorney is notified in writing of the examiner's decision. If the application if denied, the reasons for the denial must be explained in the notification letter.

No further action is required if the patent is granted. When the applicant receives a rejection letter, he may amend his application by stating that he will take care of the problems listed by the examiner, or he may request a reconsideration of the examiner's initial decision, pointing out in detail where the examiner is mistaken. If the examiner still refuses to grant the patent application after its resubmission, then the applicant may appeal his decision to the Patent Board of Appeals. But in two out of every three cases, a patent is granted by the Patent Office.

If an application is returned with a rejection letter or a request for additional information, the applicant has six months to request reconsideration or file an amended application. If the applicant doesn't respond within the six months, the application is considered abandoned and no longer pending in the Patent Office.

APPEALS

If the examiner persists in rejecting claims in the application or if his rejection is final, an applicant may appeal to the Board of Appeals in the Patent and Trademark Office. The Board of Appeals consists of the Commissioner of Patents and Trademarks, the Deputy Commissioner, Assistant Commissioners, and the Chief Examiner. Usually, each appeal is heard by a panel of three of the members.

The applicant must pay an appeal fee and file a brief to support his position. He may request a hearing. If the Board of Appeals is still adverse to the applicant, he may take his appeal to the Court of Appeals for the Federal Circuit or sue the commissioner in the U.S. District Court in Washington, D.C. If this happens, the court will review the record and either affirm the office's actions or order the Commissioner of Patents to grant a patent.

PATENT RIGHTS

A patent grants to its owner the right to exclude others from making, using, or selling the invention or process in the United States and its territories for a period of 17 years.

A patentee cannot make, use, or sell his invention if to do so would violate the law. For example, the patentee of a new airplane would not be entitled to use the patented airplane in violation of FAA regulations or any other state or federal regulations.

The patent grants the patentee the right to exclude others from commercially exploiting the invention or process. The patentee is the only one who can make, use, or sell the invention, or sell the rights to use the invention or process.

The term of the patent is for 17 years. However a maintenance fee is due and payable at the end of three and a half, seven and a half, and eleven and a half years after the original grant for all patents issued after December 19, 1980. If the maintenance fee is not paid at the specific time, the patent may expire. After the patent has expired, anyone may make, use, or sell the invention without the permission of the patentee, providing that the rights and matters covered by other unexpired patents are not used.

Recording of Assignments

The Patent Office has recorded all of the patents it has granted; therefore, if you sell your patent or buy one, the assignment should be recorded with the U.S. Patent Office.

Infringements of Patents

As noted earlier, the Patent Office has no jurisdiction over questions relating to the infringements of patents. An infringement consists of the unauthorized use, or the making or selling of a patented invention within the United States during the term of the patent. If you feel that your patent has been infringed upon, request relief in the appropriate federal court. The patent's owner may ask the court for an injunction to stop the infringement. He may also ask the court for an award of damages because of the infringement. In any infringement suit, the defendant may question the validity of the patent, in which case the validity of the patent is then decided by the court. Suits for the infringement of patents follow the rules and procedures of federal courts. From the decision of the district court, an appeal can be taken to the court of appeals for the federal circuit. From there it could be taken to the U.S. Supreme Court. The U.S. government may use any patented invention without the permission of its owner, but the owner is entitled to receive reasonable compensation for the use by or for the government.

ANSWERS TO QUESTIONS FREQUENTLY ASKED

The following questions are reprinted from a U.S. Patent Office booklet entitled *General Information Concerning Patents*.

Question 1. What do the terms "Patent Pending" and "Patent Applied for" mean?
  Answer: They are used by a manufacturer or seller to inform the public that a new application for a patent on an article is on file in the Patent Office. The law imposes a fine on those who use these terms to deceive the public.

Question 2. Is there any danger that the Patent Office will give others information in my application while it is pending?
  Answer: No. All patent applications are maintained in the strictest secrecy until the patent is issued. After the patent is issued however, the office may file all information concerning the patent. The patent application and all correspondence leading up to the issuance of the patent are made available in the search room for public inspection. Copies of these files may be purchases from the Patent Office.

Question 3. May I write to the Patent Office directly about my application after it is filed?
  Answer: The office will answer an applicant's inquiry as to the status of the ap-

plication and inform him whether his application has been rejected, allowed, or is awaiting action. However, if you have a patent attorney or agent, the office cannot correspond with both of you concerning the merits of your application. All comments concerning your invention should be forwarded through your attorney or patent agent.

Question 4. Is it necessary to go to the Patent Office to transact business concerning patent matters?

Answer: No. Most business with the office is conducted by correspondence. Interviews regarding patent applications can be arranged with examiners if necessary.

Question 5. If two or more persons work together to make an invention, to whom will the patent be granted?

Answer: If each had a share in the ideas in forming the invention, they are joint inventors and a patent will be issued to them jointly on the basis of a proper patent application filed by them jointly. If on the other hand, one of these persons has provided all of the ideas of the invention, and the other has only followed instructions in making it, the person who contributed the ideas is the sole inventor. The patent application and patent shall be in his name alone.

Question 6. If one person furnishes all ideas to make an invention and another employs him or furnishes the money for the building and testing of the invention, should the application be filed by them jointly?

Answer: No. The application must be filed by the true inventor and filed in the Patent Office in his name.

Question 7. Does the Patent Office control the fees charged by patent attorneys or agents for their services?

Answer: No. This is a matter between you and your patent agent, the office takes no part.

Question 8. Will the Patent Office help me select a patent attorney or agent to make my patent search or to prepare and prosecute my patent application?

Answer: No. The office cannot make this choice for you.

Question 9. Will the Patent Office advise me as to whether a certain patent promotion organization is reliable and trustworthy?

Answer: No. The office has no control over such organizations, and does not supply information about them.

Question 10. Are there any organizations in my area that can tell me how and where I may be able to obtain assistance in developing and marketing my invention?

Answer: Yes. In your own or neighboring communities, you may inquire of such organizations as the Chamber of Commerce, banks, and areas departments of power companies and railroads. Many communities have locally financed industrial development organizations that can help you locate manufacturers and individuals who might be interested in promoting your idea. You can also obtain assistance from one of the district offices of the U.S. Chamber of Commerce or the Small Business Administration located near you. The addresses of these offices are located in your local telephone directory.

Question 11. Are there any state government agencies that can help me in developing and marketing my invention?

Answer: Yes. In nearly every state there are state planning and development agencies or departments of commerce and industry which seek new products and new processes to assist manufacturers and communities in the state. If you do not know the names or addresses of your state organization, you can obtain this information by writing your state governor.

Question 12. Can the Patent Office assist me in developing and marketing my patent?

Answer: Only to a limited extent. The office cannot act or advise concerning the business transactions or arrangements that are involved in the making and development of an invention. However, the office will publish at the request of a patent owner a notice in the *Official Gazette* that the patent is available for licensing or sale. The fee for this service is $6.

Chapter 13

Leasing Business Property

I n this chapter, the legal problems associated with leasing business property are discussed. Before agreeing to lease any property, the business owner should be familiar with the state laws that establish the rights and liabilities of both the tenant and the landlord. The laws pertaining to this subject vary from state to state; therefore only the general principles pertaining to the subject are discussed here.

The two basic types of leases are the fixed-term lease and the periodic lease. Under a fixed-term lease, the length of the lease is set, as is the amount of rent. Except for specific reasons, neither the tenant nor the landlord may cancel the lease or vary the amount of the rent without mutual consent. A periodic lease is an open-ended agreement for an indefinite period. The lease is renewed each rent period by the payment of the rent. This type of lease is also called a "month to month."

The fixed-term lease protects you from being forced out of the premises until the lease expires and also from the rent being raised. It has the disadvantage of binding the businessperson to pay the rent for the duration of the lease, even when the business is discontinued. A periodic lease binds neither the tenant nor the landlord beyond the periodic rent period. The periodic lease, however, provides little stability for the business owner and thus should be used with caution.

Prior to signing any lease, read it carefully and make sure you understand all of its provisions, conditions, and terms. If you are in doubt, check with your attorney. Any verbal assurances by the landlord should be written out and added as a lease provision before you sign the lease agreement.

Examine the lease document for the following provisions and conditions: (It is unlikely that all of the provisions listed below may be included in the lease in a manner favorable to you. You should consider each as at least a bargaining point with the landlord.)

1. Is there a clear provision regarding the return of the security and/or cleaning deposit at the termination of the lease?

2. What are the requirements on the landlord to maintain the property according to certain standards?

3. Under what conditions may either you or the landlord cancel the lease prior to its expiration date?

4. Does the lease provide you with an option to renew the lease in order to protect your rights to stay in the same location?

5. Does the lease allow the landlord to enter the property at any time without prior notice to you?

6. Does the landlord retain a set of keys to your business?

7. Does the lease obligate you to follow any rules formulated by the landlord any time after the lease is signed?

8. Does the lease release the landlord from responsibility for any damage to your property, even if it is his fault?

9. Are you under the terms of the lease required to maintain any fixtures, appliances, or portions of the property?

10. Does the security or any other deposit that the tenant is required to post pay interest?

11. Do you have the right to sublease the premises for the duration of the lease if your business closes or if you can no longer use the property?

12. Do you have the right to put up signs for your business without the landlord's permission?

13. Can you use the property for any lawful purpose?

14. Is the landlord prohibited from renting other space in the same building to other tenants who will compete with your business?

15. What rights do you have in the use of the common property such as hallways, driveways, elevators, parking lots, etc.?

16. If the amount of your rent is based on gross receipts of your business, are provisions made for the deduction of returned merchandise, delivery or installation charges, refundable deposits, and sales tax?

17. Does the lease provide you with an option to renew the lease in order to protect your rights to stay in the same location?

PRIOR TO TAKING POSSESSION

Before you accept possession of the premises, there are certain steps you should take to protect yourself in the event any disputes occur during the term of the lease or when you vacate the premises.

1. Keep a record of all transactions between you and the landlord. This includes: copies of the lease, notices, letters between you and the landlord, receipts for rent, etc.

2. Before you move in, complete a detailed check-off list or inventory as to the condition of the premises and of any property included in the lease. Keep one copy

of this and forward one copy to the landlord. For example, if the walls need painting, make that notation on your list even if the landlord promises to paint.

3. If necessary to accurately reflect the condition of the premises, take pictures.

SECURITY DEPOSITS

In most states, state statutes have specific rules relating to the holding and return of security deposits. These statutes usually provide that the landlord may keep only that part of the deposit necessary to pay for unpaid rent, to repair any damages caused by the tenant, and to clean the building. At the end of the lease, the landlord is required to notify you in writing either by personal delivery or certified mail of any deductions for your security deposit. The burden is on the landlord to establish the right to withhold any portion of the deposit. In most states, a security or cleaning deposit cannot be nonrefundable if the tenant leaves the premises in good, clean condition, and there are no damages chargeable to him.

State statutes usually require the landlord to pay interest on security deposits. He is also required to refund the deposit or give a detailed, written explanation for withholding the deposit or any part thereof within a certain time after the lease is terminated, usually 15 to 30 days. To withhold any part of the deposit for damages caused by the tenant, the landlord must establish that the damages are in excess of those caused by the normal wear and tear. If the security deposit isn't returned as required, seek assistance from any tenant association in your area or consider using small claims court. If these are not reasonably available to you, see your attorney.

Chapter 14

Law of Agency

A gency is the legal status in which one person, an agent, is authorized to conduct business for another party, a principle. Except in the very smallest of businesses, a business owner must rely to some extent on others to conduct portions of his business. Because of this requirement the owner needs to be familiar with the laws of agency.

CREATION OF THE AGENCY

As a general rule, any person who can legally enter into a contract may be a principle in the agency relationship. However, a person may be an agent even though he can't enter into a binding contract. Thus, while a minor cannot be a principle in the agency relationship, he may be an agent. In most cases, because unincorporated associations may not enter into contracts, they cannot be principles. Individual members, acting on behalf of the associations, may in most states be principles; in which case, the individuals are personally liable on the contract.

A person is usually disqualified from being an agent if the law requires that he be licensed and he isn't, i.e., a real estate broker. An agent cannot represent both parties unless they are informed of the facts and approve the relationship. In addition, the agent cannot act secretly for his own benefit. These last two restrictions on an agent's actions are designed to ensure that the agent owes undivided loyalty to the principle.

The agency relationship may be created by either the acts of the parties or by operation of law. The usual method of creating a relationship is for the principle to appoint the agent to act on his behalf by communicating with him either verbally or in writing. This is considered actual authority. The relationship may be established by an act or apparent authority, in which the principle through a third person authorizes the agent to act on his behalf. The relationship is also established by the concept of inherent authority. In this situation, the agent has the authority to act on the behalf of the principle because of his position in relation to the principle. For example, your business manager or supervisor has the inherent authority to act in your name because of their position of authority. The agency relationship in this situation is created by operation of law to prevent fraud or injustice.

AGENT'S AUTHORITY

An agent's authority to act on behalf of his principle may be actual, apparent, or inherent. Actual authority is that authority an agent has because his principle has given it to him and he has accepted it. To have actual authority, the agent and the principle both must consent to the relationship. No consideration or payments to the agent are necessary. If the agency relationship involves buying or selling land, the agreement usually must be in writing. In most other cases, no written agreement is necessary to establish the relationship.

Implied authority of an agent is the result of authority implied by reason of the agent's relationship with the principle or the principle's business, by reason of custom and usage, and by acquiescence. To have implied authority by custom and usage, the agent must know the general custom and act in accordance with it. Implied authority by acquiescence is when the principle fails to object to the agent's actions or ratifies previous similar acts the agent has taken.

Unless he is specifically authorized by the principle, the agent cannot delegate his authority to a third person. The rationale is that their relationship is consentual in nature, and the principle has not consented to others performing the agent's functions. Exceptions to this general rule are when the acts the agent gives to a third person are purely mechanical or ministerial, when circumstances indicate that at the time the delegation was made to the agent a subagent would be necessary, and when it's a general custom of a particular business to delegate an agent's duties to a subagent.

An agent with actual authority to purchase on the principle's behalf will have the implied authority to pay for the goods either out of any of the principle's funds he has in his control, or on credit. There is also the implied authority to accept the delivery of any goods that he has the authority to purchase.

An agent who has the authority to sell the principle's property has the implied authority to give general warranties regarding the property. If the agent possesses the property, then he has the implied authority to collect payment. He must accept payment only in cash unless otherwise approved by the principle. An agent does not have the implied power to accept a check as payment for the property or sell on credit unless the principle previously approved it. An agent with the authority to sell usually has the authority to deliver the properly on receipt of payment.

Termination of the Agency

An agency relationship can be cancelled in several ways. If the agency relationship is for a specific period of time, it will automatically terminate at the end of that period. If no time period is agreed upon between the agent and his principle, then the courts will imply termination within a reasonable time unless the agent's acts are ongoing. In many cases, the agency terminates when a certain event occurs. For example, if you hire an agent to sell property for you, the agency terminates when the property is sold.

A change of circumstances that materially changes the relationship will also terminate the agency. The following changes of circumstances are sufficient to terminate the agency: destruction of the property that is the subject matter of the agency, closing of the business associated with the agency, a drastic change in business conditions, a change in laws that substantially modifies the business relationship, and insolvency of either the principle or his agent.

A major breach of an agent's fiduciary duty by the agent will terminate the relationship. The agency relationship will terminate when a party either dies or loses the capacity to enter into a contract, e.g., becomes insane. When corporations or partnerships are involved, dissolution will also terminate the agency. Either party may terminate the agency by informing the other party. The power to terminate exists even in those cases when there is a contractual agreement not to terminate. In this case, the party breaching the contract may be liable for breach of contract, but he still has the right to cancel the agency.

There are two exceptions to the unilateral right of either party to cancel the relationship. One exception is an agency "coupled with an interest." This is when the agent has an interest in the property involved. For example, a principle borrows $50,000 from an agent and gives him the authority to sell a certain piece of property and to subtract the $50,000 from the sale proceeds. In this case, because the agency is "coupled with an interest," the principle may not cancel agency unless he first repays the amount borrowed. The other exception is in those cases when the grant of authority is given to the agent or a third person to protect a debt or other obligation.

Apparent Authority

A person is usually not responsible for another's acts unless that person is authorized to act on his behalf. An exception is the "apparent authority" concept used by the courts to prevent injustice to third persons. The mere statement by a person that he is an agent of a certain person is insufficient to establish the agency. The third person has a duty to ascertain whether or not an agent has the authority to act in a particular situation. If the principle has led others to believe that the agency relationship exists, he will be bound by the acts that an agent in that situation would customarily have the authority to do.

The agency relationship would be used by the courts when the principle has a duty to deny the relationship but fails to do so. For example, if John in Joe's presence tells others that he is Joe's agent, Joe has a duty to deny the relationship. If he fails to, then any third persons present may consider that John is in fact an agent of Joe.

One may also be held to be an agent when the principle negligently allows another person to act as his agent. For example, a stranger comes into the business place and no one is present. The stranger then waits on a customer, sells a product, and pockets the money. In this case, because it was reasonable for the customer to assume that the stranger was a clerk, the business owner cannot force the customer to pay for the merchandise a second time.

If the agent's authority is stated in writing and the writing is still in the possession of the agent, a third person may reasonably assume that the agency relationship is ongoing. However, if the document has an expiration date, it would not be reasonable for a person to act on the assumption that an agency exists after that date.

A similar situation exists when an individual dies after writing some checks. The bank may continue to honor the transactions pursuant to its agreement with the individual until it receives notice of his death.

Inherent Authority

In some situations, the courts find an inherent authority for the agent to act in order to protect innocent third persons. Under this concept, a principle is liable for the wrong-doings committed by his employees if the acts were within the scope of the employee's duties. For example, a car salesman is instructed by his employer not to warrant the fitness of any of the automobiles being offered for sale. In violation of these orders, the salesman warrants the correctness of the indicated mileage on an automobile. In this case, the employer will be held to the warranty. In this regard, scope of employment means that the employee is engaged in the furtherance of his employer's business.

If the agent possesses the merchandise and is either a regular dealer in that type of merchandise or has indicia of ownership, it is assumed that he is authorized to sell the merchandise. Mere possession of the goods is insufficient to establish the right to sell.

Ratification

If an unauthorized person acts as a business owner's agent, the business owner may ratify the unauthorized transaction. If the owner does this, he is bound by the act of the unauthorized agent. To ratify the act, the principle must know of the material facts involved in the transaction and accept the entire transaction. He cannot approve the part favorable to him and deny the unfavorable portion. A principle may ratify only legal acts.

The ratification of an agent's unauthorized acts may be by express approval, by acceptance of the benefits of the act, or by silence when the principle had a duty to speak. The third person may withdraw from the transaction if he notifies the principle before the principle ratifies the transaction.

PARTIES TO AN AGENCY RELATIONSHIP

Generally speaking, the third person may not sue an agent because his contract was with the principle and not the agent. Exceptions to this general rule are when the agent fails to disclose that he is acting on behalf of a principle, or when there is a clear intent to bind the agent in the terms of the contract.

If the third person knows the principle, and the agent acted within his authority, the principle will be bound on the contract. If the principle's identity was unknown when the contract was entered into, then both the agent and the principle will be bound on the contract and the third person may sue either or both.

An agent is liable for breach of warranty when he acts on the principle's behalf without his authorization. In stating that he is acting on someone's behalf, the agent warrants the existence of the principle, that the principle has the capacity to enter into contracts, and that he has the authority to act as an agent in this situation.

If the agent fails to disclose that he is acting on behalf of a principle (undisclosed principle), the third person may sue either the agent or the principle when default occurs. The third person may sue both, but he can collect from only one. For example, if the third person sues the agent and gets a judgment against him, he can still attempt to collect from the undisclosed principle until the judgment is paid.

Because the transaction between the agent and the third person is for the principle's benefit, the agent usually cannot sue for breach of the contract. The principle may sue in these situations, unless it involves a case in which the principle has fraudulently concealed his identity.

RIGHTS AND DUTIES OF AGENT AND PRINCIPLE

The agent also has the duty of undivided loyalty toward his principle. He cannot act as an agent for more than one party or self-deal with the principle's property without the principle's expressed permission. If the agent has any interests that are adverse to those of the principle, he has a duty to disclose them.

The agent will be liable for any loss his principle suffers as the result of his failure to complete his duties or follow the reasonable directions of his principle. The agent is also obligated to perform his duties in a reasonable and prudent manner. This duty even applies to those situations in which the agent is gratuitously acting on behalf of his principle.

If the agent breaches his duties, the principle may sue him for either breach of contract or in "tort." Tort refers to a suit brought because of negligent or wrongful acts that cause injuries to others. Under a breach of contract suit, the agent may be held liable for any reasonably foreseeable damages that his principle suffers as the result of his failure to fulfill the agency contract. In a suit in tort, the principle may recover for any damages suffered because of the agent's wrongful or negligent act. In some cases the principle may also collect punitive damages. Punitive damages are those damages assessed by a court in excess of the actual damages and imposed as punishment.

If the agent makes a secret profit from the relationship, his principle may bring suit to recover it. In some situations the principle may bring a court action to force his agent to account for any funds that he received as the result of the relationship. In some cases involving agent misconduct, the principle may withhold any compensation owed to the agent.

The principle owes a duty to reasonably compensate his agent for his time and effort, unless his agent has agreed to act without pay. In addition, the principle must reimburse his agent for any reasonable expenses that he expended in the furtherance of the relationship. Additional duties may be imposed by the contract. In most situations, the agent has a lien against the property of the principle for any monies owed to him.

LIABILITY

Under the doctrine of "respondeat superior", the principle may be liable for certain acts of his agent. To be liable there must be an agency relationship, and the conduct must be within the scope of employment. To be within the scope of employment, an employment situation must exist. If the agent is an independent contractor the duties of whom the principle has no right to control, no employment situation exists and the principle is not usually liable for the acts of the agent.

To determine if an employment situation exists, the courts not only look at the degree of control that the principle has over his the agent, but also whether or not his agent is engaged in a distinct business, the degree of skill involved in the duties, and the period of employment. If the court determines that the agent is in fact an employee and not an independent contractor, the employer (principle) will be liable for the torts (misconduct and negligent acts) he committed that injured others or damaged property belonging to others.

To determine if the employee was within the scope of employment, many courts use the test: "Was the employee about the employer's business when the injury or damage occurred?" Another test commonly used is "Were the acts of the employee motivated by a desire to serve the purposes of the employer?"

Chapter 15

Business Contracts

I n this chapter, the basic laws of contracts and sales are discussed in order to give the businessperson a working knowledge of this important area of the law. No business can be conducted without entering into many contractual relationships daily.

CONTRACTS

A contract is a promise or set of promises, for which the law provides a remedy for their breach. Contracts are classified as to how they were formed. They can be expressed, implied, or in the form of a quasi-contract. An expressed contract is one formed by the expressed agreement of the parties involved. An implied contract is one in which the parties' actions form the manifestations of assent. An implied contract occurs when a person in a store picks up an item of merchandise and pays for it without any statements regarding its purchase. The customer's actions in taking the merchandise and paying for it and the business's actions in accepting his money imply by their conduct that both agreed to the sale and the purchase of the item in question. Quasi-contract is one the courts construct to prevent fraud or unjust enrichment on the part of one person.

Contracts may also be classified as to whether they are bilateral or unilateral. In a bilateral contract, each party exchanges promises—it's a promise for a promise situation. For example, X promises to buy a new car and B in return promises to pay a sum of money for the car. A unilateral contract is one in which one party promises to pay for or perform some obligation when the other party does an act. For example, X tells B that he will pay him $25 to cut his lawn. In this situation, X is asking not for a promise from B, but an act.

Contracts are also classified as to their validity. A valid contract is enforceable by both sides to the contract. A void contract is totally without legal effect. A voidable contract is one in which one party can either enforce the contract or void it. This type of situation could occur when a contract is entered into with a minor. In most cases, the minor may either enforce the contract or void it because he lacks the capacity to enter into it. Some contracts are valid, but unenforceable. For example, if the contract is required to be in writing and isn't, in most states it would be valid but unenforceable.

Formation of A Contract

To enter into a contract, there must be a mutual agreement between the parties. Mutual assent means that both parties must agree to the same bargain at the same time. There must be an offer and an acceptance of the offer. An offer is a communication to the other party that the person making the offer (offerer) wants to enter into a contractual relationship with the person to whom the offer is directed (offeree). To create a contract, the offer must be accepted by the offeree.

To be a valid offer, its terms must be definite and certain. The essential elements of an offer include:

- The identity of the person or persons to whom the offer is directed.
- The subject matter of the offer must be identified.
- The compensation to be paid for the requested performance.
- The time of performance of the contract.

The identity of the person to whom the offer is directed may be determined by the actions of the offerer or any other evidence indicating to whom the offer is intended. Only the person to whom the offer is addressed may accept it. If a third person trys to accept an offer that is not addressed to him, this attempted acceptance is considered an offer by the third person that may be accepted by the original offerer.

The subject matter of the offer is sufficiently identified if the court can ascertain the subject matter with reasonable accuracy. If the subject matter involves the sale of land, the offer must identify not only which land is involved but also the price being either offered or asked for the land. If the subject matter involves the sale of goods, the quantity must be certain or confirmable.

In many cases unspecified terms in an offer will be assumed. For example, if no time has been set for the performance of the contract, within a reasonable time is assumed. If no terms of payment are set forth, then the payment is presumed to be in cash. Often uncertain items in the offer may be cured by an acceptance which includes the missing items. In this case, the offerer must accept the new items to constitute a meeting of the minds.

Termination of An Offer

The offer must be accepted in order to have a meeting of the minds before it terminates. A rejection of the offer by the person to whom the offer is directed will terminate the offer. An answer to an offer rejecting part of the offer and adding new terms is a rejection of the original offer. But it is also considered a counteroffer that may be accepted by the original offerer. For example, X when offered an opportunity to buy land at $20,000, may counteroffer with, "Not at that price, but at $15,000." This is a rejection of the original offer and thus terminates it. However, it is a new offer addressed to the original offerer.

A mere inquiry as to better terms without rejecting the original offer is not considered a counteroffer. An example is, "I am still thinking about your offer, but would you take $15,000." In this case, the original offer has not been rejected and it can be accepted later.

An offer is automatically terminated by the death or incapacity of the parties or by the destruction of the subject matter of the contract. The offer may also be terminated by the original offerer withdrawing his offer before it is accepted. If the offer states that it will expire within a certain time, the offer is terminated at the end of that time unless it is accepted sooner.

If no time limit is included in the terms of the offer, it expires after a reasonable time. Reasonable time is determined by looking at the subject matter of the contract and considering the customs and usages in business.

Acceptance of An Offer

Acceptance is an overt indication to assent to the terms of the offer. For an acceptance to be effective, it must be communicated to the offerer and the acceptance must be unequivocal. Under the Uniform Commercial Code, some additional terms may be added to the acceptance. This concept is discussed in the Sales section of this chapter. A unilateral contract is accepted by the performance of the act requested.

Consideration

For a contract agreement to be legally enforceable, "consideration" is required. In most cases, consideration is the selling price or the act bargained for. As one court stated, "Consideration is the price for enforceability in the courts." There are two essential elements necessary to constitute consideration. First, there must be a "bargained for exchange" and second, the "bargained for exchange" must be of legal value. If X agrees to buy a car from Y for $5,000, the consideration on X's part is to pay $5,000; whereas the consideration on Y's part is to transfer ownership of the automobile.

In most cases consideration must be part of a new obligation, not one previously promised or given (past consideration). As to legal value, the courts only require that the consideration have some value. Equal value is not required. Some courts, however, have held that items of "token value" have no legal value and thus are not of sufficient legal value to uphold contracts.

As a general rule a pre-existing duty will not be considered as valid consideration. If the person promising to do an act already has a pre-existing duty to do the act, the promise is not sufficient consideration. The exceptions to this rule are when additional or different consideration is given and when the pre-existing duty is owed to a third person. Not all states accept the last exception to the pre-existing duty rule. An example of a pre-existing duty situation would be one in which a supplier, already under a duty to provide you with supplies at a contract price, refuses to deliver them unless you pay a higher price. Your agreement to pay the higher price would be unenforceable in most states for lack of consideration, because the supplier already had a duty to deliver the supplies at a contract rate.

Contractual Capacity

Certain individuals lack the capacity to enter into valid, enforceable contracts. For example a person whose mental capacity is such that he is incapable of understanding the nature and effects of his acts is also incapable of entering into a valid contract.

Minors are restricted in their ability to enter into enforceable contracts. The basic rule is that if the contract is not liable for the necessities of life, a minor can cancel any contract he enters into. However, if the minor wishes to affirm the contract, he may do so and thus force the other party to comply with the terms of the contract.

There is a conflict of authority among the states as to whether a party's intoxication at the time of his entering into a contract makes the contract void. In most states, if the other party knew of the state of intoxication, he cannot take advantage of the drunken party. If, however, the other party did not know that he was dealing with a drunken individual, then the contract is enforceable.

Defenses To Enforcement of Contracts

Several common defenses are used to prevent the enforcement of a contract. The most common is that a valid and enforceable contract was never entered into between the parties.

A mutual mistake that goes to the heart of the agreement prevents the formation of a contract because there is no meeting of the minds between the offerer and the offeree. For the mistake to be sufficient enough to prevent the existence of a legal contract, the mistake must pertain to an essential part of the contract. For example, I offer to buy Y's car for $500. Y, having two cars, thinks I am buying one car whereas I intended to buy the other car. There is a mutual mistake here as to which car I am buying, so there is no agreement and thus no contract.

If the mistake is unilateral (only by one party), it usually will not prevent the formation of a valid contract. If, however, the other party knew or should have known about the mistake, he cannot take advantage of the other person's mistake. When there is mistake as to the value of an article, the courts will usually enforce the contract because the value of the article is a common risk taken in most contracts.

Generally the courts will set aside the contract if fraud or misrepresentation concerns a material part of the agreement. Contracts that are illegal or that violate public policy are also unenforceable. Typical in this regard are gambling contracts, contracts relating to crimes, and contracts that charge an illegal interest rate.

Statute of Frauds

The statute of frauds is the common law term given to those state statutes that require certain contracts to be in writing to be enforceable. Usually verbal contracts are valid, but certain agreements must be in writing. Agreements usually required in writing are promises by an executor or administrator of an estate to pay the estate's debts out of his own funds, promises to pay the debts of another, promises made in consideration of marriage, contracts that cannot be performed within a year, sale of goods valued at $500 or more, and agreements that transfer an interest in land.

Agreements that transfer an interest in land are the most common type that has to be in writing. Leases in excess of a year are also required to be in writing. Timber, fruit, crops, or similar products are not an interest in land if they are to be severed by the seller. Mortgages and other security devices on real estate are considered as an interest in land.

To determine if a contract by its terms cannot be performed within a year, look at the date the contract was entered into. For example, a contract of employment to run from January 1 until December 30, 1986, would have to be in writing if it were entered into prior to December 29, 1985. A contract to employ someone for life can be performed within a year because the person might die within the year. This contract is not required to be in writing.

As noted above, a promise for the sale of goods of $500 or more is required to be in writing by a section of the Uniform Commercial Code. See the discussion on Sales in this chapter.

The writing that is required under the statute of frauds is acceptable if it contains the identity of parties involved, the identity of the subject matter, the terms and conditions of the agreement, consideration, and the signature of the party against whom the contract is to be enforced. This writing can involve more than one document if they are logically connected. In addition, the writing may be made after the contract is entered into. A contract that fails to comply with the statute is not void, but only unenforceable.

In many states, partial performance of the contract will remove the statute's requirement. In other states, many courts allow a reasonable recovery based on the value of the goods rather than the contract price to prevent fraud. If the party admits in court that a contract exists, this satisfies the statute of fraud.

Third Parties, Rights and Duties

The general rule is that a contract creates only rights and duties on the parties to the contract. There are several situations, however, in which a contract either creates duties or rights on persons not involved in its formation. The most common situations are those in which the contract is primarily to benefit a third person (third party beneficiary contracts), and those involving the assignments of rights in a contract.

A third party beneficiary contract is one in which one person enters into a contract with another person who is to render a benefit to a third person. For example, I want to give a new car to my son. I contract with the automobile dealer to deliver a car to my son, and I pay for it. In this case, my primary motive for entering into the contract is to benefit my son. He could sue the automobile dealer for breach of contract if the dealer fails to deliver the car without adequate justification.

To sue for the nonperformance of a contract, the third party beneficiary must be the intended beneficiary. He cannot sue if he is only an indirect or incidental beneficiary. An indirect beneficiary indirectly benefits from the contract, which was not entered into for his direct benefit. For example, I enter into a contract to buy you a new car from a local automobile dealer if you will rebuild my building. While the automobile dealer will indirectly benefit from the contract, it was not intended for his direct benefit. Thus, he cannot sue for failure of one party to perform under the contract.

Intended third party beneficiaries are grouped under two general classes, creditors and donees. A creditor beneficiary is one in which the agreement is made to pay a debt to a third person. A donee beneficiary occurs when the contract's purpose is to give a gift to a third person. The third person may enforce his rights under the contract only after he learns about it and by conduct or otherwise accepts the benefits of it. Benefits cannot be forced on third persons.

Assignments of Contracts

An assignment of a contract occurs when one party to the contract transfers his interest and rights under the contract to another person. Most contracts can be assigned. The following questions must be examined to determine if a contract can be assigned by one party to a third person:

- Is the contract of a personal nature or of the type that limits its performance to the named individuals in the contract?
- Do the contract terms permit assignment of the rights and benefits under the contract?
- Does the assignment violate law or public policy?
- Does the assignment impose additional duties, rights, or obligations on the other parties to the contract?
- Does the assignment jeopardize the rights of the other parties to the contract to receive their benefits under the contract?

In regard to the first question, an assignment of personal service contracts is usually prohibited when the nature of the services to be performed under the contract is unique. The theory behind this is that the nature of the contract is changed when the services contracted from an individual are transferred to another. This rule applies in cases involving attorneys, painters, artists, authors, doctors, teachers, etc. If the personal service to be performed is routine, then assignment is usually permitted.

Regarding the second question, a general provision that prohibits assignment in a contract is usually not enforced by the courts. Section 2-210 of the Uniform Commercial Code provides that any party may assign his rights to receive benefits under a contract, and that any prohibition of assignment in the contract will be construed as barring only a delegation of duties under the contract. The rule in most states is that an individual may assign a contract despite a provision against assignment, but the nonassigning party may sue for breach of contract. In these cases there is the power to assign, but not the right to assign.

A contract may not be assigned if the assignment is either prohibited by law or violates public policy. If the assignment would substantially modify the nonassigning party's contractual duties, the courts will refuse to enforce the assignment. For example, if you enter into a contract to supply a small grocery store with all the wrapping paper it needs for six months and the store assigns the contract to a major supermarket, the assignment would be invalid because the amount of paper needed differs substantially. Another limitation on the right to assign a contract involves those cases in which the assigned rights would substantially alter the obligor's risk.

In most cases a written agreement is usually not necessary to be an effective assignment. Usually written assignments are required only when an interest in land, the sale of goods over $500, wage assignments, and assignments used as security interests are involved. These are discussed later in this chapter.

Consideration is not necessary for a valid assignment because the assignor (one who assigns the contract) may make a gift of his rights under a contract. The assignment must indicate a present intent to transfer rights under the contract. An assignment given for consideration is usually irrevocable. However, if it is without consideration (a gift), then it is usually revocable.

The person to whom the assignment is made (the assignee) replaces the assigning party as a party to the contract, and can then sue the nonassigning party (obligor) for breach of contract directly.

The implied warranty of title and the right to assign are included in an assignment. If these warranties are violated, the assignee may sue the assignor for breach of contract (the assignment contract). Unless specifically warranted in the assignment contract, the assignor does not guarantee that the other party will perform his obligations under the contract. Rights and benefits are assigned under a contract; duties or obligations are not assigned but are delegated.

Delegation of Duties Under A Contract

As noted above, duties are not assignable, but are delegated. The key difference is that the party who delegates the duties is still liable to the other parties under the contract if the new party fails to perform the duties. The question as to what duties are delegable is also present. The usual restrictions on the delegation of duties involve personal skill and judgment, special trust, or those that change the nature of the duties under the contract.

Rights under a contract may be assigned without the delegation of the duties to perform. Unless otherwise stated, a total assignment of rights also includes the delegation of duties.

Interpretation of Contracts

There are several general rules the courts use in cases involving contract disputes. Foremost is the rule that a contract will be construed as a whole document. Specific clauses in the contract will be construed to make the contract effective as a whole. Words will be presumed to be used in accordance with their ordinary meanings unless they are given special meanings by the parties. If different provisions in the contract are inconsistent, the courts will give preference to written phrases over typed or printed ones, and typed phrases over printed ones. In cases where the parties' intentions are unclear, the courts will look to the customs and usage in the particular business and locale involved.

Parole Evidence Rule

The Parole Evidence Rule is that used in determining the parties' intentions at the time a contract was entered into. The courts will not permit parole evidence (oral statements) that conflicts with the written agreement, if the written agreement was intended to be a complete expression of the parties' agreement. For the rule to apply, the courts must first determine that the written agreement was the final expression of the agreement, and that it was intended as a complete record of the parties' agreement.

The purpose behind the Parole Evidence Rule is to prevent the parties from disputing the provisions of a written contract and thus reduce the uncertainty involved in contractual law. Exceptions to the rule are, additional agreements made after the written agreement was executed, and those agreements that do not vary the terms in the written agreement. The courts will also overlook the rule to prevent fraud.

Discharge of Contractual Duties

The usual method of discharging contractual duties is by performance. Contractual duties are also discharged if the contract becomes illegal because of a change in the law. All of the parties to the contract by agreement may cancel the contract or modify the duties under it.

A difficult question in the discharge of performance cases is when it becomes impossible to perform the duties. If no one can perform the duties, then they are usually discharged (performance is excused). If the duties are impossible to perform only by the party involved, then they usually are not excusable. Some recent court cases have excused the performance of contractual duties when performance becomes impracticable. The test for impracticability is that performance will cause an extreme and unreasonable hardship on the party to require him to perform it. A discharge by novation occurs when the parties substitute a new contract for the present agreement. In this situation, the old contract is discharged and the new assignment determines the rights, duties, and benefits of the parties.

Account Stated Contract

An account stated contract is one in which the parties agree as to the final amount one party owes to the other party. This occurs where there are several transactions between the parties, such as those in an open account. This agreement merges all the individual transactions between the parties, and discharges all rights and duties except those contained in the account stated contract.

To qualify as an account stated, there must be more than one previous transaction between the parties, and they must agree as to the amount due. This agreement may be presumed by the courts when one party sends the other a statement of balance due on the account, and the receiving party does not object within a reasonable period of time (varies in each state). To prevent an account stated contract, immediately object to any incorrect account mailed to you.

Breach of Contracts

To determine the effects of a breach of contract, it first must be decided whether it is a material or a minor breach. A minor breach does not relieve the other party from performing his duties under the contract. In minor breach cases, the only remedy is to sue for damages.

In cases involving material breaches of contract, the other party may treat the contract as ended, and sue for damages. In this case, the nonbreaching party is not obligated to perform his duties under the contract. A minor breach and a statement by the breaching party that he does not intend to complete his duties under the contract, is an anticipatory repudiation of the agreement. The nonbreaching party may then terminate the contract and sue for damages.

Whether the breach is material depends on:

- The benefits the nonbreaching party loses as the result of the breach. The larger the loss, the more likely it will be considered a material breach.
- The extent to which the injured party may be compensated for the loss by the payment of damages.
- Prior failures of the breaching party to perform to the contractual duties.
- The hardship caused to the other parties by the breach.
- Whether the breach was negligent or willful.
- The likelihood that the breaching party will perform the remainder of his duties under the contract.

Remedies for Breach of Contract

The most frequent remedy for breach of contract is the payment of damages. Compensatory damages are for reasonably foreseeable losses that you suffered as the result of the breach. Punitive damages are sometimes awarded by the courts as punishment to the breaching party. Punitive damages are usually not awarded in breach of contract cases. Nominal damages may be given in those cases where a breach of contract is established, but no damages are proven.

In certain cases, the courts will order that the breaching party specifically perform his duties under the contract. Most of the time, specific performance is available only when money damages are insufficient.

SALES

A sale is a contract governed by the law of contracts. However, the Uniform Commercial Code has established some special rules that apply to the sale of goods by merchants. Since the UCC has been adopted nationwide, Article 2 of the code is included in Appendix I.

Article 2 does not apply to the sale of land or intangibles (stocks, bonds, etc.). If you are a merchant involved in the sales of goods or if you buy your supplies from a merchant, you should refer to the provisions of Article 2. In some states minor provisions of the article were modified when they were enacted into law; therefore, before relying on the article, check with the local library to see if any modifications are in effect in your state.

SECURED TRANSACTIONS

The term "secured transaction" is used to describe the financing of the sale of goods whereby a security interest is retained by the person financing the purchase. It includes conditional sales contracts, chattel mortgages, factoring, pledges, and trust receipts. Article 9 of the UCC deals with secured transactions. It does not apply to assignments of wages, state statutory liens such as mechanics' liens (except as to the priorities of the liens), or to transfers by a government or one of its agencies.

Chapter 16

Federal Benefits Available to Small Business Owners

In this chapter some of the more popular benefits and programs available to small business owners are discussed. For specifics in each case, contact the agency concerned.

SMALL BUSINESS ADMINISTRATION

The Small Business Administration (SBA) was created by Congress in 1953 to assist, counsel, and champion American small businesses. The agency's mission is to help people enter business, help them to stay in business, help small firms obtain federal aid, and act as an advocate for small businesses. While there are other federal agencies that provide services to businesses, the SBA is the only one specifically charged with the responsibility to assist small businesses. The SBA offers four kinds of assistance:

—Financial.
—Procurement.
—Management.
—Advocacy.

Financial assistance is discussed in Chapter 2. To be considered eligible for SBA assistance, businesses must meet certain size requirements. The requirements vary by industry. Maximum sizes are:

Manufacturing. A small business if it has fewer than 500 workers, and not a small business if it has more than 1,500 employees. Between 500 and 1,500 employee limit, standards are established for certain manufacturing industries. Therefore, check with that specific industry to determine its eligibility.

Retail. A small business if its annual sales are $3.5 million or less, and a large business if its annual sales are more than $13.5 million. It can be small or large depending upon the industry if its annual sales are between $3.5 million and $13.5 million.

Wholesale. A small business if it has 500 or fewer employees, and a large business if it has more than 500 employees.

Service Industries. A small business if its annual receipts do not exceed $3.5 million, and a large business if its annual receipts exceed $14.5 million. It can be large or small depending upon the industry if annual receipts are between $3.5 million and $14.5 million.

Passenger Transportation. A small business if its annual receipts are not more than $3.5 million, except for air transportation where it is small if it has 1,500 or fewer employees.

Trucking, Warehousing, Packaging, Crafting, and Freight Forwarding. A small business if its annual receipts do not exceed $12.5 million.

General Construction. A small business if its average annual receipts are $17 million or less.

Special Trade Constructions. A small business if its annual receipts are $7 million or less.

These standards are general and subject to change, and this list is not all inclusive. If you have a question as to whether or not your business would be eligible for assistance under the Small Business Administration, contact your nearest SBA office for current standards.

Procurement

The government has established small business preference standards for the procurement of prime contracts with the government. Government procurement regulations require that a certain percentage of all government contracts be set aside for small businesses. This procurement requirement is administered and supervised by the SBA. In certain situations, preferences are given to contractors who agree to set aside a certain percentage of their subcontracts to eligible small business concerns. To facilitate the subcontracting to small businesses, the SBA publishes a free publication entitled, *Small Business Subcontracting Directory.* This directory lists the major contractors to the federal government who offer the greatest potential for subcontracting to small businesses. This directory is available from regional SBA offices.

If you are interested in either participating in a government bidding process or in subcontracting, contact your local SBA field office. There are procurement specialists in each office whose primary duties are to tell small businesses which government agencies are perspective customers, how to place their names on the bidding list, and how to obtain drawings and specifications for specific contracts. In addition, the SBA publishes two documents that should help small business owners in dealing with government contracts and subcontracts. These are the *U.S. Government Purchasing and Sales Directory,* and the *SBA's Procurement and Technical Assistance Programs.* These are available from the Superintendent of Documents, U.S. Government Printing Office, Washington, D.C. 20402.

Management Counseling

In order to provide assistance in the form of management counseling, the SBA manages a number of resource programs whose sole purpose is to counsel small business personnel in marketing, buying, producing, selling, record keeping, financial management, financing, and administration.

One of the programs developed by the SBA is SCORE (Service Core of Retired Executives). SCORE was developed by the SBA to increase management counseling to small businesses. SCORE is composed of thousands of retired business executives who volunteer their services to help small businesses solve their problems. The SBA tries to match the needs of a particular business with the expertise of a SCORE volunteer.

Another SBA program is ACE (Active Core of Executives). ACE was developed in 1969 initially to supplement the talents in the SCORE program. ACE volunteers are recruited from jobs in major industries, trade associations, educational institutions, and professional ranks. Basically, ACE consists of mid-career executives who have volunteered to provide their services on an as-needed basis.

Both SCORE and ACE provide free advice and counseling to the small businessperson who cannot afford professional consultants.

Small Business Institute (SBI)

The Small Business Institute was founded in 1972. It is basically a three-way corporation between approximately 500 colleges with schools of business administration, members of the nation's small business community, and the SBA. The SBI provides management assistance to small businesses and offers meaningful learning experiences to business owners through coordination with collegiate schools of business administration.

The SBA also has a small business development center program (SBDC). This program, started in 1976, is designed to meet the specialized needs of the small business community. Under its auspices, state and local governments, and federal agencies provide management training, counseling, and technical assistance to small businesspersons working within the resources of the SBA. Currently, 33 statewide SBDC networks coordinate the efforts of 175 individual centers. In the near future, there will be at least one SBDC in every state.

In 1982, the SBA started a series of management training seminars. The seminars include introductory training for prospective business owners, pre-business follow-up training (a more in-depth aspect of pre-business training), and a management course entitled "Back to Basics." The Back to Basics programs include small business management, business planning for the small firm, marketing and sales in small businesses, purchasing and cost control for small businesses, record keeping for small businesses, financial management for small businesses, and legal and risk management for small businesses.

The SBA also offers training in specialized topics. For these courses, the SBA "borrows" executives from federal agencies, such as the Internal Revenue Service, to conduct the specialized topics of training. For additional information regarding any of the SBA's management training or educational programs, contact the regional office of

U.S. Small Business Administration
Office of Management Assistance
115A

Business Plan
for Small
Service Firms

By Staff Members
Education Division, Office of Management Assistance,
U.S. Small Business Administration

SBA Free
Management
Assistance
Publications

Management Aids
Number 2.027

How to Get
Started with a
Small Business
Computer

Management Aids
Number 2.020

Business Plan
for Retailers

Management Aids
Number 1.003

Keep Pointed
Toward Profit

Free management assistance publications can be obtained from the Small Business Administration.

| BIDDER'S MAILING LIST APPLICATION | X | INITIAL APPLICATION | FORM APPROVED OMB NO. |
| | | REVISION | 29-R0069 |

Fill in all spaces. Insert "NA" in blocks not applicable. Type or print all entries. See reverse for instructions.

TO (Enter name and address of Federal agency to which form is submitted. Include ZIP Code)

General Services Administration, Washington, D.C. 20380

DATE

July 7, 1986

1. APPLICANT'S NAME AND ADDRESS (Include county and ZIP Code)

Joe's Small Business
740 Level Street
Anytown, USA 00000

2. ADDRESS (Include county and ZIP Code) TO WHICH SOLICITATIONS ARE TO BE MAILED (If different from item 1)

Joe's Small Business
P.O. Box 3233
Anytown, USA 00000

3. TYPE OF ORGANIZATION (Check one)

| X INDIVIDUAL | PARTNERSHIP | NON-PROFIT ORGANIZATION |

CORPORATION, INCORPORATED UNDER THE LAWS OF THE STATE OF

4. HOW LONG IN PRESENT BUSINESS

two years

5. NAMES OF OFFICERS, OWNERS, OR PARTNERS

PRESIDENT	VICE PRESIDENT	SECRETARY
Joe Owner	Jane Owner	none
TREASURER	OWNERS OR PARTNERS	
none	Joe & Jane Owner	

6. AFFILIATES OF APPLICANT (Names, locations and nature of affiliation. See definition on reverse)

7. PERSONS AUTHORIZED TO SIGN BIDS, OFFERS, AND CONTRACTS IN YOUR NAME (Indicate if agent)

NAME	OFFICIAL CAPACITY	TEL. NO. (Incl. area code)
Joe Owner	Owner, President	(502) 000-0000
Jane Owner	Owner, Vice President	(502) 000-0000

8. IDENTIFY EQUIPMENT, SUPPLIES, MATERIALS, AND/OR SERVICES ON WHICH YOU DESIRE TO BID (See attached Federal agency's supplemental listing and instructions, if any)

Office Cleaning Equipment

9. TYPE OF OWNERSHIP (See definitions on reverse)

| MINORITY BUSINESS ENTERPRISE | X OTHER THAN MINORITY BUSINESS ENTERPRISE |

10. TYPE OF BUSINESS (See definitions on reverse)

| MANUFACTURER OR PRODUCER | X REGULAR DEALER (Type 1) | REGULAR DEALER (Type 2) |
| SERVICE ESTABLISHMENT | CONSTRUCTION CONCERN | RESEARCH AND DEVELOPMENT FIRM |

☐ SURPLUS DEALER (Check this box if you are also a dealer in surplus goods)

11. SIZE OF BUSINESS (See definitions on reverse)

| X SMALL BUSINESS CONCERN* | OTHER THAN SMALL BUSINESS CONCERN |

*If you are a small business concern, fill in (a) and (b):

| (a) AVERAGE NUMBER OF EMPLOYEES (Including affiliates) FOR FOUR PRECEDING CALENDAR QUARTERS | (b) AVERAGE ANNUAL SALES OR RECEIPTS FOR PRECEDING THREE FISCAL YEARS |
| five | $125,000.00 |

12. FLOOR SPACE (Square feet)

| MANUFACTURING | WAREHOUSE |
| | 2,500 |

13. DATE _____ AMOUNT _____

NET WORTH $250,000.00

14. SECURITY CLEARANCE (If applicable, check highest clearance authorized)

FOR	TOP SECRET	SECRET	CONFIDENTIAL	NAMES OF AGENCIES WHICH GRANTED SECURITY CLEARANCES (Include dates)
KEY PERSONNEL				none
PLANT ONLY				

THIS SPACE FOR USE BY THE GOVERNMENT

CERTIFICATION

I certify that information supplied herein (Including all pages attached) is correct and that neither the applicant nor any person (Or concern) in any connection with the applicant as a principal or officer, so far as is known, is now debarred or otherwise declared ineligible by any agency of the Federal Government from bidding for furnishing materials, supplies, or services to the Government or any agency thereof.

SIGNATURE

NAME AND TITLE OF PERSON AUTHORIZED TO SIGN (Type or print)

129–105

STANDARD FORM 129 (REV. 2–77)
Prescribed by GSA, FPR (41 CFR) 1–16.802

A copy of a bidder's mailing list application. To receive copies of various federal agencies' requests for bids, the businessperson should file an application with each federal agency that he or she wishes to do business with.

the SBA or the Director of the Small Business Administration at the address in Appendix G.

Management Assistance Publications

The Small Business Administration publishes a wide range of materials for both established small businesses and small business planning. You can get a free SBA publications catalog by writing the SBA, P.O. Box 15434, Fort Worth, Texas 76119.

Advocacy

One of the duties of the SBA is to provide advocacy for small businesses. The SBA acts as the primary spokesman for small businesses and represents its views and interests before Congress and other federal bodies. It is required to examine the role of small businesses in the American economy with regard to competition, innovation, productivity, and entrepreneurship, and to report its findings to the President and Congress.

The Office of Advocacy within the SBA was established to protect, strengthen, and effectively represent small businesses within the federal government. To accomplish this mission, the Office of Advocacy maintains an information and referral service. The

The suite of government offices in Austin, Texas. There are government offices in all major cities in the United States. A visit to them may provide you with potential customers for your products or services.

toll free number of this service is 1-800-365-5855, or in Washington, D.C., 202-653-7561. The information desk is staffed Monday through Friday from 9:00 A.M. to 5:00 P.M. Eastern standard time. In addition, the Office of Advocacy has 12 regional offices which serve as the Chief Counsel's direct link to the nation's small business community. They are charged with the duty of maintaining contact with local businesses, regional business groups, SBA district offices, and state and local government officials.

DEPARTMENT OF DEFENSE

The Department of Defense, being the largest purchaser of supplies, services, and construction in the federal government, provides a good opportunity for small business. Each military branch and the Defense Logistics Agency maintains small business assistance offices in the Washington, D.C., area.

The headquarters of the small business offices are; U.S. Army—Director of Small and Disadvantage Business Utilization, Office of the Secretary of the Army, Pentagon, Washington, D.C. 20310. Navy—Director of Small and Disadvantage Business Utilization, Office of the Secretary of the Navy, Chrystal Plaza #6, Washington, D.C. 20360; Air Force—Director of Small and Disadvantage Business Utilization, Office of the Secretary of the Air Force, Pentagon, Washington, D.C. 20230; Defense Logistics Agency—Staff Director of Small and Disadvantage Business Utilization, Defense Logistics Agency, Cameron Station, Alexandria, Virginia 22314.

At each major military procurement office in the military services and the Defense Logistics Agency you will find a small and disadvantage business utilization specialist to assist small businesses in obtaining contracts with the Department of Defense and the military services.

DEPARTMENT OF ENERGY

The Department of Energy has appointed a Director for the Office of Small and Disadvantage Business Utilization. The director is the focal point and advocate for preference programs for small businesses and women-owned business firms in their dealings with the department. The office screens planned procurement requests to make sure preference programs to small businesses and disadvantaged businesses are given adequate consideration before bids are requested. Information relating to small business procurement activities and assistance in the Department of Energy may be obtained by contacting the Office of Small and Disadvantage Business Utilization, Department of Energy, 1000 Independence Avenue SW, Washington, D.C. 20585.

EXPORT-IMPORT BANK OF THE UNITED STATES

The Export-Import Bank of the United States has a small business credit program that helps small business companies get low interest export loans or medium-term loans from commercial banks. The purpose of this program is to encourage and assist small businesses in dealing with export-import types of business. For additional information on this program, call the Export-Import Bank for the address of the nearest office in your area. Their toll free number is 1-800-424-5201.

GENERAL SERVICES ADMINISTRATION

The General Services Administration (GSA) also provides opportunities for many small businesses to sell their products directly to the federal government. To encourage small business involvement in government purchases, the GSA operates business service centers in 12 major metropolitan areas throughout the United States. Business service center counselors can advise you on the General Services Administration's contracting opportunities, and answer all but the most technical questions concerning the government's buying, leasing, and sales programs.

The GSA actively supports small businesses through its preferential procurement programs. Among those are small business set-asides whereby certain contracts are set aside for exclusive competition among small businesses. Labor surplus areas are set-asides whereby certain contracts are restricted to firms that agree to perform most of the contract work in labor surplus areas. Similar contract set-asides are provided for socially and economically disadvantaged businesses, women-owned businesses, and businesses owned by Vietnam veterans.

In this chapter, only highlights of the federal programs available to assist small business persons are included. There are numerous other programs and this is an area of constant change; therefore, your attention is directed to those selected federal agencies listed in Appendix G under Federal Information Centers, whose telephone numbers are included in Appendix H. A prudent businessperson would check for any possible government assistance as a part of his planning process for either starting a new business or expanding his present business.

Chapter 17

Closing or Transferring Business Ownership

L egal problems and concepts associated with the closing or transfer of a business are discussed in this chapter. In this regard, the reader should refer to Chapter 2 to the discussion on buying a business. Many of the principles stated in that chapter are applicable in this area, such as in buying a business, or in selling or transferring a business planning counts. It should be planned much the same way as the planning processes recommended in purchasing or starting a business. For example, the buy and sell agreement in Appendix A may also be used in selling or transferring ownership of your business.

If you are transferring your business from a sole proprietorship to a partnership or closed corporation of which you will be a principal member, I strongly recommend that the formal requirements of a transfer or the selling of a business interest be effected. Follow these requirements even though you may be the principal stockholder in the corporation or the managing partner of the partnership. If you follow this procedure, there will be no question as to which assets remain yours and which now belong to the association. This is especially recommended when you sell or transfer a sole proprietorship to a corporation. You will eventually need to establish exactly what belongs to the corporation and what belongs to you.

One of the biggest problems with the sale or transfer of ownership is evaluating the business. Those concepts, discussed in Chapter 2, are once again referred to. It is especially important that persons dealing with the business, such as suppliers, customers, etc., know that a change of ownership has occurred. This will help reduce your potential liability. When regulated businesses are involved, a report of the change of ownership should be forwarded to the regulatory agency.

In selling your business interest, consider the tax consequences of the sale. For example, a strictly cash settlement in most cases will have the highest tax consequences to the seller, and a tax free exchange the least.

BANKRUPTCY

Bankruptcy is an unpleasant subject to talk about, however since approximately 50 percent of new businesses fail in their first year of operation, it is necessary to consider the aspects and the possibility of bankruptcy. The Supreme Court in 1934 in one famous case stated that the primary purposes of the Federal Bankruptcy Act are to relieve the honest debtor from the weight of oppressive indebtedness and to permit him to start afresh. Pursuant to a provision in the Constitution, bankruptcy is controlled almost exclusively by the federal government. The primary source of statutory authority for bankruptcy is the Bankruptcy Reform Act of 1978 (BRA). It is Title XI of the United States Code. That act also provides the Supreme Court with the authority to make rules for situations the statutes don't cover.

There are two types of bankruptcy proceedings, liquidation under Chapter 7, and reorganization under Chapters 11 and 13. In liquidation proceedings the trustee collects the nonexempt property of the debtor, converts the property to cash, and distributes the cash to his creditors. The debtor gives up all nonexempt property in return for a discharge of his debts. Most bankruptcy proceedings are Chapter 7 liquidation cases.

Chapters 11 and 13 deal with the reorganization of a debtors' debts. In reorganization proceedings, the creditors usually look to the future earnings of the debtor, not to the property or when the proceedings to satisfy their claims began. Under reorganization, the debtor retains his assets and makes payments to the creditor usually from a post petition earnings pursuant to a court-approved plan.

Bankruptcy proceedings begin with the filing of a petition with the Federal Bankruptcy Court. In most cases the debtor files the petition. Such debtor-initiated proceedings are referred to as voluntary proceedings. In certain cases, creditors have the right to initiate involuntary bankruptcy proceedings against a debtor under either Chapter 7 or 11.

Voluntary Bankruptcy

In order for a debtor to apply for voluntary bankruptcy under Chapter 7, the debtor must be a person. A person as defined under the act includes partnerships and corporations. A sole proprietorship is not considered a person, and therefore cannot commence voluntary bankruptcy proceedings unless its owner files bankruptcy as to his total assets.

Railroads, insurance companies, or banking institutions may not initiate voluntary bankruptcy proceedings under Chapter 7. Any person eligible to file a petition under Chapter 7 may also file a petition for reorganization under Chapter 11, with the exception of stockbrokers and commodity brokers.

In order to file for reorganization under Chapter 13, the debtor must be an individual. He must have an income that is sufficiently stable and regular to make individual payments under a Chapter 13 plan. Thus, Chapter 13's primary purpose is to cover wage earners; whereas, mainly businesses are covered under Chapter 11. An additional

FORM NO. 1 Voluntary Petition Individual or Joint Petition

(CLERK'S STAMP)

Name __Cliff Roberson__
Attorney for Petitioner

Address __P.O. Box 3893__

_____Pinedale, Ca. 93650_____

Telephone: ____(209) 294-2305____

[**NOTE:** These official forms should be observed and used with such alterations as may be appropriate to suit the circumstances. See Rule 9009.]

VOLUNTARY PETITION

☒ **INDIVIDUAL**   ☐ **JOINT PETITION**

UNITED STATES BANKRUPTCY COURT FOR THE

...Central.................. DISTRICT OF .California.................

In re

Joe A. Debtor

Debtor [set forth here all names including trade names used by Debtor within last 6 years].
Social Security Number ....435-45-6679...................
and Debtor's Employer's Tax Identification No. ....none.........
Social Security Number ....
and Debtor's Employer's Tax Identification No. ....

FOR COURT USE ONLY

Date Petition Filed

Case No.

Bankruptcy Judge

VOLUNTARY PETITION

1. Petitioner's(s') mailing address, including county, is .....540 .West .Street,. Pinedale, .Ca.93640.........
....

2. Petitioner(s') has (have) resided [or has had his (their) domicile or has had his (their) principal place of business or has had his (their) principal assets] within this district for the preceding 180 days [or for a longer portion of the preceding 180 days than in any other district].

3. Petitioner(s) is (are) qualified to file this petition and is (are) entitled to the benefits of title 11, United States Code as a voluntary debtor(s).

4. [If appropriate] A copy of petitioner's(s) proposed plan, dated ...., is attached [or Petitioner(s) intends to file a plan pursuant to chapter 11 or chapter 13] of title 11, United States Code.

5. [If Petitioner(s) is (are) a Corporation] Exhibit "A" is attached to and made part of this petition.

6. [If Petitioner(s) is (are) (an) individual(s) whose debts are primarily consumer debts.] Petitioner(s) is (are) aware that [he or she] may proceed under chapter 7 or 13 of title 11, United States Code, understands the relief available under each such chapter, and chooses to proceed under chapter 7 or such title.

7. [If Petitioner(s) is (are) (an) individual(s) whose debts are primarily consumer debts and such petitioner(s) is (are) represented by an attorney.] A declaration or an affidavit in the form of Exhibit "B" is attached to and made a part of this petition.

WHEREFORE, petitioner(s) prays for relief in accordance with chapter 7 [or chapter 11 or chapter 13] of title 11, United States Code.

Signed: ....
[Attorney for Petitioner(s)]

Address: P.O. Box 3893, Pinedale, Ca. 93650 ....

....

[Petitioner(s) signs if not represented by attorney.]

....
Petitioner

....
Petitioner

I/We,........ Joe A. Debtor .... the petitioner(s) named in the foregoing petition, declare under penalty of perjury that the foregoing is true and correct.

Executed on . June 3, 19XX .   . . . . .   Signature . . . .
Petitioner

Signature . . . .

An example of a petition for reorganization.

limitation under Chapter 13 is that the debtor must have unsecured debts totaling less than $100,000 and secured debts totaling less than $350,000. If the debtor does not meet the requirements under Chapter 13, he still may be eligible for bankruptcy under 7 or 11.

Insolvency is not a requirement prior to petitioning for voluntary bankruptcy. In the case of a husband and wife, they may file a single petition for voluntary relief under any chapter available to each spouse. If the husband and wife file together under Chapter 13, their aggregate debts are subject to the monetary limitations of $100,000 for unsecured debts and $350,000 for secured debts. A debtor who files a bankruptcy petition must pay a $60 filing fee for Chapters 7 and 13, and a $200 filing fee for Chapter 11. Bankruptcy fees cannot be waived. A voluntary bankruptcy case is started with the filing of a petition by an eligible debtor. No formal adjudication is necessary to start the proceedings.

Involuntary Bankruptcy

Under certain conditions creditors may file involuntary petitions for bankruptcy against a debtor under either Chapter 7 or 11, but not under Chapter 13. Certain debtors, such as railroads, insurance companies, banking institutions, and farmers, are protected from involuntary petitions. For a creditor to file a petition in bankruptcy, generally three creditors with unsecured claims totaling at least $5,000 must join in the petition. If, however, the creditor has less than 12 unsecured creditors, a single creditor with an unsecured claim of $5,000 is sufficient to file the petition.

The basis for involuntary relief is that the debtor is generally not paying his debts as they become due. This is often referred to as equitable insolvency. An alternate basis for involuntary proceedings is that within 120 days before the petition was filed, a receiver, assignee, or custodian took possession of virtually all of the debtor's property or was appointed to take charge of a substantial part of the debtor's property.

Unlike a voluntary petition, an involuntary petition does not operate as adjudication or as an order for relief. The debtor has a right to file an answer contesting the involuntary proceedings.

If the judge dismisses the petition upon the request of the debtor, the court may grant judgment for the debtor against the petitioning creditors for all costs and reasonable attorney fees. If the creditor's petition was filed in bad faith, the court may also award punitive damages.

Stays In Debt Collection Proceedings

When a debtor who files a bankruptcy petition or a court sustains an involuntary petition, an automatic stay is issued. The stay virtually bars all debt collection efforts and permits the bankruptcy trustee the time necessary to collect the property of the estate. The stay acts to restrain creditors from taking any further action to enforce their claims or liens during the period of the stay. This means that the creditors cannot foreclose on any property in the hands of the debtor during the period of the stay, except where permitted by a court order. The bankruptcy court may order an end to the stay, and it automatically terminates when the bankruptcy proceedings are closed or dismissed, or the debtor receives or is denied a discharge.

A creditor who has a secured interest in a debtor's property may, under certain circumstances, request that the court grant relief from the stay and allow him to attach the property.

Property of the Estate

Property of the estate includes all of the debtor's property as of the time the petition was filed. The property of the estate includes both real and personal property, changeable property, and intangible property either in the debtor's possession or for any property he has a right to possess. Property the debtor acquires after the petition is filed remains his with the exception of property he becomes entitled to by inheritance, property settlement of a divorce decree, or beneficiary of a life insurance policy within 180 days after the filing of the petition. Property of the estate also includes the earnings from the property of the estate, and property received from a conversion of the property of the estate.

Exempt property is that which an individual debtor may assert as an exemption that they are entitled to under the laws of the state where he lives. Instead of taking the exempt property, the debtor may claim a federal exemption. The usual exemptions include a portion of the homestead, an automobile, household furnishings, and property of a personal or sentimental value. To determine what property is exempt, check your state statutes and compare those to the federal exemptions. Then decide which exemption would be more favorable in your particular circumstances.

Discharge in Bankruptcy

A discharge in bankruptcy in a Chapter 7 liquidation proceeding releases the debtor from personal liability for debts that he incurred before the date the bankruptcy petition was filed. Exceptions to this are all income and excise taxes for three years immediately preceding bankruptcy, and those taxes more than three years old if a tax return was not filed, if a return was filed within two years of the filing of the bankruptcy petition, or if a fraudulent return was filed.

The act also accepts from discharge debts for money, property, or services obtained through fraud, false misrepresentation, or false pretenses. One section of the code specifically deals with obtaining credit through the use of false financial statements, and provides that a materially false, written statement respecting the debtor's financial condition and his intent to deceive will prevent the debt from being discharged in bankruptcy. Note that in this regard merely establishing the falsity of the debtor's financial data is not sufficient. The creditor must also establish his reliance on it, the reasonableness of his reliance, and the debtor's intent to deceive.

Other nondischargeable debts include debts not listed in the bankruptcy proceedings schedule of debts, debts incurred by fraudulent acts while acting in a fiduciary capacity, child support, alimony from the support of a spouse, and any debts arising from the debtor's willful and malicious injury to the person or property of another. Fines, penalties, or forfeitures owed to a government entity are usually nondischargeable.

UNIFORM FRAUDULENT CONVEYANCE ACT

The purpose of the Uniform Fraudulent Conveyance Act is to prevent debtors from fraudulently conveying property to the detriment of his creditors.

Section 5 of the Uniform Fraudulent Conveyance Act provides that every conveyance a businessperson makes that doesn't leave him enough capital to pay his debts as they mature is fraudulent both to his present and future creditors, and therefore can be set aside. The purpose behind the Uniform Fraudulent Conveyance Act is to prevent debtors from giving away or selling their property at a lower than market price and thereby defrauding creditors. Any creditor who can establish that a transfer of property was made by a debtor without fair consideration may take judicial action to have the transfer set aside. He also may disregard the transfer and attach a levy upon the property conveyed.

The Uniform Fraudulent Conveyance Act does not apply if fair consideration is given for the property. Fair consideration is defined as the exchange for such property, obligations, or monetary amounts as the fair equivalent thereof. Therefore, the selling of property by a debtor for a reasonable market price would not be considered in the Uniform Fraudulent Conveyance Act.

Appendix A

Sample Business Buy-Sell Contract

THIS AGREEMENT is made and entered into on this _____ day of _____, 198____, between _____, hereinafter referred to as the Seller, and _____, hereinafter referred to as the Buyer.

Whereas the Seller is the present owner of a business using the trade name of _____, located at (address of business including the city and state), and the Seller wishes to sell to the buyer (his or her) rights, title and interests in the business including the goodwill therein, and the Buyer is willing to purchase the same on the terms and conditions hereinafter provided in this contract, it is agreed as follows:

I

SALE OF BUSINESS

The Seller shall sell and the Buyer shall buy, free from all liabilities and encumbrances except as hereinafter provided, the business owned and conducted by the Seller at the premises known as (address), including the goodwill as a going business, the lease (or building) to such premises, stock in trade, furniture, fixtures, equipment and supplies, all of which are listed in Schedule A attached to this agreement.

II

PURCHASE PRICE

The purchase price for the assets referred to in paragraph I shall be (enter entire purchase price) and allocable as follows:

Lease (or building)	$ _____
Goodwill	$ _____
Fixtures and equipment	$ _____
Inventory	$ _____
Supplies	$ _____
Total	$ _____

III

METHOD OF PAYMENT

The Buyer shall pay to the Seller the purchase price as stated above in the following manner: (a) $_____ by certified or cashier's check upon the execution of this contract, receipt of which is hereby acknowledged by the Seller, this check will be held in escrow by _____, attorney for the Seller, as provided in paragraph XII; (b) $_____ by certified or cashier's check at the time of closing, subject to any adjustments provided for in paragraph IV; (c) the balance of $_____ in monthly installments of $_____ each, payable on the first day of each month and beginning the first day of _____, 198____, together with interest at _____ percent per annum. Upon the default in the payment of an installment payment for a period of longer than 30 days the Seller or his assigns may declare the remaining balance due and payable. As security for the payment of the unpaid balance, the Buyer shall execute and deliver to the Seller at closing a chattel mortgage upon the inventory, fixtures and equipment described in Schedule A.

IV

ADJUSTMENTS

Adjustments shall be made at the time of closing for the following: inventory sold, insurance premiums, rent, deposits with utility companies, payroll, payroll taxes and missing fixtures or equipment. The net amount of the adjustments shall be added or subtracted from the amount due at the time of closing.

V

ASSUMPTION OF CONTRACTS AND LIABILITIES

If the business is transferred by the Seller to the Buyer, the Buyer shall be bound by and does assume the terms of the following contracts:

(1) Lease of business premises dated _____.
(List all other contracts and leases that Buyer assumes) The Buyer shall indemnify

the Seller against any liabilities or expenses arising out of any breach of any above listed contract occurring after the closing.

VI

SELLER'S WARRANTIES

The Seller warrants and represents the following:

(1) He is the owner of and has good and marketable title to all the assets specifically listed in Schedule A, free from all debts and encumbrances except as noted.

(2) The financial statements which are attached to this contract as Schedule B have been prepared in conformity with generally accepted accounting principles and are a true and correct statement of the financial condition of said business as of their respective dates.

(3) There are no business liabilities or obligations of any nature, whether absolute, accrued, contingent or otherwise, except as reflected in the financial statements attached as Schedule B.

(4) There are no pending litigation, governmental proceedings or investigations or to the knowledge of the Seller are any threatened or in prospect, against or relating to the business.

(5) The statements made and the information given by the Seller to the Buyer regarding the business are true and accurate and no material facts have been withheld from the Buyer.

(6) The Seller has no knowledge of any developments or threatened developments of any kind that would be materially adverse to the business.

VII

COVENANT NOT TO COMPETE

The Seller covenants to and with the Buyer and Buyer's Successors and Assigns that for a period of five years from and after closing that the Seller will not, directly or indirectly, in any capacity, engage in any business similar to or in competition with the business sold, within a 100 mile radius of the present business location.

VIII

SELLER'S OBLIGATIONS PENDING CLOSING

The Seller covenants and agrees with the Buyer as follows:

(1) The Seller shall conduct business in a normal and regular manner up to the date of closing and shall use his best efforts to retain the business in its present state, to preserve the business's goodwill, customers and suppliers.

(2) The Seller shall give the Buyer or the Buyer's representative full access dur-

ing regular business hours to the Seller's books, records, etc.

(3) The Seller shall comply with the Bulk Sales Act.

(4) The Seller shall deliver to the Buyer for examination and approval prior to closing date any bills of sale, titles and instruments necessary to establish the Seller's marketable title.

(5) The Seller shall maintain an accurate record of the inventory sold in the ordinary course of business from the date this agreement is signed until the date of closing.

IX

RISK OF LOSS

The Seller assumes all risks of destruction, loss or damage due to fire or any other casualty until closing. If any destruction, loss or damage occurs that materially affect the operation of the business, the Buyer has the option to cancel the sale and receive a return of all moneys, property, etc. advanced under the terms of the contract. If any loss, damage or destruction occurs that does not materially affect the operation of the business; the purchase price shall be adjusted accordingly.

X

CONDITIONS PRECEDENT TO CLOSING

The Buyer's obligation at closing are subject to the fulfillment prior to or at closing of the following conditions:

(1) All the Seller's representations and warranties contained in this agreement shall be true as of the time of closing.

(2) The Seller will have complied with and performed all agreements and other terms required by this contract.

XI

CLOSING

The closing of this sale shall take place at the office of _____ on _____ day of _____ 198____ at (time). At that time the Buyer shall take possession of the business, all necessary instruments and documents shall be delivered to the Buyer and the Buyer will receive the keys to the premises at that time.

XII

SELLER'S SECURITY

As security for the indemnities specified in paragraph 8, the Seller shall furnish a bond in the amount of $_____ from an approved bonding company or in lieu of a bond, shall deposit $_____ with _____ to hold in escrow for a period of one year from the date closing.

XIII

INDEMNIFICATION BY THE SELLER

The Seller shall indemnify and hold the buyer harmless and will reimburse the Buyer on demand for any payments made by the Buyer after closing in regards to any liabilities and obligations of the Seller not expressly assumed by the Buyer and for any damage resulting from misrepresentations, breeches of warranty or nonfulfillment of the terms of this contract.

XIV

ARBITRATION

All controversies arising under this contract or relating to any of its terms shall be submitted to a panel of three arbitrators. Such panel to be selected by each party selecting one arbitrator and the two selected arbitrators selecting a third arbitrator. The recommendations of the panel of arbitrators shall be conclusive and binding on each party. The arbitrators shall also designate the party or parties to pay the expenses incurred in the arbitration process.

IN WITNESS WHEREOF, each party hereby sets their signature to this contract on this _____ day of _____, 198____.
(SIGNED by both parties and witnessed)

Appendix B

Uniform Partnership Act

(Courtesy of National Conference of Commissioners on Uniform State Laws)

PART I

Section 1. Name. This act may be cited as the Uniform Partnership Act.

Section 2. Definitions. In this act, "Court" includes every court and judge having jurisdiction in the case.

"Business" includes every trade, occupation or profession.

"Person" includes individuals, partnerships, corporations and any other associations.

"Bankrupt" includes bankrupt under the Federal Bankruptcy Act or insolvent under any state insolvent acts.

"Conveyance" includes every assignment, lease, mortgage or encumbrance.

"Real Property" includes land and any interest or estate in land.

Section 3. Knowledge and Notice. (1) A person has "knowledge" of a fact within the meaning of the act not only when he has actual knowledge thereof, but also when he has knowledge of such other facts as in the circumstances shows bad faith.

(2) A person has "notice" of a fact within the meaning of this act when the person who claims the benefit of the notice:

(a) States the fact to such person, or

(b) Delivers through the mail, or by other means of communication, a written statement of the fact to such person or to a proper person at his place of business or residence.

Section 4. Construction. (1) The rule that statutes in derogation of the common law are to be strictly construed shall have no application to this act.

(2) The law of estoppel shall apply under this act.

(3) The law of agency shall apply under this act.

(4) This act shall be so interpreted and construed as to effect its general purpose to make uniform the law of those states which enact.

(5) This act shall not be construed so as to impair the obligations of any contract existing when the act goes into effect, nor to affect any action or proceedings begun or right accrued before this act takes effect.

Section 5. Cases Not Provided for in this Act. In any case not provided for in this act the rules of law and equity, including the law merchant, shall govern.

PART II

Nature of a Partnership

Section 6. Defined. (1) A partnership is an association of two or more persons to carry on as co-owners a business for profit.

(2) But any association formed under any other statute of this state, or any statute adopted by authority, other than the authority of this state, is not a partnership under this act, unless such association would have been a partnership in this state prior to the adoption of this act; but this act shall apply to limited partnerships except in so far as the statutes relating to such partnerships are inconsistent herewith.

Section 7. Existence of Partnership. In determining whether a partnership exists, these rules shall apply:

(1) Except as provided by Section 16 persons who are not partners as to each other are not partners as to third persons.

(2) Joint tenancy, tenancy in common, tenancy by the entireties, joint property, common property, or part ownership does not of itself establish a partnership, whether such co-owners do or do not share any profits made by the use of the property.

(3) The sharing of gross returns does not of itself establish a partnership, whether or not the persons sharing them have a joint or common right or interest in any property from which the returns are derived.

(4) The receipt by a person of a share of the profits of a business is prima facie evidence that he is a partner in the business, but no such inference shall be made if such profits are payment:

(a) As a debt by installments or otherwise,

(b) As wages of an employee or rent to a landlord,

(c) As an annuity to a widow or representative of a deceased partner,

(d) As interest on a loan, though the amount of payment vary with the profits of the business.

(e) As the consideration for the sale of a good-will of a business or other property by installments or otherwise.

Section 8. Property of the Partnership (1) All property originally brought into the partnership stock or subsequently acquired by purchase or otherwise, on account of the partnership, is partnership property.

(2) Unless the contrary intention appears, property acquired with partnership funds is partnership property.

(3) Any estate in real property may be acquired in the partnership name. Title so acquired can be conveyed only in the partnership name.

(4) A conveyance to a partnership in the partnership name, though without words of inheritance, passes the entire estate of the grantor unless a contrary intent appears.

PART III

Relations of Partners to Persons Dealing with Partnership

Section 9. Partner Agent of Partnership (1) Every partner is an agent of the partnership for the purpose of its business, and the act of every partner, including the execution in the partnership name of any instrument, for apparently carrying on in the usual way the business of the partnership of which he is a member binds the partnership, unless the partner so acting has in fact no authority to act for the partnership in the particular matter, and the person with whom he is dealing has knowledge of the fact that he has no such authority.

(2) An act of a partner which is not apparently for the carrying on of the business of the partnership in the usual way does not bind the partnership unless authorized by the other partners.

(3) Unless authorized by the other partners or unless they have abandoned the business, one or more but less than all the partners have no authority to:

(a) Assign the partnership property in trust for creditors or on the assignee's promise to pay the debts of the partnership,

(b) Dispose of the good-will of the business,

(c) Do any other act which would make it impossible to carry on the ordinary business of a partnership,

(d) Confess a judgment,

(e) Submit a partnership claim or liability to arbitration or reference.

(4) No act of a partner in contravention of a restriction on authority shall bind the partnership to persons having knowledge of the restriction.

Section 10. Conveyance of Real Property. (1) Where title to real property is in the partnership name, any partner may convey title to such property by a conveyance executed in the partnership name; but the partnership may recover such property unless the partner's act binds the partnership under the provisions of paragraph (1) of section 9 or unless such property has been conveyed by the grantee or a person claiming through such grantee to a holder for value without knowledge that the partner, in making the conveyance, has exceeded his authority.

(2) Where title to real property is in the name of the partnership, a conveyance executed by a partner, in his own name, passes the equitable interest of the partner-

ship, provided the act is one within the authority of the partner under the provisions of paragraph (1) of section 9.

(3) Where title to real property is in the name of one or more but not all the partners, and the record does not disclose the right of the partnership, the partners in whose name the title stands may convey title to such property, but the partnership under the provisions of paragraph (1) of section 9, unless the purchaser, or his assignee, is a holder for value, without knowledge.

(4) Where the title to real property is in the name of one or more or all partners, or in a third person in trust for the partnership, a conveyance executed by a partner in the partnership name, or in his own name, passes the equitable interest of the partnership, provided the act is one within the authority of the partner under the provisions of paragraph (1) of section 9.

(5) Where the title to real property is in the names of all the partners, a conveyance executed by all partners passes all their rights in such property.

Section 11. Admission of Partner. An admission or representation made by any partner concerning the partnership affairs within the scope of his authority as conferred by this act is evidence against the partnership.

Section 12. Notice to Partnership. Notice to any partner of any matter relating to the partnership affairs, and the knowledge of the partner acting in the particular matter, acquired while a partner or then present to his mind, and the knowledge of any other partner who reasonably could and should have communicated it to the acting partner, operate as notice to or knowledge of the partnership, except in the case of a fraud on the partnership committed by or with the consent of that partner.

Section 13. Partner's Wrongful Act. Where, by any wrongful act or omission of any partner acting in the ordinary course of the business of the partnership or with the authority of his co-partners, loss or injury is caused to any person, not being a partner in the partnership, or any penalty is incurred, the partnership is liable therefor to the same extent as the partner so acting or omitting to act.

Section 14. Partner's Breach of Trust. The partnership is bound to make good the loss:

(a) Where one partner acting within the scope of his apparent authority receives money or property of a third person and misapplies it; and

(b) Where the partnership in the course of its business receives money or property of a third person and it is misapplied by any partner while it is in the custody of the partnership.

Section 15. Partner's Liability. All partners are liable

(a) Jointly and severally for everything chargeable to the partnership under sections 13 and 14.

(b) Jointly for all other debts and obligations of the partnership; but any partner may enter into a separate obligation to perform a partnership contract.

Section 16. Partnership by estoppel. (1) When a person, by words spoken or written or by conduct, represents himself, or consents to another representing him to any one, as a partner in an existing partnership or with one or more persons not actual partners, he is liable to any such person to whom such representation has been made, who has, on the faith of such representation, given credit to the actual or apparent partnership, and if he has made such representation or consented to its being made in a public manner he is liable to such person, whether the representation has or has not been made or communicated to such person so giving credit by or with the knowledge of the apparent partner making the representation or consenting to its being made.

(a) When a partnership liability results, he is liable as though he were an actual member of the partnership.

(b) When no partnership liability results, he is liable jointly with the other persons, if any, so consenting to the contract or representation as to incur liability, otherwise separately.

(2) When a person, has been thus represented to be a partner in an existing partnership, or with one or more persons not actual partners, he is an agent of the persons consenting to such representation to bind them to the same extent and in the same manner as though he were a partner in fact, with respect to persons who rely upon the representation. Where all the members of the existing partnership consent to the representation, a partnership act or obligation results; but in all other cases it is the joint act or obligation of the person acting and the persons consenting to the representation.

Section 17. Liability of New Partner. A person admitted as a partner into an existing partnership is liable for all the obligations of the partnership arising before his admission as though he had been a partner when such obligations were incurred, except that this liability shall be satisfied only out of partnership property.

PART IV

Relations to Each Other

Section 18. Rights and Duties of Partners. The rights and duties of the partners in relation to the partnership shall be determined, subject to any agreement between them, by the following rules:

(a) Each partner shall be repaid this contributions, whether by way of capital or advances to the partnership property and share equally in the profits and surplus remaining after all liabilities, including those to partners, are satisfied; and must contribute towards the losses, whether of capital or otherwise, sustained by the partnership according to his share in the profits.

(b) The partnership must indemnify every partner in respect of payments made and personal liabilities reasonably incurred by him in the ordinary and proper conduct of its business, or for the preservation of its business or property.

(c) A partner, who in the aid of the partnership makes any payment or advance beyond the amount of capital which he agreed to contribute, shall be paid interest from the date of the payment or advance.

(d) A partner shall receive interest on the capital contributed by him only from the date when repayment should be made.

(e) All partners have equal rights in the management and conduct of the partnership business.

(f) No partner is entitled to remuneration for acting in the partnership business, except that a surviving partner is entitled to reasonable compensation for his services in winding up the partnership affairs.

(g) No person can become a member of a partnership without the consent of all the partners.

(h) Any difference arising as to ordinary matters connected with the partnership business may be decided by a majority of the partners; but no act in contravention of any agreement between the partners may be done rightfully without the consent of all the partners.

Section 19. Books of Partnership. The partnership books shall be kept, subject to any agreement between the partners, at the principal place of business of the partnership, and every partner shall at all times have access to and may inspect and copy any of them.

Section 20. Information. Partners shall render on demand true and full information of all things affecting the partnership to any partner or the legal representative of any deceased partner or partner under legal disability.

Section 21. Fiduciary Relationship. (1) Every partner must account to the partnership for any benefit, and hold as trustee for it any profits derived by him without the consent of the other partners from any transaction connected with the formation, conduct, or liquidation of the partnership or from any use by him of its property.

(2) This section applies also to the representatives of a deceased partner engaged in the liquidation of the affairs of the partnership as the personal representatives of the last surviving partner.

Section 22. Accounting. Any partner shall have the right to a formal account as to partnership affairs:

(a) If he is wrongfully excluded from the partnership business or possession of its property by his co-partners,

(b) If the right exists under the terms of any agreement,

(c) As provided by section 21,

(d) Whenever other circumstances render it just and reasonable.

Section 23. Partnership Continuation. (1) When a partnership for a fixed term or particular undertaking is continued after the termination of such term or particular undertaking without any express agreement, the rights and duties of the partners remain the same as they were at such termination, so far as is consistent with a partnership at will.

(2) A continuation of the business by the partners or such of them as habitually acted therein during the term, without any settlement or liquidation of the partnership affairs, is prima facie evidence of a continuation of the partnership.

PART V

Property Rights of a Partner

Section 24. Property Rights of a Partner. The property rights of a partner are (1) his rights in specific partnership property, (2) his interest in the partnership, and (3) his right to participate in the management.

Section 25. Property Rights in Specific Property. (1) A partner is co-owner with his partners of specific partnership property holding as a tenant in partnership.

(2) The incidents of this tenancy are such that:

(a) A partner, subject to the provisions of this act and to any agreement between the partners, has an equal right with his partners to possess specific partnership property for partnership purposes; but he has no right to possess such property for any other purpose without the consent of his partners.

(b) A partner's right in specific property is not assignable except in connection with the assignment of rights of all the partners in the same property.

(c) A partner's right in specific partnership property is not subject to attachment or execution, except on a claim against the partnership. When partnership property is attached for a partnership debt the partners, or any of them, or the representatives of a deceased partner, can not claim any right under the homestead or exemption laws.

(d) On the death of a partner his right in specific partnership property vests in the surviving partner or partners, except where the deceased was the last surviving partner, then his right in such property vests in his legal representative. Such surviving partner or partners, or the legal representative of the last surviving partner, has no right to possess the partnership property for any but a partnership purpose.

(e) A partner's right in specific partnership property is not subject to allowances to widows, heirs or next of kin.

Section 26. Nature of Partner's Interest. A partner's interest in the partnership is his share of the profits and surplus, and the same is personal property.

Section 27. Assignment of Partner's Interest. (1) A conveyance by a partner of his interest in the partnership does not of itself dissolve the partnership, nor, as against the other partners in the absence of agreement, entitle the assignee, during the continuance of the partnership, to interfere in the management or administration of the partnership business or affairs, or to inspect any information or account of partnership transactions, or to inspect the partnership books; but it merely entitles the assignees to receive in accordance with his contract the profits to which the assigning partner would otherwise be entitled.

Section 28. Partner's Interest Subject to Charging Order. On due application to a competent court by any judgment creditor of a partner, the court which entered the judgment, order, or decree, or any other court, may charge the interest of the debtor partner with payment of the unsatisfied amount of such judgment debt with interest thereon; and may then or later appoint a receiver of his share of the profits, and of any other money due or to fall due to him in respect of the partnership, and make all other orders, directions, accounts and inquires which the debtor partner might have made, or which the circumstances of the case may require.

(2) The interest charged may be redeemed at any time before foreclosure, or in case of a sale being directed by the court may be purchased without thereby causing a dissolution:

(a) With separate property, by any one or more of the partners, or

(b) With partnership property, by any one or more of the partners with the consent of all the partners whose interests are not so charged or sold.

(3) Nothing in this act shall be held to deprive a partner of his right, if any, under the exemption laws, as regards his interest in the partnership.

PART VI

Dissolution and Winding Up

Section 29. Dissolution Defined. The dissolution of a partnership is the change in the relation of the partners caused by any partner ceasing to be associated in the carrying on as distinguished from the winding up of the business.

Section 30. Partnership Not Terminated by Dissolution. On dissolution the partnership is not terminated, but continues until the winding up of partnership affairs is completed.

Section 31. Causes of Dissolution. Dissolution is caused: (1) Without violation of the agreement between the partners,

(a) By the termination of the definite term or particular undertaking specified in the agreement,

(b) By the express will of any partner when no definite term or particular undertaking is specified,

(c) By the express will of all the partners who have not assigned their interests or suffered them to be charged for their separate debts, either before or after the termination of any specified term or particular undertaking,

(d) By the expulsion of any partner from the business bona fide in accordance with such a power conferred by agreement between the partners;

(2) In contravention of the agreement between the partners, where the circumstances do not permit a dissolution under any other provision of this section, by the express will of any partner at any time;

(3) By any event which makes it unlawful for the business of the partnership to be carried on or for the members to carry it on in partnership;

(4) By the death of any partner;

(5) By the bankruptcy of any partner or the partnership;

(6) By decree of the court under section 32.

Section 32. Dissolution by Decree of Court. (1) On application by or for a partner the court shall decree a dissolution whenever:

(a) A partner has been declared a lunatic in any judicial proceeding or is shown to be of unsound mind,

(b) A partner becomes in any other way incapable of performing his part of the partnership contract,

(c) A partner has been guilty of such conduct as tends to affect prejudicially the carrying on of the business,

(d) A partner wilfully or persistently commits a breach of the partnership agreement, or otherwise so conducts himself in matters relating to the partnership business that it is not reasonably practicable to carry on the business in partnership with him,

(e) The business of the partnership can only be carried on at a loss,

(f) Other circumstances render a dissolution equitable.

(2) On the application of the purchaser of a partner's interest under sections 27 or 28.

(a) After the termination of the specified term or particular undertaking,

(b) At any time if the partnership was a partnership at will when the interest was assigned or when the charging order was issued.

Section 33. General Effect of Dissolution on Authority of Partner. Except so far as may be necessary to wind up partnership affairs or to complete transactions begun but not then finished, dissolution terminates all authority of any partner to act for the partnership,

(1) With respect to the partners

(a) When the dissolution is not by act, bankruptcy or death of a partner; or

(b) When the dissolution is by such act, bankruptcy or death of a partner, in cases where section 34 so requires.

(2) With respect to persons not partners, as declared in section 35.

Section 34. Right of Partner to Contribution From Copartners After Dissolution. Where the dissolution is caused by the act, death or bankruptcy of a partner, each partner is liable to his copartners for his share of any liability created by any partner acting for the partnership as if the partnership had not been dissolved unless

(a) The dissolution being by act of any partner, the partner acting for the partnership had knowledge of the dissolution, or

(b) The dissolution being by the death or bankruptcy of a partner, the partner acting for the partnership had knowledge or notice of the death or bankruptcy.

Section 35. Power of Partner to Bind Partnership to Third Persons After Dissolution. (1) After dissolution a partner can bind the partnership except as provided in Paragraph (3)

(a) By any act appropriate for winding up partnership affairs or completing transaction unfinished at dissolution;

(b) By any transaction which would bind the partnership if dissolution had not taken place, provided the other party to the transaction

(I) Had extended credit to the partnership prior to dissolution and had no knowledge or notice of the dissolution; or

(II) Though he had not so extended credit, had nevertheless known of the partnership prior to dissolution, and having no knowledge or notice of dissolution, the fact of dissolution had not been advertised in a newspaper of general circulation in the place (or in each place if more than one) at which the partnership business was regularly carried on.

(2) The liability of a partner under paragraph (1b) shall be satisfied out of partnership assets alone when such partner had been prior to dissolution

(a) Unknown as a partner to the person with whom the contract is made; and

(b) So far unknown and inactive partnership affairs that the business reputation of the partnership could not be said to have been in any degree due to his connection with it.

(3) The partnership is in no case bound by any act of a partner after dissolution

(a) Where the partnership is dissolved because it is unlawful to carry on the business, unless the act is appropriate for winding up partnership affairs; or

(b) Where the partner had become bankrupt; or

(c) Where the partner has no authority to wind up partnership affairs; except by a transaction with one who

(I) Had extended credit to the partnership prior to dissolution and had no knowledge or notice of his want of authority; or

(II) Had not extended credit to the partnership prior to dissolution, and, having no knowledge or notice of his want of authority has not been advertised in the manner provided for advertising the fact of dissolution in paragraph (1bII).

(4) Nothing in this section shall affect the liability under section 16 of any person who after dissolution represents himself or consents to another representing him as a partner in a partnership engaged in carrying on business.

Section 36. Effect of Dissolution on Partner's Existing Liability. (1) The dissolution of the partnership does not itself discharge the existing liability of any partner.

(2) A partner is discharged from any existing liability upon dissolution of the partnership by an agreement to that effect between himself, the partnership creditor and the person or partnership continuing the business; and such agreement may be inferred from the course of dealing between the creditor having knowledge of the dissolution and the person or partnership continuing the business.

(3) Where a person agrees to assume the existing obligations of a dissolved partnership, the partners whose obligations have been assumed shall be discharged from any liability to any creditor of the partnership who, knowing of the agreement, consents to a material alteration in the nature or time of payment of such obligations.

(4) The individual property of a deceased partner shall be liable for all obligations of the partnership incurred while he was a partner but subject to the prior payment of his separate debts.

Section 37. Right to Wind Up. Unless otherwise agreed the partners who have not wrongfully dissolved the partnership or the legal representative of the last surviving partner, not bankrupt, had the right to wind up the partnership affairs; provided, however, that any partner, his legal representative or his assignee, upon cause shown, may obtain winding up the court.

Section 38. Rights of Partners to Application of Partnership Property. (1) When dissolution is caused in any way, except in contravention of the partnership agreement, each partner as against his co-partners and all persons claiming through them in respect of their interests in the partnership, unless otherwise agreed, may have the partnership property applied to discharge its liabilities, and the surplus applied to pay in cash the net amount owing to the respective partners. But if dissolution is caused by expulsion of a partner, bona fide under the partnership agreement and if the expelled partner is discharged from all partnership liabilities, either by payment or agreement under section 36(2), he shall receive in cash only the net amount due him from the partnership.

(2) When dissolution is caused in contravention of the partnership agreement the rights of the partners shall be as follows:

(a) Each partner who has not caused dissolution wrongfully shall have,

(I) All the rights specified in paragraph (1) of this section, and

(II) The right, as against each partner who has caused the dissolution wrongfully, to damages for breach of the agreement.

(b) The partners who have not caused the dissolution wrongfully, if they all desire to continue the business in the same name, either by themselves or jointly with others, may do so, during the agreed term for the partnership and for that purpose may possess the partnership property, provided they secure the payment by bond approved by the court, or pay any partner who has caused the dissolution wrongfully, the value of his interest in the partnership at the dissolution, less any damages recoverable under clause (2aII) of this section, and in like manner indemnify him against all present or future partnership liabilities.

(c) A partner who has caused the dissolution wrongfully shall have: (I) If the business is not continued under the provisions of paragraph (2b) all the rights of a partner under paragraph (1), subject to clause (2aII), of this section,

(II) If the business is continued under paragraph (2B) of this section the right as against his co-partners and all claiming through them in respect of their interests in the partnership, to have the value of his interest in the partnership, less any damages caused to his co-partners by the dissolution, ascertained and paid to him in cash, or the payment secured by bond approved by the court, and to be released from all existing liabilities of the partnership, but in ascertaining the value of the partner's interest the value of the good-will of the business shall not be considered.

Section 39. Rights Where Partnership is Dissolved for Fraud or Misrepresentation. Where a partnership contract is rescinded on the ground of the fraud or misrepresentation of one of the parties thereto, the party entitled to rescind is, without prejudice to any other right, entitled,

(a) To a lien on, or right of retention of, the surplus of the partnership property after satisfying the partnership liabilities to third persons for any sum of money paid by him for the purchase of an interest in the partnership and for any capital or advances contributed by him; and

(b) To stand, after all liabilities to third persons have been satisfied, in the place of the creditors of the partnership for any payments made by him in respect of the partnership liabilities; and

(c) To be indemnified by the person guilty of the fraud or making the representation against all debts and liabilities of the partnership.

Section 40. Rules for Distribution. In settling accounts between the partners after dissolution, the following rules shall be observed, subject to any agreement to the contrary:

(a) The assets of the partnership are:

(I) The partnership property,

(II) The contributions of the partners necessary for the payment of all liabilities specified in clause (b) of this paragraph.

(b) The liabilities of the partnership shall rank in order of payment, as follows:

(I) Those owing to creditors other than partners,

(II) Those owing to partners other than for capital and profits,

(III) Those owing to partners in respect of capital,

(IV) Those owing to partners in respect of profits.

(c) The assets shall be applied in the order of their declaration in clause (a) of this paragraph to the satisfaction of the liabilities.

(d) The partners shall contribute, as provided by section 18(a) the amount necessary to satisfy the liabilities; but if any, but not all, of the partners are insolvent, or, not being subject to process, refuse to contribute, the other parties shall contribute their share of the liabilities, and, in the relative proportions in which they share the profits, the additional amount necessary to pay the liabilities.

(e) An assignee for the benefit of creditors or any person appointed by the court shall have the right to enforce the contributions specified in clause (d) of this paragraph.

(f) Any partner or his legal representative shall have the right to enforce the contributions specified in clause (d) of this paragraph, to the extent of the amount which he has paid in excess of his share of the liability.

(g) The individual property of a deceased partner shall be liable for the contributions specified in clause (d) of this paragraph.

(h) When partnership property and the individual properties of the partners are in possession of a court for distribution, partnership creditors shall have priority on partnership property and separate creditors on individual property, saving the rights of lien or secured creditors as heretofore.

(i) Where a partner has become bankrupt or his estate is insolvent the claims against his separate property shall rank in the following order:

(I) Those owing to separate creditors,

(II) Those owing to partnership creditors,

(III) Those owing to partners by way of contribution.

Section 41. Liability of Persons Continuing the Business in Certain Cases. (1) When any new partner is admitted into an existing partnership, or when any partner retires and assigns (or the representative of the deceased partner assigns) his rights in partnership property to two or more of the partners, or to one or more of the partners and one or more third persons, if the business is continued without liquidation of the partnership affairs, creditors of the first or dissolved partnership are also creditors of the partnership so continuing the business.

(2) When all but one partner retire and assign (or the representative of a deceased partner assigns) their rights in partnership property to the remaining partner, who continues the business without liquidation of partnership affairs, either alone or with others, creditors of the dissolved partnership are also creditors of the person or partnership so continuing the business.

(3) When any partner retires or dies and the business of the dissolved partnership is continued as set forth in paragraphs (1) and (2) of this section, with the consent of the retired partners or the representatives of a deceased partner, but without any assignment of his right in partnership property, rights of creditors of the dissolved partnership and of the creditors of the person or partnership continuing the business shall be as if such assignment has been made.

(4) When all the partners or their representatives assign their rights in partnership property to one or more third persons who promise to pay the debts and who continue the business of the dissolved partnership, creditors of the dissolved partnership are also creditors of the person or partnership continuing the business.

(5) When any partner wrongfully causes a dissolution and the remaining partners continue the business under the provisions of section 38(2B), either alone or with others, and without liquidation of the partnership affairs, creditors of the dissolved partnership are also creditors of the person or partnership continuing the business.

(6) When a partner is expelled and the remaining partners continue the business either alone or with others, without liquidation of the partnership affairs, creditors of the dissolved partnership continuing the business.

(7) The liability of a third person becoming a partner in the partnership continuing the business, under this section, to the creditors of the dissolved partnership shall be satisfied out of the partnership property only.

(8) When the business of a partnership after dissolution is continued under any conditions set forth in this section the creditors of the dissolved partnership, as against the separate creditors of the retiring or deceased partner or the representative of the deceased partner, have a prior right to any claim of the retired partner or the representative of the deceased partner against the person or partnership continuing the business, on account of the retired or deceased partner's interest in the dissolved partnership or on account of any consideration promised for such interest or for his right in partnership property.

(9) Nothing in this section shall be held to modify any right of creditors to set aside any assignment on the ground of fraud.

(10) The use by the person or partnership continuing the business of the partnership name, or the name of a deceased partner as part thereof, shall not of itself make the individual property of the deceased partner liable for any debts contracted by such person or partnership.

Section 42. Rights of Retiring Partner When the Business is Continued. When any partner retires or dies, and the business is continued under any of the conditions set forth in section 41 (1, 2, 3, 5, 6) or section 38(2b), without any settlement of accounts as between him or his estate and the person or partnership continuing the business, unless otherwise agreed, he or his legal representative as against such persons or partnership may have the value of his interest at the date of dissolution ascertained, and shall receive as an ordinary creditor an amount equal to the value of his interest in the dissolved partnership with interest, or, at his option or at the option of his legal representative, in lieu of interest, the profits attributable to the use of his right in the property of the dissolved partnership; provided that the creditors of the dissolved partnership as against the separate creditors, or the representative of the retired or deceased partner, shall have priority on any claim arising under this section, as provided by section 41(8) of this act.

Section 43. Accrual of Actions. The right to an account of his interest shall accrue to any partner, or his legal representative, as against the winding up partners or the surviving partners or the person or partnership continuing the business, at the date of dissolution, in the absence of any agreement to the contrary.

Appendix C

Sample

Partnership Agreement

On this date, (date) at the City of (city), County of (county), State of (state) this partnership agreement is hereby entered into, by and between the below listed partners:

Name   Address

In consideration of the mutual promises contained in this agreement, the above-named persons agreed to and do hereby form a partnership under the Uniform Partnership Act of the State of (state) and the terms of this agreement.

The name of the partnership shall be (name). Its principal place of business shall be at (address) or any other place as mutually agreed on by the partners. Other places of business of the partnership shall be mutually agreed to by the partners.

The business to be carried on by the partnership is that of (state type of business).

The partnership shall commence on (date) and shall continue until dissolved by mutual agreement of the partners.

The initial capital of the partnership will be (state total value in dollars and cents including value of non-cash assets invested). Of this amount invested (amount of cash invested) is in cash and (value of non-cash property) is in property.

The below listed partners will contribute the following amounts of cash:

Name   Amount

The below listed partners will contribute the following non-cash assets:

Name   Description of property   Value

The contributions and transfer to the partnership of all non-cash assets must be made on or before (date) or this agreement is null and void.

Each of the partners shall share in the profits and losses of the partnership in the following manner: (set out in detail the agreement as to sharing profits and losses).

Each of the partners will give his undivided attention time and attention to the partnership business and shall to the best of his ability promote the interests of the partnership. (If one or more partners will not devote full-time employment to the partnership, include that fact in this paragraph.)

Partners (will not receive) or (will receive the following) salary for work devoted to the partnership business.

Partners [may not draw any advances of expected profits] or [may draw the following advances of expected profits for living expenses every (time period). These advances will be charged against their share of the profits of the partnership. If profits are not as expected, partners may be required to re-emburse the partnership for any advances they have taken].

The books of the partnership shall be kept at (location) and shall be open for inspection by any partner during normal business hours. The fiscal year of the partnership shall be the normal tax year of all the partners.

All partners shall have equal rights in the management of the partnership and the conduct of the business of the partnership. Decisions shall be by majority vote of the partners, except as noted below. (Note any special situations below.)

No partner will, without the consent of all the partners, sell or dispose of the capital assets or property of the partnership.

On the death of a partner or the withdrawal of any partner, the partners desiring to continue the business shall pay to the estate of the dead partner or to the withdrawing partner the cash value of his interest in the partnership. If necessary to prevent economic strain on the business, the partners desiring to continue the business may delay the distribution of assets for a period of not longer than 180 days. If there is a dispute as to the value of the withdrawing or deceased partner's in the partnership, an independent and neutral appraiser will be appointed.

In the event that the majority of partners shall agree to dissolve the partnership, the business shall be wound up, debts paid and the surplus divided among the partners in accordance with ratio of their share of the investment in the partnership at the time the dissolution is started.

This agreement may be amended by the two-thirds vote of the partners as measured by their interest in the sharing of the profits and losses.

Executed at (place) on the date first above written.

(signatures of each partner)

Appendix D

Uniform Limited Partnership Act

(Courtesy of National Conference of Commissioners on Uniform State Laws)

Section 1. (Limited Partnership Defined.) A limited partnership is a partnership formed by two or more persons under the provisions of Section 2, having as members one or more general partners and one or more limited partners. The limited partners as such shall not be bound by the obligations of the partnership.

Section 2. (Formation.) (1) Two or more persons desiring to form a limited partnership shall

(a) Sign and swear to a certificate, which shall state
    I. The name of the partnership,
    II. The character of the business,
    III. The location of the principal place of business,
    IV. The name and place of residence of each member; general and limited partners being respectively designated,
    V. The term for which the partnership is to exist,
    VI. The amount of cash and a description of and the agreed value of the other property contributed by each limited partner.
    VII. The additional contributions, if any, agreed to be made by each limited partner and the times at which or events on the happening of which they shall be made,

VIII. The time, if agreed upon, when the contribution of each limited partner is to be returned,

IX. The share of the profits or the other compensation by way of income which each limited partner shall receive by reason of his contribution,

X. The right, if given, of a limited partner to substitute an assignee as contributor in his place, and the terms and conditions of the substitution,

XI. The right, if given, of one or more of the limited partners to admit additional partners,

XII. The right, if given, of one or more of the limited partners to priority over other limited partners, as to contributions or as to compensation by way of income, and the nature of such priority,

XIII. The right, if given, of the remaining general partner or partners to continue the business on the death, retirement or insanity of a general partner, and

XIV. The right, if given, of a limiter partner to demand and receive property other than cash in return for his contribution.

(b) File for record the certificate in the office of (here designate the proper office).

(2) A limited partnership is formed if there has been substantial compliance in good faith with the requirements of paragraph (1).

Section 3. (Business Which May Be Carried On.) A limited partnership may carry on any business which a partnership without limited partners may carry on, except (here designate the business to be prohibited).

Section 4. (Character of Limited Partner's Contribution.) The contributions of a limited partner may be cash or other property, but not services.

Section 5. (A Name Not To Contain Surname of Limited Partner; Exceptions.) (1) The surname of a limited partner shall not appear in the partnership name, unless

(a) It is also the surname of a general partner, or

(b) Prior to the time when the limited partner became such the business had been carried on under a name in which his surname appeared.

(2) A limited partner whose name appears in a partnership name contrary to the provisions of paragraph (1) is liable as a general partner to partnership creditors who extend credit to the partnership without actual knowledge that he is not a general partner.

Section 6. (Liability for False Statements in Certificate.) If the certificate contains a false statement, one who suffers loss by reliance on such statement may hold liable any party to the certificate who knew the statement to be false

(a) At the time he signed the certificate, or

(b) Subsequently, but within a sufficient time before the statement was relied upon to enable him to cancel or amend the certificate, or to file a petition for its cancellation or amendment as provided in Section 25(3).

Section 7. (Limited Partner Not Liable to Creditors.) A limited partner shall not become liable as a general partner unless, in addition to the exercise of his rights and powers as a limited partner, he takes part in the control of the business.

Section 8. (Admission of Additional Limited Partners.) After the formation of a limited partnership, additional limited partners may be admitted upon filing an amendment to the original certificate in accordance with the requirements of Section 25.

Section 9. (Rights, Powers and Liabilities of a General Partner.) (1) A general partner shall have all the rights and powers and be subject to all the restrictions and liabilities of a partner in a partnership without limited partners, except that without the written consent or ratification of the specific act by all the limited partners, a general partner or all of the general partners have no authority to

(a) Do any act in contravention of the certificate,

(b) Do any act which would make it impossible to carry on the ordinary business of the partnership,

(c) Confess a judgment against the partnership,

(d) Possess partnership property, or assign their rights in specific partnership property, for other than a partnership purpose,

(e) Admit a person as a general partner,

(f) Admit a person as a limited partner, unless the right so to do is given in the certificate,

(g) Continue the business with partnership property on the death, retirement or insanity of a general partner, unless the right so to do is given in the certificate.

Section 10. (Rights of a Limited Partner.) (1) A limited partner shall have the same rights as a general partner to

(a) Have the partnership books kept at the principal place of business of the partnership, and at all times to inspect and copy any of them,

(b) Have on demand true and full information of all things affecting the partnership, and a formal account of partnership affairs, whenever circumstances render it just and reasonable, and

(c) Have dissolution and winding up by decree of court.

(2) A limited partner shall have the right to receive a share of the profits or other compensation by way of income, and to the return of his contribution as provided in Sections 15 and 16.

Section 11. (Status of Person Erroneously Believing Himself a Limited Partner.) A person who has contributed to the capital of a business conducted by a person or partnership erroneously believing that he has become a limited partner in a limited partnership, is not, by reason of his exercise of the rights of a limited partner, a general partner with the person or in the partnership carrying on the business, or bound by the obligations of such person or partnership; provided that on ascertaining the mistake he promptly renounces his interest in the profits of the business, or other compensation by way of income.

Section 12. (One Person both General and Limited Partner.) (1) A person may be a general partner and a limited partner in the same partnership at the same time.

(2) A person who is a general, and also at the same time a limited partner, shall have all the rights and powers and be subject to all the restrictions of a general partner; except that, in respect to his contribution, he shall have the rights against the other members which he would have had if he were not also a general partner.

Section 13. (Loans and Other Business Transactions with Limited Partner.) (1) A limited partner also may loan money to and transact other business with the partnership, and, unless he is also a general partner, receive on account of resulting claims against the partnership, with general creditors, a pro rata share of the assets. No limited partner shall in respect to any such claim

(a) Receive or hold as collateral security any partnership property, or

(b) Receive from a general partner or the partnership any payment, conveyance, or release from liability, if at the time the assets of the partnership are not sufficient to discharge partnership liabilities to persons not claiming as general or limited partners,

(2) The receiving of collateral security, or a payment, conveyance, or release in violation of the provisions of paragraph (1) is a fraud on the creditors of the partnership.

Section 14. (Relation of Limited Partners Inter Se.) Where there are several limited partners the members may agree that one or more of the limited partners shall have a priority over other limited partners as to the return of their contributions, as to their compensation by way of income, or as to any other matter. If such an agreement is made it shall be stated in the certificate, and in the absence of such a statement all the limited partners shall stand upon equal footing.

Section 15. (Compensation of Limited Partner.) A limited partner may receive from the partnership the share of the profits or the compensation by way of income stipulated for in the certificate; provided, that after such payment is made, whether from the property of the partnership or that of a general partner, the partnership assets are in excess of all liabilities of the partnership except liabilities to limited partners on account of their contributions and to general partners.

Section 16. (Withdrawal or Reduction of Limited Partner's Contribution.) (1) A limited partner shall not receive from a general partner or out of partnership property any part of his contribution until

(a) All liabilities of the partnership, except liabilities to general partners and to limited partners on account of their contributions, have been paid or there remains property of the partnership sufficient to pay them,

(b) The consent of all members is had, unless the return of the contribution may be rightfully demanded under the provisions of paragraph (2), and

(c) The certificate is cancelled or so amended as to set forth the withdrawal or reduction.

(2) Subject to the provisions of paragraph (1) a limited partner may rightfully demand the return of his contribution

(a) On the dissolution of a partnership, or

(b) When the date specified in the certificate for its return has arrived, or

(c) After he has given six months' notice in writing to all other members, if no time is specified in the certificate either for the return of the contribution or for the dissolution of the partnership.

(3) In the absence of any statement in the certificate to the contrary or the consent of all members, a limited partner, irrespective of the nature of his contribution, has only the right to demand and receive cash in return for his contribution.

(4) A limited partner may have the partnership dissolved and its affairs wound up when

(a) He rightfully but unsuccessfully demands the return of his contribution, or

(b) The other liabilities of the partnership have not been paid, or the partnership property is insufficient for their payment as required by paragraph (1a) and the limited partner would otherwise be entitled to the return of his contribution.

Section 17. (Liability of Limited Partner to Partnership.) (1) A limited partner is liable to the partnership

(a) For the difference between his contribution as actually made, and that stated in the certificate as having been made, and

(b) For any unpaid contribution which he agreed in the certificate to make in the future at the time and on the conditions stated in the certificate.

(2) A limited partner holds as trustee for the partnership

(a) Specific property stated in the certificate as contributed by him, but which was not contributed or which has been wrongfully returned, and

(b) Money or other property wrongfully paid or conveyed to him on account of his contribution.

(3) The liabilities of a limited partner as set forth in this section can be waived or compromised only by the consent of all members; but a waiver or compromise shall not affect the right of a creditor of a partnership, who extended credit or whose claim arose after the filing and before a cancellation or amendment of the certificate, to enforce such liabilities.

(4) When a contributor has rightfully received the return in whole or in part of the capital of his contribution, he is nevertheless liable to the partnership for any sum, not in excess of such return with interest, necessary to discharge its liabilities to all creditors who extended credit or whose claims arose before such return.

Section 18. (Nature of Limited Partner's Interest in Partnership.) A limited partner's interest in the partnership is personal property.

Section 19. (Assignment of Limited Partner's Interest.) (1) A limited partner's interest is assignable.

(2) A substituted limited partner is a person admitted to all the rights of a limited partner who has died or has assigned his interest in a partnership.

(3) An assignee, who does not become a substituted limited partner, has no right to require any information or account of the partnership transactions or to inspect the partnership books; he is only entitled to receive the share of the profits or other compensation by way of income, or the return of his contribution, to which his assignor would otherwise be entitled.

(4) An assignee shall have the right to become a substituted limited partner if all the members (except the assignor) consent thereto or if the assignor, being there unto empowered by the certificate, gives the assignee that right.

(5) An assignee becomes a substituted limited partner when the certificate is appropriately amended in accordance with Section 25.

(6) The substituted limited partner has all the rights and powers, and is subject to all the restrictions and liabilities of his assignor, except those liabilities of which he was ignorant at the time he became a limited partner and which could not be ascertained from the certificate.

(7) The substitution of the assignee as a limited partner does not release the assignor from liability to the partnership under Section 6 and 17.

Section 20. (Effect of Retirement, Death or Insanity of a General Partner.) The retirement, death or insanity of a general partner dissolves the partnership, unless the business is continued by the remaining general partners

(a) Under a right so to do stated in the certificate, or

(b) With the consent of all members.

Section 21. (Death of Limited Partner.) (1) On the death of a limited partner his executor or administrator shall have all the rights of a limited partner for the purpose of settling his estate, and such power as the deceased had to constitute his assignee a substituted limited partner.

(2) The estate of a deceased limited partner shall be liable for all his liabilities as a limited partner.

Section 22. (Rights of Creditors of Limited Partner.) (1) On due application to a court of competent jurisdiction by any judgment creditor of a limited partner, the court may charge the interest of the indebted limited partner with payment of the unsatisfied amount of the judgment debt; and may appoint a receiver, and make all other orders, directions, and inquiries which the circumstances of the case may require.

(2) The interest may be redeemed with the separate property of any general partner, but may not be redeemed with partnership property.

(3) The remedies conferred by paragraph (1) shall not be deemed exclusive of others which may exist.

(4) Nothing in this act shall be held to deprive a limited partner of his statutory exemption.

Section 23. (Distribution of Assets.) (1) In setting accounts after dissolution the liabilities of the partnership shall be entitled to payment in the following order:

(a) Those to creditors, in the order of priority as provided by law, except those to limited partners on account of their contributions, and to general partners,

(b) Those to limited partners in respect to their share of the profits and other compensation by way of income on their contributions,

(c) Those to limited partners in respect to the capital of their contributions,

(d) Those to general partners other than for capital and profits,

(e) Those to general partners in respect to profits,

(f) Those to general partners in respect to capital,

(2) Subject to any statement in the certificate or to subsequent agreement, limited partners share in the partnership assets in respect to their claims for capital, and in respect to their claims for profits or for compensation by way of income on their contributions respectively, in proportion to their respective amounts of such claims.

Section 24. (When Certificate Shall be Cancelled or Amended.) (1) The certificate shall be cancelled when the partnership is dissolved or all limited partners cease to be such.

(2) A certificate shall be amended when

(a) There is a change in the name of the partnership or in the amount or character of the contribution of any limited partner,

(b) A person is substituted as a limited partner,

(c) An additional limited partner is admitted,

(d) A person is admitted as a general partner,

(e) A general partner retires, dies or becomes insane, and the business is continued under Section 20.

(f) There is a change in the character of the business of the partnership,

(g) There is a false or erroneous statement in the certificate,

(h) There is a change in the time as stated in the certificate for the dissolution of the partnership or for the return of a contribution,

(i) A time is fixed for the dissolution of the partnership, or the return of a contribution, no time having been specified in the certificate, or

(j) The members desire to make a change in any other statement in the certificate in order that it shall accurately represent the agreement between them.

Section 25. (Requirements for Amendment and for Cancellation of Certificate.) (1) The writing to amend a certificate shall

(a) Conform to the requirement of Section 2(1a) as far as necessary to set forth clearly the change in the certificate which it is desired to make, and

(b) Be signed and sworn to by all members, and an amendment substituting a limited partner or adding a limited or general partner shall be signed also by the member to be substituted or added, and when a limited partner is to be substituted, the amendment shall also be signed by the assigning limited partner.

(2) The writing to cancel a certificate shall be signed by all members.

(3) A person desiring the cancellation or amendment of a certificate, if any person designated in paragraphs (1) and (2) as a person who must execute the writing refuses to do so, and may petition the (here designate the proper court) to direct a cancellation or amendment thereof.

(4) If the court finds that the petitioner has a right to have the writing executed by a person who refuses to do so, it shall order the (here designate the responsible official in the office designated in Section 2) in the office where the certificate is recorded to record the cancellation or amendment of the certificate; and where the certificate is to be amended, the court shall also cause to be filed for record in said office a certified copy of its decree setting forth the amendment.

(5) A certificate is amended or cancelled when there is filed for record in the office (here designate the office designated in Section 2) where the certificate is recorded

(a) A writing in accordance with the provisions of paragraph (1), or (2) or

(b) A certified copy of the order of court in accordance with the provisions of paragraph (4).

(6) After the certificate is duly amended in accordance with this section, the amended certificate shall thereafter by for all purposes the certificate provided for by this act.

Section 26. (Parties to Actions.) A contributor, unless he is a general partner, is not a proper party to proceedings by or against a partnership, except where the object is to enforce a limited partner's right against or liability to the partnership.

Section 27. (Name of Act.) This act may be cited as The Uniform Limited Partnership Act.

Section 28. (Rules of Construction.) (1) The rule that statutes in derogation of the common law are to be strictly construed shall have no application to this act.

(2) This act shall be so interpreted and construed as to effect its general purpose to make uniform the law of those states which enact it.

(3) This act shall not be so construed as to impair the obligations of any contract existing when the act goes into effect, nor to affect any action on proceedings begun or right accrued before this act takes effect.

Section 29. (Rules for Cases not Provided for in this Act.) In any case not provided for in this act the rules of law and equity, including the law merchant, shall govern.

Section 30. (Provisions for Existing Limited Partnerships.) (1) A limited partnership formed under any statute of this state prior to the adoption of this act, may become a limited partnership under this act by complying with the provisions of Section 2; provided the certificates sets forth

(a) The amount of the original contribution of each limited partner, and the time when the contribution was made, and

(b) That the property of the partnership exceeds the amount sufficient to discharge its liabilities to persons not claiming as general or limited partners by an amount greater than the sum of the contributions of its limited partners.

(2) A limited partnership formed under any statute of this state prior to the adoption of this act, until or unless it becomes a limited partnership under this act, shall continue to be governed by the provisions of (here insert proper reference to the existing limited partnership act or acts), except that such partnership shall not be renewed unless so provided in the original agreement.

Appendix E

Articles of Incorporation of All Business Company, Inc.

We, the undersigned incorporators, hereby certify and file this Certificate of Incorporation under the provisions and subject to the laws of the State of _____, particularly (at this point insert the specific state statute under which the corporation is incorporated) for the purposes of the transaction of business and conduct and promotion of the objects and purposes stated in this document.

The name of the incorporation (hereinafter called the Corporation) is ALL BUSINESS COMPANY, INC.

The Corporation's principal place of business is located in the City of _____, in the County of _____, in the State of _____, at the street and number of _____. (If the principal place of business is outside the state include this phrase: The address of resident agent of the Corporation is _____)

The nature of the business and the purposes to be conducted and promoted by the Corporation are _____. In addition, to the authority to promote any lawful purpose and to engage in any lawful activity for which corporations may be organized under the General Corporation Laws of the State of _____.

The names and addresses of each of the incorporators:

The names and addresses of the original directors are:

The Corporation shall have perpetual existence.
The total number of shares of stock which the corporation is authorized to issue

is _____ with a par value of $_____ each. All shares of stock shall be of one class and are Common Stock. The number of shares of stock originally issued are _____.

The effective date of the articles of incorporation of the Corporation, and the date upon which the existence of the corporation shall commence is _____ 19____.

IN WITNESS WHEREOF, we, the undersigned incorporators, do hereby further certify that the facts hereinabove stated are truly set forth and have set our respective signatures and seals.

Dated at (place) (month, day, year):

_____(seal)

_____(seal)

_____(seal)]

(STATE OF _____

COUNTY OF _____)

On the below listed date, the following persons personally appeared before me (list names of incorporators here), all incorporators who sign the foregoing Articles of Incorporation, known to me personally to be such and are familiar with the provisions and contents of the Articles of Incorporation, they acknowledged the act of signing their names and state that the facts of the above document are truly set forth.

Given under my hand and seal of office this _____ day of _____, 198____

_____

Notary Public

Appendix F

Summary of Small Claims Courts' Rules by State

ALABAMA

The Alabama small claims court is a branch of the district court. The maximum dollar limit for which an individual may be sued is $500.00. Attorneys are allowed to present cases in small claims court. Either party who is unhappy with the decision of the small claims court may appeal within fourteen days to the circuit court for a new trial. The defendant may be sued in the county or district where he resides or where the injury or property damage occurred. A corporation may be sued in any county which it does business. The service of process in Alabama is either by certified mail or sheriff's constable or by disinterested adult.

ALASKA

The small claims court of Alaska is part of the district court. The maximum dollar amount an individual may be sued for is $2,000.00. The defendant may be sued in the county of his residence, of his place of employment or business or in which injury or property damage occurred. Service of process in Alaska may be by registered or certified mail or a peace officer may serve it. Attorneys are allowed to practice in small claims court in Alaska. Either party is allowed to appeal the decision of the small claims court within 30 days on any claim over $50.00 to the superior court. Appeals in small claims court in Alaska is based solely on the law, not the facts. The defendant has 20 days from the date of service to file a written answer to a petition under small claims court.

ARIZONA

Arizona has no formal small claims court system. Small claims, however, may be handled by the justice court. The maximum dollar limit is $2,500.00. The defendant may be sued in any precinct in which he resides, where any act or mission or obligation was to be performed; and corporations may be sued in any precinct wherein they have an agent, representative or conduct any business. The service of process in the Arizona justice court is by sheriff, constable or disinterested adults with the courts permission. Attorneys are allowed to practice in the justice court in Arizona. Appeals are allowed by either party if appealed within 10 days of the small claims court's decision. The appeal must be based solely on the law, not on facts.

ARKANSAS

The small claims courts in Arkansas are a branch of the municipal court; or in rural areas, the justice of the peace; or in Boone County, a branch of the Boone County Circuit Court. The maximum dollar limit for which a person may sue in small claims court in Arkansas is $300.00 except for the small claims court in Boone County. In that county, the maximum limit is $500.00. A defendant may be sued in any county in which the defendant resides, in any county in which an act or omission occurred or an obligation was to be performed. Either party may appeal any decision to the circuit court within 30 days of notification of the small claims court decision.

CALIFORNIA

The small claims courts of California are a department of either the municipal court in urban areas or the justice court in rural areas. The maximum dollar limit is $1,500.00. The defendant may be sued in any judicial district where the defendant resides and in any judicial district where an act, or omission, or an obligation was to be performed. A corporation may be sued in the county where its principal place of business is located. The service of process in the California small claims courts may be by sheriff, certified or registered mail, or disinterested adult. Attorneys are not allowed to practice in small claims courts in California. Only by the defendant can appeal.

COLORADO

The small claims courts in Colorado are a branch of the county courts. The maximum dollar amount which anyone can sue in small claims courts is $1,000.00. The defendant may be sued in any county where the defendant resides or in any county where the plantiff resides if the defendant is personally served in that county; or in any county in which a contract or obligation was entered into. The service of process in Colorado may be by sheriff, certified mail or disinterested adult. Attorneys are allowed in small claims court only if the attorney is the plaintiff or defendant or a full-time employee of the plaintiff or defendant. Either party may appeal to the district court within 10 days of being notified of the small claims courts decision.

CONNECTICUT

The Connecticut small claims courts are a division of their superior courts. The maximum dollar limit for which anyone may sue in a small claims court in Connecticut is $1,000.00. The defendant may be sued in the county or judicial district where he resides or does business or in any county in which an act or omission in question occurred. The service of process must be either by a disinterested adult or a peace officer. Attorneys are allowed to practice in small claims court. No appeals are permitted.

DELAWARE

Delaware, like Arizona, has no formal small claims system. However, a person may sue in a justice of peace court where the maximum dollar limit is $1,500.00. A person may be sued anywhere in the state of Delaware. Service of process may be by either certified mail, sheriff or constable. Attorneys are allowed to practice in the small claims court. Either party may appeal within 15 days after notification of the decision in the small claims court.

DISTRICT OF COLUMBIA

The small claims courts in the District of Columbia are a part of the superior court system. The maximum dollar limit for which a person may be sued in the District of Columbia is $750.00. Since there is only one small claims court in the District of Columbia located on G Street, NW, that is the only place where the defendant can be sued. In order to sue a defendant in the small claims court of the District, the defendant must be served within the boundaries of the District of Columbia. Service of process may be by disinterested adult, certified or registered mail, or U.S. Marshall. Attorneys are allowed to practice in the small claims courts. Either party can appeal. The time limit for appeals is only three days after notification of the small claims decision.

FLORIDA

The small claims courts in Florida are a branch of the county court system. The maximum dollar limit for which an individual may be sued is $1,500.00. The defendant may be sued in any county in which he resides; any county in which an act or omission occurred under the contract. A corporation may be sued in any county in which it keeps an office for transactions of business. The service of process is by registered mail, disinterested adult or a peace officer. Attorneys are allowed to practice before the small claims courts in Florida. Either party may appeal a decision of the small claims court within 30 days after notification to the circuit court. Appeals are only on questions of law. Either party has a right to a jury trial.

GEORGIA

The Georgia small claims courts varies according to counties, and the rules are different for each county. In Fulton County (Atlanta), the maximum dollar amount for which an individual may be sued is $200.00. Service of process must be by the constable, and attorneys are allowed. Either party can appeal within 30 days to the superior court for a new trial.

HAWAII

The small claims courts in Hawaii are a part of the district court. The maximum dollar limit for which a defendant may be sued in a Hawaiian small claims court is $1,000.00. The defendant may be sued in the judicial district where he resides or in the case of more than one defendant, where a majority of the defendants reside, or in a judicial district where any omission or act under the contract occurred. Attorneys are allowed to practice in the Hawaiian small claims courts. There are no appeals of the decisions of the small claims courts.

IDAHO

The Idaho small claims court is a division of the district court. The maximum amount for which anyone may be sued in Idaho is $2,000.00. The defendant may be sued in the county where he resides only. A corporation may be sued in the county where its principal place of business is located. Service of process may be either by registered or certified mail, disinterested adult or the sheriff. Attorneys are not allowed to practice in the Idaho small claims court. Either party may appeal the decision of the small claims court to the district court within 30 days after notification of the decision.

ILLINOIS

There are some differences in the various small claims courts in Illinois. Normally, the small claims courts are in the circuit courts, except in Cook County where the small claims court is considered the "Pro Se" Branch of the Cook County Court system. The maximum amount an individual may be sued for in most small claims courts in Illinois is $1,000.00. In Cook County it is $2,500.00. This amount varies in individual counties; therefore, make sure you check your county. Normally, the defendant may be sued within any county he resides, conducts business, has an office or any county in which act or admission under the contract in question occurred. The service of process may be by disinterested adults, by the sheriff or certified mail for service within the county only. Attorneys allowed in the normal small claims courts. In the Cook County pro se small claims branch of the court, attorneys are not allowed. Appeals are permitted by either party to the Appellate Court within 30 days after notification of the small claims court decision. The parties may appeal on issues of law only.

INDIANA

The Indiana small claims court is a branch of the circuit court, county court or superior court. It varies throughout the state. The maximum dollar amount is $2,000.00 in most small claims courts. However, for those small claims courts that are a part of the superior court, the maximum amount is $1,500.00. The defendant may be sued in any county in which the defendant resides, in which he is employed, or in which an act, omission or obligation under the contract has occurred or the county in which the contract was to be performed by the defendant. Service of process may be by either by registered mail, sheriff or police officer. Attorneys are allowed, and appeals may be taken by either party to the Court of Appeals.

IOWA

The Iowa small claims court is a part of the district court. The maximum dollar limit is $1,000.00. The defendant may be sued in any county in which the defendant resides, any county in which an act or admission or obligation was to be performed that is an issue. The service of process may be by disinterested adult, certified mail, or a peace officer. Attorneys are allowed to practice in the Iowa small claims court. Appeals are allowed to either party within 10 days on legal issues only.

KANSAS

The Kansas small claims courts are a part of the district courts. The maximum dollar amount in Kansas is $500.00. The defendant may be sued in any county in which he resides or any county in which he can be served if the defendant is employed or conducts business in that county, or in the county in which the plaintiff resides if the defendant can be served in that county. The service of process can be served by disinterested adult or the sheriff only. Attorneys are not allowed to practice in the Kansas small claims courts. Appeals are permitted by either party within 10 days after notification of the small claims courts decision.

KENTUCKY

The small claims courts in Kentucky are a division of the state district court system. The maximum amount for which an individual may be sued for in small claims court is $1,000.00. The defendant may be sued only in the judicial district where he resides or where he or his agent is doing business. The service of process must be either by registered mail, sheriff or constable. Attorneys are permitted to practice in the small claims courts. Either party may appeal to the circuit court within 10 days on legal issues only.

LOUISIANA

In the urban areas of Louisiana the small claims courts are a part of the city courts; and in the rural areas, they are part of the justice of peace courts. The maximum dollar amount for which anyone may be sued in Louisiana is in city court $1,500, and in the justice of peace courts $1,200. The defendant may be sued only in the parish in which he resides. A corporation or a partnership may also be sued in any district in which they have an office or business establishment. The service of process is by certified mail or sheriff or constable. Attorneys are allowed to practice in the small claims courts in Louisiana. Appeals are allowed by either party only in justice of the peace courts to the district court. In the small claim cases tried in city courts, no appeals are allowed.

MAINE

The small claims court system in Maine is a part of the district court. The maximum dollar amount for which anyone may be sued in the small claims court in Maine is $1,000.00. The defendant may be sued in the district in which the defendant resides or has a place of business. A corporation may be sued in any district in which it has either a place of business or where its resident agent resides. The service of process may either be by the sheriff or certified mail. Attorneys are allowed to practice in small claims court in Maine. Either party can appeal a decision of small claims court to the superior court on issues of law within 10 days after notification of the small claims court decision.

MARYLAND

The small claims court in Maryland is a branch of the district court. The maximum amount for which an individual may be sued in the small claims court in Maryland is $1,000.00. The defendant may be sued in any county in which he resides, in which he is employed, in which he does business or where the injury to person or property in question occurred. The service of process must either be by the sheriff or constable. Attorneys are allowed to practice in the small claims court in Maryland. Either party may appeal within 30 days to either the Baltimore City Court if inside Baltimore or the circuit court if outside of Baltimore. The appeal is basically a request for a new trial.

MASSACHUSETTS

In Boston, the small claims court is a part of the municipal court. Elsewhere in Massachusetts, it is part of the district court. The maximum dollar limit for which an individual may be sued in the small claims court in Massachusetts is $750.00 except on cases involving consumer complaints against businesses. In those cases, the maximum amount is $2,250.00. The defendant may be sued in any judicial district in which the defendant resides, is employed or does business. The service of process may be by registered mail, sheriff, or constable. Attorneys are allowed, and either party may appeal to the superior court within 10 days after notification of the small claims court decision.

MICHIGAN

The Michigan small claims court is a branch of the district court. The maximum dollar amount for which an individual may be sued in the small claims courts are $600.00. The defendant may be sued in any district in which he resides, has a place of business, conducts business or in any county in which an act or omission is question occurred. The service of process is by disinterested adult, sheriff, or certified mail. Attorneys are not permitted to practice in the small claims courts. Neither party may appeal the decision of the small claims court.

MINNESOTA

The Minnesota small claims court is part of the conciliation court and a branch of either the municipal or county court. The maximum amount for which an individual may be sued in the Minnesota courts is in the municipal court for $1,000.00 and in county court for $500.00. The defendant may be sued in any county in which he resides. A corporation may be sued in any county in which it has an office or place of business. The service of process may be by disinterested adults, registered or certified mail, police officer, sheriff, and in some cases service may be by a municipal court clerk who may orally or by telephone affect service. Attorneys are permitted to practice in the

Minneapolis and St. Paul's small claims courts only. Either party may appeal within 10 days of notification of the decision of the small claims court to municipal court or county court for a new trial.

MISSISSIPPI

The maximum amount for which an individual may be sued in a small claims court in the state of Mississippi is $750.00. The Mississippi small claims courts are a part of the justice of peace courts. The defendant may be sued in any county in which he resides, in any county in which an act or omission occurred, or the obligation entered into which is the subject of the law suit. A corporation may be sued in any county where it has an office. The service of process is normally by the sheriff or constable only. Attorneys are allowed, and either party may appeal within 10 days to the circuit court for a new trial.

MISSOURI

The small claims courts of Missouri are a part of the circuit court system. The maximum amount for which an individual may sue in the small claims courts in Missouri is $1,000. The defendant may be sued in any county in which he resides, or if served in the county where the plaintiff lives, or in any county where an act or admission in question occurred. A corporation may be sued in any county where it has an office or agent for the transaction of usual or customary business. The service of process may be by either certified mail or sheriff. Attorneys are allowed, and either party may appeal within 10 days of notification of small claims court decision to the circuit court judge for a new trial.

MONTANA

The Montana small claims court is part of the district or justice court. The maximum dollar amount in the Montana small claims is $1,500 in city courts and $750 in justice courts. The defendant may be sued in any judicial district or county in which the defendant resides, in any county in which an obligation in question was to be performed. Service of process may be by the sheriff, constable, or disinterested adult. Service of process must be limited, however, to within the county's boundary. Attorneys are not permitted unless all parties present have an attorney. Either party may appeal within 10 days to the district court.

NEBRASKA

The Nebraska small claims courts are a part of either the county or municipal court. The maximum dollar amount for which an individual may be sued in Nebraska is $1,000. The defendant may be sued in any county in which he resides or in any county in which an injury or property damage occurred. A corporation may be sued in any county where it regularly does business. Service of process may be by certified or registered mail. Attorneys are not allowed to practice in the Nebraska small claims courts. Either party may appeal within 10 days to the district court requesting a new trial.

NEVADA

The Nevada small claims court is part of the justice court. The maximum dollar limit in the Nevada small claims courts are $1,000. The defendant may be sued in any city or township in which he resides. Service of process may be by disinterested adult or certified or registered mail. Attorneys are permitted to practice in the small claims courts. Appeals may be taken by either party to the district court on legal issues only within five days after the notification of the small claims judgment.

NEW HAMPSHIRE

The New Hampshire small claims courts are a part of the district or municipal courts. The maximum dollar limit is $500. The defendant may be sued in any city or town for municipal court or any county for district court in which the defendant resides. Service of process is normally by registered mail. Attorneys are allowed to practice in small claims court and either party may appeal on legal issues to the New Hampshire Supreme Court.

NEW JERSEY

The New Jersey small claims court is part of the county district court. The maximum dollar amount for which an individual may be sued in the New Jersey small claims court is $1,000. The defendant may be sued in any county in which he resides. A corporation may be sued in any county in which it is actually doing business. Either part may appeal the judgement of the small claims court within 45 days of notification of the decision to the appellate division of the superior court on legal issues only.

NEW MEXICO

The New Mexico small claims courts vary. Generally, the maximum dollar limit is $2,000. The defendant can be sued in the county in which he is served, the county in which he resides or in the county where an act or omission in question has occurred. Attorneys are allowed to practice in the New Mexico small claims courts. Either party may appeal a decision of the small claims court to the district court on issues of law, if appealed within 30 days of notification of the small claims court decision.

NEW YORK

The small claims courts vary in New York. The general rule is that they are a part of either the city courts or the district courts, or in some areas the justice courts. The maximum amount is $1,500. Normally, the defendant can be sued in any political subdivision in which the defendant resides, in which the defendant is employed, or has a business office. The service of process is normally by registered or certified mail. Attorneys are allowed to practice in the New York small claims court. Limited appeals are allowed. It varies per district.

NORTH CAROLINA

The maximum dollar amount for which an individual may be sued in North Carolina is $1,000.00. The North Carolina small claims courts are a part of the North Carolina District Court system. The defendant may be sued only in the county in which he resides. A corporation can be sued in any county in which it maintains a place of business. The service of process is by either certified mail or Sheriff's Office. Attorneys are allowed to practice in the small claims courts. Either party may appeal within 10 days of the decision to the district court, Division of the Superior Court, and request a new trial.

NORTH DAKOTA

The small claims courts of North Dakota are either a part of the county justice or the county courts. The maximum dollar amount varies in different counties with the normal maximum amount being $1,000. The defendant may be sued only in the county in which he resides. Corporations and other business associations may be sued in the county in which the corporation or partnership, etc. has a place of business. Attorneys are allowed to practice in the small claims court. There are no appeals from the North Dakota small claims court decisions.

OHIO

The small claims courts in Ohio are a part of the county or municipal court system. The maximum dollar amount for which a defendant may be sued is $1,000. In Ohio, the defendant may be sued in the county in which he resides or in the county in which an obligation was occurred that is in question. Service of process is by disinterested adult or certified mail. Attorneys are allowed to practice in the small claims courts. Either party may appeal within 30 days of notice of the small claims court decision to the Court of Common Pleas on legal issues only.

OKLAHOMA

The Oklahoma small claims court are a part of the district court system. The maximum dollar limit is $1,000. A defendant may be sued in the county in which the defendant resides, or in which an obligation was entered into. A corporation may be sued in any county in which it has an office. Attorneys are allowed to practice in the Oklahoma small claims court. Appeals are allowed by either party to the Oklahoma Supreme Court on legal issues only.

OREGON

The Oregon small claims courts are either a part of the district court or the justice court. The maximum amount for which a defendant may be sued for in a small claims court which is a division of the justice court is $500 and $700 in the small claims courts which are a part of the district court. The defendant can be sued only in the county in which he resides or in the county in which the plaintiff resides if the defendant can be served in that county. Service of process is normally by the sheriff, disinterested adult, or in cases of claims under $50 by certified mail. Attorneys are not allowed to practice in the Oregon small claims courts without the judge's consent.

PENNSYLVANIA

In Pennsylvania, there are two separate systems. One is the small claims court in Philadelphia which is a part of the Philadelphia Municipal Court. The small claims courts elsewhere in the state are a part of the district justice courts. The maximum amount an individual may be sued for throughout the state is $2,000; except, in Philadelphia where it is $1,000. The service of process in Philadelphia is by municipal court writ servers. Outside the county, service is by certified mail. Attorneys are allowed to practice in both systems. Appeals are permitted by either party within 30 days of notification of the small claims court decision. The appeals are made to the Court of Common Pleas on both issues of law and questions of fact.

PUERTO RICO

The Puerto Rican small claims court is part of the district court system. The maximum dollar amount for which an individual may be sued is $500. A defendant may be sued in any judicial district in which the defendant resides. Corporations, partnerships and other business associations may be sued in any district in which they do business or in any district where an obligation under the contract occurred. Service of process is normally by certified mail. Attorneys are permitted to practice in their small claims courts. Either party may appeal a decision of the small claims court to the superior court within 10 days of notification. Appeals are on issues of law only.

RHODE ISLAND

Rhode Island small claims court is part of the district court. The maximum dollar amount for which a person may be sued in small claims court is $1,000. The service of process is normally by certified or registered mail. Attorneys are permitted to practice in the small claims court. A defendant may appeal to the superior court requesting a new trial. Plaintiffs are not allowed to appeal a small claims court judgement.

SOUTH CAROLINA

The small claims court system is part of the magistrate's court. The maximum amount for which an individual may be sued is $1,000. The defendant may be sued in the county or township in which he resides. A corporation can be sued in any county in which it does business. The service of process is normally either by the sheriff or a disinterested adult. Attorneys are permitted to practice in South Carolina's small claims courts. Either party may appeal a decision of the small claims court to the county or circuit court on legal issues only.

SOUTH DAKOTA

The South Dakota small claims court is part of the circuit or magistrate court. The dollar limit for which someone may be sued in small claims court in South Dakota is $1,000. The defendant may be sued in any county in which he resides, in any county in which injury or property damage in question occurred. A corporation may be sued in the county where it has its principal place of business. Service of process is normally by certified or registered mail. Attorneys are permitted to practice in the South Dakota small claims court. There are no appeals from the decisions of the small claims court.

TENNESSEE

Tennessee small claims courts are a part of the Court of General Sessions, or in rural areas the Justice of Peace Court. The small claims court in Tennessee allows suits up to $10,000. The defendant may be sued in any county in which he resides, or in case of a debt in a county in which the obligation occurred. The service of process must either be by the sheriff or constable. Attorneys are permitted in the Tennessee small claims courts. Appeals are permitted by either party to the circuit court for a new trial if appealed within 10 days of notification of the small claims decision.

TEXAS

The Texas small claims courts are a part of the Justice of Peace Courts. The maximum dollar limit in Texas is a $500. The defendant may be sued in the precinct where he resides, or where the obligation is to be performed. Service of process must be by either sheriff or constable. Attorneys are permitted. Either party may appeal the decision of the small claims court to the county court or county court at law requesting a new trial if appealed within 10 days of notice of decision.

UTAH

The small claims courts in Utah are part of the circuit or justice court. The maximum dollar amount in Utah is $400. The defendant may be sued in any political subdivision in which he lives or in which an act or omission occurred. Service of process is either by the sheriff or disinterested adult. Attorneys are permitted to practice in the Utah small claims court. Only a defendant may appeal a decision of the small claims court. The appeals by the defendants are to the district court for a new trial.

VERMONT

The Vermont small claims courts are a part of the district court. The maximum amount for which an individual may be sued in small claims court is $500. The individual may be sued in any territorial unit in which the defendant resides or in any unit in which the plaintiff resides or where an act or admission in question under the suit occurred. Attorneys are permitted to practice in the Vermont small claims court. Any party may appeal a decision of the small claims court within 30 days to the Vermont Supreme Court on legal issues only.

VIRGINIA

The small claims courts of Virginia are a part of the general district court system. The maximum dollar amount for which an individual may be sued for is $7,000. The defendant may be sued in any district in which he resides, which he is employed in, or regularly and systematically conducts business in, or in any county in which act or omission under question occurred. Service of process is by either the sheriff or disinterested adult. Attorneys are permitted to practice in Virginia small claims court. Either party can appeal the decision to circuit court requesting a new trial.

WASHINGTON

The Washington small claims courts are part of the justice or district courts. The maximum dollar limit varies from $1,000 in the larger counties and $500 elsewhere. Attorneys are allowed to practice with the judge's consent. The defendant may be sued in the city, town or district in which he lives. A corporation may be sued in any district where it transacts business or has an office.

WEST VIRGINIA

The West Virginia small claims courts are a part of the magistrate courts. The maximum dollar amount in West Virginia is $1,500. The defendant may be sued in any county in which he resides, any county in which he can be served; and if the defendant is a corporation, in any county in which the corporation does business. Service of process is by either the sheriff or disinterested adult. Attorneys are permitted to practice in the West Virginia small claims court. Either party may appeal a decision within 20 days of notification to the circuit court requesting a new trial.

WISCONSIN

The Wisconsin small claims courts are part of the county court system. The maximum dollar limit for which an individual may be sued is $1,000. The defendant may be sued in any county in which he resides, or in any county in which injury or property damage occurred. A corporation may be sued in any county in which it has a place of business. The service of process is normally by the sheriff, disinterested adult, or registered mail. Attorneys are permitted to practice in the Wisconsin small claims courts. Either party may appeal within 45 days of a small claims court decision to the Court of Appeals on legal issues only.

WYOMING

The Wyoming small claims courts are a part of the county court or Justice of Peace Courts. The maximum dollar amount is $1,000. The defendant may be sued in any county in which the defendant resides or in which he is served. Service of process is normally by the sheriff, constable or disinterested adult. Attorneys are permitted to practice in the Wyoming small claims court. Appeals are permitted by either party to the district court on legal issues only.

Appendix G

Selected Federal Agencies

The following is a list of selected federal agencies that the business owner may contact when additional information is needed in the selected area:

Administrative Conference of the United States, Public Information Officer, 2120 L Street, N.W., Room 500, Washington, D.C. 20037, (202)254-7065.

Amtrak, Customer Relations, P.O. Box 2709, Washington, D.C. 20013, (202)363-2121.

Civil Aeronautics Board, Office of Congressional, Community and Consumer Affairs, Washington, D.C. 20428, (202)673-6047.

Commission on Civil Rights, Assistant Staff Directory, 1121 Vermont Avenue, N.W., Room 500, Washington, D.C. 20425, (202)254-6345.

Commodity Futures Trading Commission, Office of Governmental Affairs, 2033 K Street, N.W., Washington, D.C. 20581, (202)254-6090.

Consumer Product Safety Commission, Office of the Secretary, Washington, D.C. 20207, (202)492-6800 (District of Columbia), (800)638-2772 (toll free elsewhere).

Department of Agriculture, Agricultural Marketing Service, Washington, D.C. 20250, (202)447-7589.

Farmers Home Administration, Department of Agriculture, Washington, D.C. 20250, (202)447-4323.

Federal Crop Insurance Corporation, Department of Agriculture, South Building, Washington, D.C. 20250, (202)447-3287.

Food and Nutrition Service, Department of Agriculture, Room 512, 3101 Park Office Center Drive, Alexandria, Virginia 22302, (703)756-3276.

Meat and Poultry Hotline, Food Safety and Inspection Service, Department of Agriculture, Washington, D.C. 20250, (202)472-4485.

Office of the Consumer Advisor, Department of Agriculture, Administration Building, Washington, D.C. 20250, (202)382-9681.

Department of Commerce, Commissioner of Patents and Trademarks, Washington, D.C. 20231, (703)557-3428.

Office of Consumer Affairs, Room 5725, Department of Commerce, Washington, D.C. 20230, (202)377-5001.

Office of the Solicitor, Patent and Trademark Office, Department of Commerce, Washington, D.C. 20231, (703)557-3525.

Office of Utilization Research, National Marine Fisheries Service, Department of Commerce, Washington, D.C. 20235, (202)634-7458.

Office of Weights and Measures, National Bureau of Standards, Department of Commerce, Washington, D.C. 20234, (301)921-2401.

Department of Education, Clearing House on the Handicapped, 330 C Street, S.W., Mail Stop 2319, Washington, D.C. 20202, (202)245-0080.

Federal Student Financial Aid Program, Department of Education, Department CY184, Pueblo, Colorado 81009, (800)492-6602 (toll free—Maryland), (800)638-6700 (toll free elsewhere).

Office of Public Participation and Special Concerns, Department of Education, 400 Maryland Avenue, S.W., Reporters Building, Room 505, Washington, D.C. 20202, (202)447-9043.

Department of Energy, Conservation and Renewable Energy Inquiry and Referral Service, (phone only), (800)462-4983 (toll free—Pennsylvania), (800)523-2929 (toll free—continental U.S.), (800)233-3071 (toll free—Alaska and Hawaii).

Consumer Inquiries, Weatherization Assistance, Office of Conservation and Renewable Energy, Department of Energy, Washington, D.C. 20585, (202)252-2207.

Office of Consumer Affairs, Department of Energy, Washington, D.C. 20585, (202)252-5373.

Manager, Technical Information Center, P.O. Box 62, Oak Ridge, Tennessee 37830, (written complaints and inquiries only).

Department of Health and Human Services, AIDS Hotline, (202)646-8182 (District of Columbia), (800)342-AIDS (toll free elsewhere).

Public Inquiries, Administration on Aging, Department of Health and Human Services, Washington, D.C. 20201, (202)245-2158.

Cancer Hotline, (202)636-5700 (District of Columbia), (800)254-1234 (Hawaii), (212)794-7982 (New York City), (800)638-6070 (toll free—Alaska), (800)4-CANCER (toll free elsewhere).

Centers for Disease Control, Atlanta, Georgia 30333.

Division of Long-Term Care, Health Care Financing Administration, Department of Health and Human Services, 1849 Gwyn Oak Avenue, Dogwood East Building, Baltimore, Maryland 21207, (301)594-3642.

Food and Drug Administration, Look in your telephone directory under "U.S. Government, Health and Human Services Department, Food and Drug Administration." If it does not appear, contact the Federal Information Center (FIC) nearest you. If the FIC is unable to help you, write or call:

Consumer Affairs and Small Business Staff (HFO-22), Food and Drug Administration, Department of Health and Human Services, 5600 Fishers Lane, Room 13-55, Rockville, Maryland 20857, (301)443-4166.

Health Care Financing Administration, Department of Health and Human Services, 6325 Security Boulevard, Baltimore, Maryland 21207, (301)594-9086, (301)594-9016 TTY for the deaf.

Health Maintenance Organizations, Divisions of Private Sector Initiatives, Room 17A55, Parklawn Building, 5600 Fishers Lane, Rockville, Maryland 20857, (301)443-2778.

Inspector General's Hotline, (202)472-4222 (District of Columbia), (800)368-5779 (toll free elsewhere).

National Health Information Clearinghouse, Suite 600, 1555 Wilson Blvd., Rosslyn, Virginia 22209, (703)522-2590 (District of Columbia), (800)336-4797 (toll free elsewhere).

Office of Program Operations, Office for Civil Rights, Department of Health and Human Services, Washington, D.C. 20201, (202)245-6118.

Social Security Administration—Look in your telephone directory under "U.S. Government, Health and Human Services Department, Social Security Administration."

Department of Housing and Urban Development, Mobile Home Standards Division, 451 7th Street, S.W., Room 3234, Washington, D.C. 20410, (202)755-6590.

Office of Fair Housing and Equal Opportunity, Department of Housing and Urban Development, 451 7th Street, S.W., Room 5100, Washington, D.C. 20410, (202)755-7252 (District of Columbia), (800)424-8590 (toll free elsewhere).

Office of Interstate Land Sales, Department of Housing and Urban Development, 451 7th Street, S.W., Room 4108, Washington, D.C. 20410, (202)755-8182.

Federal Communications Commission, Consumer Assistance and Small Business Office, 1919 M Street, N.W., Room 252, Washington, D.C. 20554, (202)632-7000.

For complaints about radio, TV or telephone interference: Look in your telephone directory under "U.S. Government, Federal Communications Commission." If it does not appear, contact the Federal Information Center (FIC) nearest you. If the FIC is unable to help you, write or call the office listed above.

Federal Deposit Insurance Corporation—Look in your telephone directory under "U.S. Government, Federal Deposit Insurance Corporation." If it does not appear, contact the Federal Information Center (FIC) nearest you. If the FIC is unable to help you, write or call:

Office of Consumer Programs, Federal Deposit Insurance Corporation, 550 17th Street, N.W., Washington, D.C. 20429, (202)389-4353 (District of Columbia), (800)424-5488 (toll free elsewhere).

Federal Emergency Management Agency, Federal Insurance Administration, Washington, D.C. 20472, (202)287-0750 (District of Columbia), (800)638-6620 (toll free elsewhere).

Office of Disaster Assistance Programs—Look in your telephone directory under U.S. Government, Federal Emergency Management Agency. If it does not appear, contact the Federal Information Center (FIC) nearest you. If the FIC is unable to help you, write or call:

Office of Disaster Assistance Programs, Federal Emergency Management Agency, Washington, D.C. 20472, (202)287-0550.

Emergency Preparedness, Self-Protection—Look in your telephone directory under U.S. Government, Federal Emergency Management Agency. If it does not appear, contact the Federal Information Center (FIC) nearest you. If the FIC is unable to help you, write or call:

Office of Public Affairs, Federal Emergency Management Agency, Washington, D.C. 20472, (202)287-0300.

U.S. Fire Administration, Federal Emergency Management Agency, National Emergency Training Center, 16825 S. Seton Avenue, Emmitsburg, Maryland 21727, (301)652-6080 or 6180.

Federal Energy Regulatory Commission, Division of Intergovernmental Affairs, 825 North Capitol Street, N.E., Room 9200, Washington, D.C. 20426, (202)357-8392.

Federal Home Loan Bank Board—Look in your telephone directory under "U.S. Government, Federal Home Loan Bank Board, Office of Examination and Supervision." If it does not appear, contact the Federal Information Center (FIC) nearest you. If the FIC is unable to help you, write or call:

Department of Consumer and Civil Rights, Office of Community Investment, Federal Home Loan Bank Board, 1700 G Street, N.W., Fifth Floor, Washington, D.C. 20552, (202)377-6211.

Federal Maritime Commission, Office of Informal Inquiries and Complaints, 1100 L Street, N.W., Washington, D.C. 20573, (202)523-5807.

Federal Reserve System, Board of Governors of the—Look in your telephone directory under "U.S. Government, Federal Reserve System, Board of Governors of the." If it does not appear, contact the Federal Information Center (FIC) nearest you. If the FIC is unable to help you, write or call:

Federal Trade Commission—Look in your telephone directory under "U.S. Government, Federal Trade Commission." If it does not appear, contact the Federal Information Center (FIC) nearest you. If the FIC is unable to help you, write or call:

Correspondence Office, Federal Trade Commission, 6th and Pennsylvania Avenue, N.W., Room 701, Washington, D.C. 20580, (202)523-3567.

Correspondence Office, Federal Trade Commission, 6th and Pennsylvania Avenue, N.W., Room 701, Washington, D.C. 20580, (202)523-3567.

General Services Administration—Look in your telephone directory under "U.S. Government, General Services Administration." If it does not appear, contact the Federal Information Center (FIC) nearest you.

Government Printing Office, Government Publications, Superintendent of Documents, Publications Service Section, Washington, D.C. 20401, (202)275-3050.

Subscriptions, Superintendent of Documents, Subscription Research Section, Government Printing Office, Washington, D.C. 20402, (202)275-3054.

International Trade Commission, 701 E Street, N.W., Room 156, Washington, D.C. 20436, (202)523-0161.

Interstate Commerce Commission, Office of Compliance and Consumer Assistance, Interstate Commerce Commission, Washington, D.C. 20423, (202)275-7148.

National Consumer Cooperative Bank, Information Officer, 1630 Connecticut Avenue, N.W., Washington, D.C. 20009, (202)745-4757 (District of Columbia), (800)424-2481 (toll free elsewhere).

National Credit Union Administration—Look in your telephone directory under "U.S. Government, National Credit Union Administration." If it does not appear, contact the Federal Information Center (FIC) nearest you. If the FIC is unable to help you, write or call:

National Credit Union Administration, 1776 G Street, N.W., Washington, D.C. 20456, (202)375-1000.

National Labor Relations Board, Office of the Executive Secretary, Room 701, 1717 Pennsylvania Avenue, N.W., Washington, D.C. 20570, (202)254-9430.

National Transportation Safety Board, 800 Independence Avenue, S.W., Room 808, Washington, D.C. 20594, (202)382-6606.

Nuclear Regulatory Commission, Office of Public Affairs, Washington, D.C. 20555, (301)492-7715.

Office of the Federal Register, National Archives and Record Service, Washington, D.C. 20408, (202)523-5240.

Pension Benefit Guaranty Corporation, Suite 700, 2020 K Street, N.W., Washington, D.C. 20006, (202)254-4817.

Postal Rate Commission, Office of the Consumer Advocate, Washington, D.C. 20268, (202)254-3840.

President's Committee on Employment of the Handicapped, Public Relations Office, 1111 20th Street, N.W., Washington, D.C. 20036, (202)653-5044.

Railroad Retirement Board, 425 13th Street, N.W., Room 622, Washington, D.C. 20004, (202)724-0894 (between 9:00 a.m. and 3:30 p.m. Eastern time).

Securities and Exchange Commission, Office of Consumer Affairs and Information Service, 450 5th Street, N.W., Washington, D.C. 20549, (202)272-7440.

Small Business Administration, Office of Consumer Affairs, 1441 L Street, N.W., Room 503-D, Washington, D.C. 20416, (202)653-6076.

Tennessee Valley Authority, Citizen Action Office, West Summit Hill Drive, Knoxville, Tennessee 37902, (615)632-4402, (800)362-9250 (toll free—Tennessee), (800)251-9242 (toll free—Alabama, Arkansas, Georgia, Kentucky, Mississippi, North Carolina, Virginia).

United States Postal Service, Chief Postal Inspector, Washington, D.C. 20260, (202)245-5445.

For the consumer's convenience, all Postal Offices and mail carriers have postage-free Consumer Service Cards available for reporting mail problems and submitting comments and suggestions. If the problem cannot be resolved using the Consumer Service Card or through direct contact with the local Post Office, then contact:

Consumer Advocate, United States Postal Service, Washington, D.C. 20260, (202)245-4514.

Veterans Administration—Look in your telephone directory under "U.S. Government, Veterans Administration (VA)" for the nearest VA Regional Office or VA Medical Center. If it does not appear, contact the Federal Information Center (FIC) nearest you. If the FIC is unable to help you, contact:

Consumer Affairs Staff, Veterans Administration, Washington, D.C. 20420, (202)389-2843.

Department of Memorial Affairs, Cemetery Service, Veterans Administration, Washington, D.C. 20420, (202)275-1459.

Department of Memorial Affairs, Monuments Service, Veterans Administration, Washington, D.C. 20420, (202)275-1493.

For information about VA medical care, contact any VA facility (consult your telephone directory for care facility serving your area) or contact:

The Inquiries Unit (101B3), Veterans Administration, Washington, D.C. 20420, (202)389-3314.

Veterans Assistance Service, Veterans Administration, Washington, D.C. 20420, (202)389-2567.

Office of Real Estate Practices, Department of Housing and Urban Development, 451 7th Street, S.W., Room 9266, Washington, D.C. 20410, (202)426-0070.

Office of Single Family Housing, Federal Housing Administration, Department of Housing and Urban Development, 451 7th Street, S.W., Room 9278, Washington, D.C. 20410, (202)755-3046.

Office of Title Insurance Loans, Department of Housing and Urban Development, 451 7th Street, S.W., Room 9160, Washington, D.C. 20410, (202)755-6680.

Office of Urban Rehabilitation, Department of Housing and Urban Development, 451 7th Street, S.W., Room 7168, Washington, D.C. 20410, (202)755-5685.

Department of the Interior, Bureau of Indian Affairs, Washington, D.C. 20240, (202)343-7445.

National Park Service, Department of the Interior, Washington, D.C. 20240, (202)343-4621.

Division of Law Enforcement, United States Fish and Wildlife Service, Department of the Interior, P.O. Box 28006, Washington, D.C. 20005, (202)343-9242.

Department of Justice, Antitrust Division—Look in your telephone directory under "U.S. Government, Department of Justice, Antitrust Division." If it does not appear, contact the Federal Information Center (FIC) nearest you. If the FIC is unable to help you, write or call:

Office of Consumer Litigation, Civil Division, Department of Justice, Washington, D.C. 20530, (202)724-6786.

Civil Rights Division—Look in your telephone directory under "U.S. Government, Department of Justice, Civil Rights Division." If it does not appear, contact the Federal Information Center (FIC) nearest you. If the FIC is unable to help you, write or call:

Civil Rights Division, Department of Justice, Main Justice Building, Washington, D.C. 20530, (202)633-3847.

Drug Enforcement Administration—Look in your telephone directory under "U.S. Government, Department of Justice, Drug Enforcement Division." If it does not appear, contact the Federal Information Center (FIC) nearest you. If the FIC is unable to help you, write or call:

Drug Enforcement Administration, Department of Justice, 400 6th Street, S W., Room 2558, Washington, D.C. 20024, (202)633-1000.

Immigration and Naturalization Service—Look in your telephone directory under "U.S. Government, Department of Justice, Immigration and Naturalization Service.' If it does not appear, contact the Federal Information Center (FIC) nearest you. If the FIC is unable to help you, write or call:

Immigration and Naturalization Service, Department of Justice, 25 E Street, N.W., Washington, D.C. 20538, (202)724-7796.

Department of Labor, General Inquiries, Coordinator of Consumer Affairs, Room S-1032, Washington, D.C. 20210, (202)523-6060.

Employment and Training Administration—Look in your telephone directory under "U.S. Government, Department of Labor, Employment and Training Administration." If it does not appear, contact the Federal Information Center (FIC) nearest you. If the FIC is unable to help you, write or call:

Director, Office of Public Affairs, Employment and Training Administration, Department of Labor, 601 D Street, N.W., Room 10418, Washington, D.C. 20530, (202)376-6270.

Employment Standards Administration—Look in your telephone directory under "U.S. Government, Department of Labor, Employment Standards Administration." If it does not appear, contact the Federal Information Center (FIC) nearest you. If the FIC is unable to help you, write or call:

Office of Information and Consumer Service, Employment Standards Administration, Department of Labor, Washington, D.C. 20210, (202)523-8743.

Labor Management Services Administration—Look in your telephone directory under "U.S. Government, Department of Labor, Labor Management Services Administration." If it does not appear, contact the Federal Information Center (FIC) nearest you. If the FIC is unable to help you, write or call:

Office of Information, Labor Management Service Administration, Department of Labor, Washington, D.C. 20210, (202)523-7408.

Office of Information and Public Affairs, Mine Safety and Health Administration, Department of Labor, Ballston Towers #3, Arlington, Virginia 22203, (703)235-1452.

Occupational Safety and Health Administration—Look in your telephone directory under "U.S. Government, Department of Labor, Occupational Safety and Health Administration." If it does not appear, contact the Federal Information Center (FIC) nearest you. If the FIC is unable to help you, write or call:

Office of Information, Occupational Safety and Health Administration, Department of Labor, Washington, D.C. 20210, (202)523-8151.

Veterans' Employment Training, Office of the Assistant Secretary for Veterans' Employment and Training, Department of Labor, Room S-1315, Washington, D.C. 20210, (202)523-9116.

Department of State, Overseas Citizens Services, Room 4811, Washington, D.C. 20520, (202)632-3444 (for non-emergencies), (202)632-5225 (for emergencies).

Passport Services, Department of State, Washington, D.C. 20520, (202)532-4328.

Visa Services, Department of State, Washington, D.C. 20520, (202)632-1972.

Department of Transportation, Auto Safety Hotline, Washington, D.C. 20590, (202)426-0123 (District of Columbia), (800)424-9393 (toll free elsewhere).

Consumer Affairs Officer, Department of Transportation, Washington, D.C. 20590, (202)426-4518.

Community and Consumer Liaison Division, (APA-400), Federal Aviation Administration, Department of Transportation, Washington, D.C. 20591, (202)-426-1960.

National Ride Sharing Information Center, Federal Highway Administration, Department of Transportation, Washington, D.C. 20590, (202)426-0210.

Office of Public Affairs and Consumer Participation (NOA-42), National Highway Traffic Safety Administration, Department of Transportation, Washington, D.C. 20590, (202)-426-0670.

National Response Center, (oil and chemical spills), Department of Transportation, Washington, D.C. 20590, (202)426-2675 (District of Columbia), (800)424-8802 (toll free elsewhere).

Office of Boating, Public and Consumer Affairs (G-B), United States Coast Guard, Department of Transportation, Washington, D.C. 20593, (202)472-2384.

Office of Public Affairs (UPA-1), Urban Mass Transportation Administration, Department of Transportation, Washington, D.C. 20590, (202)426-4043.

Department of the Treasury, Bureau of Alcohol, Tobacco and Firearms, Room 4216, 1200 Pennsylvania Avenue, N.W., Washington, D.C. 20226, (202)566-9100.

Bureau of the Mint, Consumer Affairs, Department of the Treasury, Room 1021, 501 13th Street, N.W., Washington, D.C. 20220, (202)376-0461.

Comptroller of the Currency, Director, Consumer Examinations, Department of the Treasury, 490 L'Enfant Plaza, S.W., Washington, D.C. 20219, (202)447-1600.

Internal Revenue Service—Look in your telephone directory under "U.S. Government, Department of the Treasury, Internal Revenue Service." If it does not appear, contact the Federal Information Center (FIC) nearest you.

United States Customs Service—Look in your telephone directory under "U.S. Government, Department of the Treasury, U.S. Customs Service." If it does not appear, contact the Federal Information Center (FIC) nearest you. If the FIC is unable to help you, write or call:

Office of Inspection and Control, United States Customs Service, Department of the Treasury, 1301 Constitution Avenue, N.W., Washington, D.C. 20229, (202)566-8157.

Environmental Protection Agency, Office of Emergency and Remedia Response, Washington, D.C. 20460, (202)382-7917.

Emission Control Standards, Office of Mobile Source Air Pollution Control, Environmental Protection Agency, Washington, D.C. 20460, (202)382-7645.

Office of Public Affairs, Environmental Protection Agency, Washington, D.C. 20460, (202)382-4355.

Public Inquiries Center, Environmental Protection Agency, Washington, D.C. 20460, (202)382-7550.

Toxic Substances Control Act (TSCA) Assistance Office (phone only), (202)554-1404 (District of Columbia), (800)424-9065 (toll free elsewhere).

Equal Employment Opportunity Commission—Look in your telephone directory under "U.S. Government, Equal Employment Opportunity Commission." If it does not appear, contact the Federal Information Center (FIC) nearest you. If the FIC is unable to help you, contact or call:

Office of Program Operations, Equal Employment Opportunity Commission, Washington, D.C. 20506, (202)634-6831.

Appendix H

Federal Information Centers

For information about any service or agency in the Federal Government, call the Federal Information Center (FIC) nearest you.

Alabama, Birmingham (205)322-8591, Mobile (205)438-1421.

Alaska, Anchorage (907)271-3650.

Arizona, Phoenix (602)261-3313.

Arkansas, Little Rock (501)378-6177.

California, Los Angeles (213)688-3800, Sacramento (916)440-3344, San Diego (619)293-6030, San Francisco (415)556-6600, Santa Ana (714)836-2386.

Colorado, Colorado Springs (303)471-9491, Denver (303)234-7181, Pueblo (303)544-9523.

Connecticut, Hartford (203)527-2617, New Haven (203)624-4720.

Florida, Ft. Lauderdale (305)522-8531, Jacksonville (904)354-4756, Miami (305)350-4155, Orlando (305)422-1800, St. Petersburg (813)893-3495, Tampa (813)229-7911, West Palm Beach (305)833-7566.

Hawaii, Honolulu (808)546-8620.

Illinois, Chicago (312)353-4242.

Indiana, Gary (219)883-4110, Indianapolis (317)269-7373.

Iowa, From any Iowa location (800)532-1556 (toll free).

Kansas, From any Kansas location (800)432-2934 (toll free).

Kentucky, Louisville (502)582-6261.

Louisiana, New Orleans (504)589-6696.

Maryland, Baltimore (301)962-4980.

Massachusetts, Boston (617)223-7121.

Michigan, Detroit (313)226-7016, Grand Rapids (616)451-2628.

Minnesota, Minneapolis (612)349-5333.

Missouri, St. Louis (314)425-4106, From other Missouri locations (800)392-7711 (toll free).

Nebraska, Omaha (402)221-3353, From other Nebraska locations (800)642-8383 (toll free).

New Jersey, Newark (201)645-3600, Trenton (609)396-4400.

New Mexico, Albuquerque (505)766-3091.

New York, Albany (518)463-4421, Buffalo (716)846-4010, New York (212)264-4464, Rochester (716)546-5075, Syracuse (315)476-8545.

North Carolina, Charlotte (704)376-3600.

Ohio, Akron (216)375-5638, Cincinnati (513)684-2801, Cleveland (216)522-4040, Columbus (614)221-1014, Dayton (513)223-7377, Toledo (419)241-3223.

Oklahoma, Oklahoma City (405)231-4868, Tulsa (918)584-4193.

Oregon, Portland (503)221-2222.

Pennsylvania, Philadelphia (215)597-7042, Pittsburgh (412)644-3456.

Rhode Island, Providence (401)331-5565.

Tennessee, Chattanooga (615)265-8231, Memphis (901)521-3285, Nashville (615)242-5056.

Texas, Austin (512)472-5494, Dallas (214)767-8585, Fort Worth (817)334-3624, Houston (713)229-2552, San Antonio (512)224-4471.

Utah, Salt Lake City (801)524-5353.

Virginia, Norfolk (804)441-3101, Richmond (804)643-4928, Roanoke (703)982-8591.

Washington, Seattle (206)442-0570, Tacoma (206)383-5230.

Wisconsin, Milwaukee (414)271-2273.

Appendix I

Uniform Commercial Code

(Courtesy of National Conference of Commissioners on Uniform State Laws)

ARTICLE 2

SALES

PART 1. SHORT TITLE, GENERAL CONSTRUCTION
AND SUBJECT MATTER

Section

PART 2. FORM, FORMATION AND READ-JUSTMENT OF CONTRACT

PART 3. GENERAL OBLIGATION AND CONSTRUCTION OF CONTRACT

PART 1

SHORT TITLE, GENERAL CONSTRUCTION AND SUBJECT MATTER

§ 2—101. Short Title

This Article shall be known and may be cited as Uniform Commercial Code—Sales.

§ 2—102. Scope; Certain Security and Other Transactions Excluded From This Article

Unless the context otherwise requires this Article applies to transactions in goods; it does not apply to any transaction which although in the form of an unconditional contract to sell or present sale is intended to operate only as a security transaction nor does this Article impair or repeal any statute regulating sales to consumers, farmers or other specified classes of buyers.

§ 2—103. Definitions and Index of Definitions

(1) In this Article unless the context otherwise requires
  (a) "Buyer" means a person who buys or contracts to buy goods.
  (b) "Good faith" in the case of a merchant means honesty in fact and the observance of reasonable commercial standards of fair dealing in the trade.
  (c) "Receipt" of goods means taking physical possession of them.
  (d) "Seller" means a person who sells or contracts to sell goods.

(2) Other definitions applying to this Article or to specified Parts thereof, and the sections in which they appear are:
  "Acceptance". Section 2—606.
  "Banker's credit". Section 2—325.
  "Between merchants". Section 2—104.
  "Cancellation". Section 2—106(4).

§ 2—103 UNIFORM COMMERCIAL CODE

  "Commercial unit". Section 2—105.
  "Confirmed credit". Section 2—325.
  "Conforming to contract". Section 2—106.
  "Contract for sale". Section 2—106.
  "Cover". Section 2—712.
  "Entrusting". Section 2—403.
  "Financing agency". Section 2—104.
  "Future goods". Section 2—105.
  "Goods". Section 2—105.
  "Identification". Section 2—501.
  "Installment contract". Section 2—612.
  "Letter of Credit". Section 2—325.
  "Lot". Section 2—105.
  "Merchant". Section 2—104.
  "Overseas". Section 2—323.
  "Person in position of seller". Section 2—707.
  "Present sale". Section 2—106.
  "Sale". Section 2—106.
  "Sale on approval". Section 2—326.

"Sale or return". Section 2—326.

"Termination". Section 2—106.

(3) The following definitions in other Articles apply to this Article:

"Check". Section 3—104.

"Consignee". Section 7—102.

"Consignor". Section 7—102.

"Consumer goods". Section 9—109.

"Dishonor". Section 3—507.

"Draft". Section 3—104.

(4) In addition Article 1 contains general definitions and principles of construction and interpretation applicable throughout this Article.

§ 2-104. Definitions: "Merchant"; "Between Merchants"; "Financing Agency"

(1) "Merchant" means a person who deals in goods of the kind or otherwise by his occupation holds himself out as having knowledge or skill peculiar to the practices or goods involved in the transaction or to whom such knowledge or skill may be attributed by his employment of an agent or broker or other intermediary who by his occupation holds himself out as having such knowledge or skill.

(2) "Financing agency" means a bank, finance company or other person who in the ordinary course of business makes advances against goods or documents of title or who by arrangement with either the seller or the buyer intervenes in ordinary course to make or collect payment due or claimed under the contract for sale, as by purchasing or paying the seller's draft or making advances against it or by merely taking it for collection whether or not documents of title accompany the draft. "Financing agency" includes also a bank or other person who similarly intervenes between persons who are in the position of seller and buyer in respect to the goods (Section 2—707).

(3) "Between merchants" means in any transaction with respect to which both parties are chargeable with the knowledge or skill of merchants.

§ 2—105. Definitions: Transferability; "Goods"; "Future" Goods; "Lot"; "Commercial Unit"

(1) "Goods" means all things (including specially manufactured goods) which are movable at the time of identification to the contract for sale other than the money in which the price is to be paid, investment securities (Article 8) and things in action. "Goods" also includes the unborn young of animals and growing crops and other identified things attached to realty as described in the section on goods to be severed from realty (Section 2—107).

(2) Goods must be both existing and identified before any interest in them can pass. Goods which are not both existing and identified are "future" goods. A purported present sale of future goods or of any interest therein operates as a contract to sell.

(3) There may be a sale of a part interest in existing identified goods.

(4) An undivided share in an identified bulk of fungible goods is sufficiently identified to be sold although the quantity of the bulk is not determined. Any agreed proportion of such a bulk or any quantity thereof agreed upon by number, weight or other

measure may to the extent of the seller's interest in the bulk be sold to the buyer who then becomes an owner in common.

(5) "Lot" means a parcel or a single article which is the subject matter of a separate sale or delivery, whether or not it is sufficient to perform the contract.

(6) "Commercial unit" means such a unit of goods as by commercial usage is a single whole for purposes of sale and division of which materially impairs its character or value on the market or in use. A commercial unit may be a single article (as a machine) or a set of articles (as a suite of furniture or an assortment of sizes) or a quantity (as a bale, gross, or carload) or any other unit treated in use or in the relevant market as a single whole.

§ 2—106.　Definitions: "Contract"; "Agreement"; "Contract for Sale"; "Sale"; "Present Sale"; "Conforming" to Contract; "Termination"; "Cancellation"

(1) In this Article unless the context otherwise requires "contract" and "agreement" are limited to those relating to the present or future sale of goods. "Contract for sale" includes both a present sale of goods and a contract to sell goods at a future time. A "sale" consists in the passing of title from the seller to the buyer for a price (Section 2—401). A "present sale" means a sale which is accomplished by the making of the contract.

(2) Goods or conduct including any part of a performance are "conforming" or conform to the contract when they are in accordance with the obligations under the contract.

(3) "Termination" occurs when either party pursuant to a power created by agreement or law puts an end to the contract otherwise than for its breach. On "termination" all obligations which are still executory on both sides are discharged but any right based on prior breach or performance survives.

(4) "Cancellation" occurs when either party puts an end to the contract for breach by the other and its effect is the same as that of "termination" except that the cancelling party also retains any remedy for breach of the whole contract or any unperformed balance.

§ 2—107.　Goods to Be Severed From Realty: Recording

(1) A contract for the sale of minerals or the like (including oil and gas) or a structure or its materials to be removed from realty is a contract for the sale of goods within this Article if they are to be severed by the seller but until severance a purported present sale thereof which is not effective as a transfer of an interest in land is effective only as a contract to sell.

(2) A contract for the sale apart from the land of growing crops or other things attached to realty and capable of severance without material harm thereto but not described in subsection (1) or of timber to be cut is a contract for the sale of goods within this Article whether the subject matter is to be severed by the buyer or by the seller even though it forms part of the realty at the time of contracting, and the parties can by identification effect a present sale before severance.

(3) The provisions of this section are subject to any third party rights provided by the law relating to realty records, and the contract for sale may be executed and recorded

as a document transferring an interest in land and shall then constitute notice to third parties of the buyer's rights under the contract for sale.

PART 2

FORM, FORMATION AND READJUSTMENT OF CONTRACT

§ 2—201. Formal Requirements; Statute of Frauds

(1) Except as otherwise provided in this section a contract for the sale of goods for the price of $500 or more is not enforceable by way of action or defense unless there is some writing sufficient to indicate that a contract for sale has been made between the parties and signed by the party against whom enforcement is sought or by his authorized agent or broker. A writing is not insufficient because it omits or incorrectly states a term agreed upon but the contract is not enforceable under this paragraph beyond the quantity of goods shown in such writing.

(2) Between merchants if within a reasonable time a writing in confirmation of the contract and sufficient against the sender is received and the party receiving it has reason to know its contents, it satisfies the requirements of subsection (1) against such party unless written notice of objection to its contents is given within 10 days after it is received.

(3) A contract which does not satisfy the requirements of subsection (1) but which is valid in other respects is enforceable

    (a) if the goods are to be specially manufactured for the buyer and are not suitable for sale to others in the ordinary course of the seller's business and the seller, before notice of repudiation is received and under circumstances which reasonably indicate that the goods are for the buyer, has made either a substantial beginning of their manufacture or commitments for their procurement; or

    (b) if the party against whom enforement is sought admits in his pleading, testimony or otherwise in court that a contract for sale was made, but the contract is not enforceable under this provision beyond the quantity of goods admitted; or

    (c) with respect to goods for which payment has been made and accepted or which have been received and accepted (Sec. 2—606).

§ 2—202. Final Written Expression: Parol or Extrinsic Evidence

Terms with respect to which the confirmatory memoranda of the parties agree or which are otherwise set forth in a writing intended by the parties as a final expression of their agreement with respect to such terms as are included therein may not be contradicted by evidence of any prior agreement or of a contemporaneous oral agreement but may be explained or supplemented

    (a) by course of dealing or usage of trade (Section 1—205) or by course of performance (Section 2—208); and

    (b) by evidence of consistent additional terms unless the court finds the writing to have been intended also as a complete and exclusive statement of the terms of the agreement.

§ 2—203. Seals Inoperative

The affixing of a seal to a writing evidencing a contract for sale or an offer to buy or sell goods does not constitute the writing a sealed instrument and the law with respect to sealed instruments does not apply to such a contract or offer.

§ 2—204. Formation in General

(1) A contract for sale of goods may be made in any manner sufficient to show agreement, including conduct by both parties which recognizes the existence of such a contract.

(2) An agreement sufficient to constitute a contract for sale may be found even though the moment of its making is undetermined.

(3) Even though one or more terms are left open a contract for sale does not fail for indefiniteness if the parties have intended to make a contract and there is a reasonably certain basis for giving an appropriate remedy.

§ 2—205. Firm Offers

An offer by a merchant to buy or sell goods in a signed writing which by its terms gives assurance that it will be held open is not revocable, for lack of consideration, during the time stated or if not time is stated for a reasonable time, but in no event may such period of irrevocability exceed three months; but any such term of assurance on a form supplied by the offeree must be separately signed by the offeror.

§ 2—206. Offer and Acceptance in Formation of Contract

(1) Unless otherwise unambiguously indicated by the language or circumstances

  (a) an offer to make a contract shall be construed as inviting acceptance in any manner and by any medium reasonable in the circumstances;

  (b) an order or other offer to buy goods for prompt or current shipment shall be construed as inviting acceptance either by a prompt promise to ship or by the prompt or current shipment of conforming or non-conforming goods, but such a shipment of non-conforming goods does not constitute an acceptance if the seller seasonably notifies the buyer that the shipment is offered only as an accommodation to the buyer.

(2) Where the beginning of a requested performance is a reasonable mode of acceptance an offeror who is not notified of acceptance within a reasonable time may treat the offer as having lapsed before acceptance.

§ 2—207. Additional Terms in Acceptance or Confirmation

(1) A definite and seasonable expression of acceptance or a written confirmation which is sent within a reasonable time operates as an acceptance even though it states terms additional to or different from those offered or agreed upon, unless acceptance is expressly made conditional on assent to the additional or different terms.

(2) The additional terms are to be construed as proposals for addition to the contract. Between merchants such terms become part of the contract unless:

  (a) the offer expressly limits acceptance to the terms of the offer;

  (b) they materially alter it; or

(c) notification of objection to them has already been given or is given within a reasonable time after notice of them is received.

(3) Conduct by both parties which recognizes the existence of a contract is sufficient to establish a contract for sale although the writings of the parties do not otherwise establish a contract. In such a case the terms of the particular contract consist of those terms on which the writings of the parties agree, together with any supplementary terms incorporated under any other provisions of this Act.

§ 2—208. Course of Performance or Practical Construction

(1) Where the contract for sale involves repeated occasions for performance by either party with knowledge of the nature of the performance and opportunity for objection to it by the other, any course of performance accepted or acquiesced in without objection shall be relevant to determine the meaning of the agreement.

(2) The express terms of the agreement and any such course of performance, as well as any course of dealing and usage of trade, shall be construed whenever reasonable as consistent with each other; but when such construction is unreasonable, express terms shall control course of performance and course of performance shall control both course of dealing and usage of trade (Section 1—205).

(3) Subject to the provisions of the next section on modification and waiver, such course of performance shall be relevant to show a waiver or modification of any term inconsistent with such course of performance.

§ 2—209. Modification, Rescission and Waiver

(1) An agreement modifying a contract within this Article needs no consideration to be binding.

(2) A signed agreement which excludes modification or rescission except by a signed writing cannot be otherwise modified or rescinded, but except as between merchants such a requirement on a form supplied by the merchant must be separately signed by the other party.

(3) The requirements of the statute of frauds section of this Article (Section 2—201) must be satisfied if the contract as modified is within its provisions.

(4) Although an attempt at modification or recission does not satisfy the requirements of subsection (2) or (3) it can operate as a waiver.

(5) A party who has made a waiver affecting an executory portion of the contract may retract the waiver by reasonable notification received by the other party that strict performance will be required of any term waived, unless the retraction would be unjust in view of a material change of position in reliance of the waiver.

§ 2—210. Delegation of Performance; Assignment of Rights

(1) A party may perform his duty through a delegate unless otherwise agreed or unless the other party has a substantial interest in having his original promisor perform or control the acts required by the contract. No delegation of performance relieves the party delegating of any duty to perform or any liability for breach.

(2) Unless otherwise agreed all rights of either seller or buyer can be assigned except where the assignment would materially change the duty of the other party, or in-

crease materially the burden or risk imposed on him by his contract, or impair materially his chance of obtaining return performance. A right to damages for breach of the whole contract or a right arising out of the assignor's due performance of his entire obligation can be assigned despite agreement otherwise.

(3) Unless the circumstances indicate the contrary a prohibition of assignment of "the contract" is to be construed as barring only the delegation to the assignee of the assignor's performance.

(4) An assignment of "the contract" or of "all my rights under the contract" or an assignment in similar general terms is an assignment of rights and unless the language or the circumstances (as in an assignment for security) indicate the contrary, it is a delegation of performance of the duties of the assignor and its acceptance by the assignee constitutes a promise by him to perform those duties. This promise is enforceable by either the assignor or the other party to the original contract.

(5) The other party may treat any assignment which delegates performance as creating reasonable grounds for insecurity and may without prejudice to his rights against the assignor demand assurances from the assignee (Section 2—609).

PART 3

GENERAL OBLIGATION AND CONSTRUCTION OF CONTRACT

§ 2—301. General Obligations of Parties

The obligation of the seller is to transfer and deliver and that of the buyer is to accept and pay in accordance with the contract.

§ 2—302. Unconscionable Contract or Clause

(1) If the court as a matter of law finds the contract or any clause of the contract to have been unconscionable at the time it was made the court may refuse to enforce the contract, or it may enforce the remainder of the contract without the unconscionable clause, or it may so limit the application of any unconscionable clause as to avoid any unconscionable result.

(2) When it is claimed or appears to the court that the contract or any clause thereof may be unconscionable the parties shall be afforded a reasonable opportunity to present evidence as to its commercial setting, purpose and effect to aid the court in making the determination.

§ 2—303. Allocation or Division of Risks

Where this Article allocates a risk or a burden as between the parties "unless otherwise agreed", the agreement may not only shift the allocation but may also divide the risk or burden.

§ 2—304. Price Payable in Money, Goods, Realty, or Otherwise

(1) The price can be made payable in money or otherwise. If it is payable in whole or in part in goods each party is a seller of the goods which he is to transfer.

(2) Even though all or part of the price is payable in an interest in realty the transfer of the goods and the seller's obligations with reference to them are subject to this Article, but not the transfer of the interest in realty or the transferor's obligations in connection therewith.

§ 2—305. Open Price Term

(1) The parties if they so intend can conclude a contract for sale even though the price is not settled. In such a case the price is a reasonable price at the time for delivery if

(a) nothing is said as to price; or

(b) the price is left to be agreed by the parties and they fail to agree; or

(c) the price is to be fixed in terms of some agreed market or other standard as set or recorded by a third person or agency and it is not so set or recorded.

(2) A price to be fixed by the seller or by the buyer means a price for him to fix in good faith.

(3) When a price left to be fixed otherwise than by agreement of the parties fails to be fixed through fault of one party the other may at his option treat the contract as cancelled or himself fix a reasonable price.

(4) Where, however, the parties intend not to be bound unless the price be fixed or agreed and it is not fixed or agreed there is no contract. In such a case the buyer must return any goods already received or if unable so to do must pay their reasonable value at the time of delivery and the seller must return any portion of the price paid on account.

§ 2—306. Output, Requirements and Exclusive Dealings

(1) A term which measures the quantity by the output of the seller or the requirements of the buyer means such actual output or requirements as may occur in good faith, except that no quantity unreasonably disproportionate to any stated estimate or in the absence of a stated estimate to any normal or otherwise comparable prior output or requirements may be tendered or demanded.

(2) A lawful agreement by either the seller or the buyer for exclusive dealing in the kind of goods concerned imposes unless otherwise agreed an obligation by the seller to use best efforts to supply the goods and by the buyer to use best efforts to promote their sale.

§ 2—307. Delivery in Single Lot or Several Lots

Unless otherwise agreed all goods called for by a contract for sale must be tendered in a single delivery and payment is due only on such tender but where the circumstances give either party the right to make or demand delivery in lots the price if it can be apportioned may be demanded for each lot.

§ 2—308. Absence of Specified Place for Delivery

Unless otherwise agreed

(a) the place for delivery of goods is the seller's place of business or if he has none his residence; but

(b) in a contract for sale of identified goods which to the knowledge of the parties at the time of contracting are in some other place, that place is the place for their delivery; and

(c) documents of title may be delivered through customary banking channels.

§ 2—309. Absence of Specific Time Provisions; Notice of Termination

(1) The time for shipment or delivery or any other action under a contract if not provided in this Article or agreed upon shall be a reasonable time.

(2) Where the contract provides for successive performances but is indefinite in duration it is valid for a reasonable time but unless otherwise agreed may be terminated at any time by either party.

(3) Termination of a contract by one party except on the happening of an agreed event requires that reasonable notification be received by the other party and an agreement dispensing with notification is invalid if its operation would be unconscionable.

§ 2—310. Open Time for Payment or Running of Credit; Authority to Ship Under Reservation

Unless otherwise agreed

(a) payment is due at the time and place at which the buyer is to receive the goods even though the place of shipment is the place of delivery; and

(b) if the seller is authorized to send the goods he may ship them under reservation, and may tender the documents of title, but the buyer may inspect the goods after their arrival before payment is due unless such inspection is inconsistent with the terms of the contract (Section 2—513); and

(c) if delivery is authorized and made by way of documents of title otherwise than by subsection (b) then payment is due at the time and place at which the buyer is to receive the documents regardless of where the goods are to be received; and

(d) where the seller is required or authorized to ship the goods on credit the credit period runs from the time of shipment but post-dating the invoice or delaying its dispatch will correspondingly delay the starting of the credit period.

§ 2—311. Options and Cooperation Respecting Performance

(1) An agreement for sale which is otherwise sufficiently definite (subsection (3) of Section 2—204) to be a contract is not made invalid by the fact that it leaves particulars of performance to be specified by one of the parties. Any such specification must be made in good faith and within limits set by commercial reasonableness.

(2) Unless otherwise agreed specifications relating to assortment of the goods are at the buyer's option and except as otherwise provided in subsections (1) (c) and (3) of Section 2—319 specifications or arrangements relating to shipment are at the seller's option.

(3) Where such specification would materially affect the other party's performance but is not seasonably made or where one party's cooperation is necessary to the agreed performance of the other but is not seasonably forthcoming, the other party in addition to all other remedies

(a) is excused for any resulting delay in his own performance; and

(b) may also either proceed to perform in any reasonable manner or after the time for a material part of his own performance treat the failure to specify or to cooperate as a breach by failure to deliver or accept the goods.

§ 2—312. Warranty of Title and Against Infringement; Buyer's Obligation Against Infringement

(1) Subject to subsection (2) there is in a contract for sale a warranty by the seller that

(a) the title conveyed shall be good, and its transfer rightful; and

(b) the goods shall be delivered free from any security interest or other lien or encumbrance of which the buyer at the time of contracting has no knowledge

(2) A warranty under subsection (1) will be excluded or modified only by specific language or by circumstances which give the buyer reason to know that the person selling does not claim title in himself or that he is purporting to sell only such right or title as he or a third person may have.

(3) Unless otherwise agreed a seller who is a merchant regularly dealing in goods of the kind warrants that the goods shall be delivered free of the rightful claim of any third person by way of infringement or the like but a buyer who furnishes specifications to the seller must hold the seller harmless against any such claim which arises out of compliance with the specifications.

§ 2—313. Express Warranties by Affirmation, Promise, Description, Sample

(1) Express warranties by the seller are created as follows:

(a) Any affirmation of fact or promise made by the seller to the buyer which relates to the goods and becomes part of the basis of the bargain creates an express warranty that the goods shall conform to the affirmation or promise.

(b) Any description of the goods which is made part of the basis of the bargain creates an express warranty that the goods shall conform to the description.

(c) Any sample or model which is made part of the basis of the bargain creates an express warranty that the whole of the goods shall conform to the sample or model.

(2) It is not necessary to the creation of an express warranty that the seller use formal words such as "warrant" or "guarantee" or that he have a specific intention to make a warranty, but an affirmation merely of the value of the goods or a statement purporting to be merely the seller's opinion or commendation of the goods does not create a warranty.

§ 2—314. Implied Warranty: Merchantability; Usage of Trade

(1) Unless excluded or modified (Section 2—316), a warranty that the goods shall be merchantable is implied in a contract for their sale if the seller is a merchant with respect to goods of that kind. Under this section the serving for value of food or drink to be consumed either on the premises or elsewhere is a sale.

(2) Goods to be merchantable must be at least such as

(a) pass without objection in the trade under the contract description; and

(b) in the case of fungible goods, are of fair average quality within the description; and

(c) are fit for the ordinary purposes for which such goods are used; and

(d) run, within the variations permitted by the agreement, of even kind, quality and quantity within each unit and among all units involved; and

(e) are adequately contained, packaged, and labeled as the agreement may require; and

(f) conform to the promises or affirmations of fact made on the container or label if any.

(3) Unless excluded or modified (Section 2—316) other implied warranties may arise from course of dealing or usage or trade.

§ 2—315.   Implied Warranty: Fitness for Particular Purpose

Where the seller at the time of contracting has reason to know any particular purpose for which the goods are required and that the buyer is relying on the seller's skill or judgment to select or furnish suitable goods, there is unless excluded or modified under the next section an implied warranty that the goods shall be fit for such purpose.

§ 2—316.   Exclusion or Modification of Warranties

(1) Words or conduct relevant to the creation of an express warranty and words or conduct tending to negate or limit warranty shall be construed wherever reasonable as consistent with each other; but subject to the provisions of this Article on parol or extrinsic evidence (Section 2—202) negation or limitation is inoperative to the extent that such construction is unreasonable.

(2) Subject to subsection (3), to exclude or modify the implied warranty of merchantability or any part of it the language must mention merchantability and in case of a writing must be conspicuous, and to exclude or modify any implied warranty of fitness the exclusion must be by a writing and conspicuous. Language to exclude all implied warranties of fitness is sufficient if it states, for example, that "There are no warranties which extend beyond the description on the face hereof."

(3) Notwithstanding subsection (2)

(a) unless the circumstances indicate otherwise, all implied warranties are excluded by expressions like "as is", "with all faults" or other language which in common understanding calls the buyer's attention to the exclusion of warranties and makes plain that there is no implied warranty; and

(b) when the buyer before entering into the contract has examined the goods or the sample or model as fully as he desired or has refused to examine the goods there is no implied warranty with regard to defects which an examination ought in the circumstances to have revealed to him; and

(c) an implied warranty can also be excluded or modified by course of dealing or course of performance or usage of trade.

(4) Remedies for breach of warranty can be limited in accordance with the provisions of this Article on liquidation or limitation of damages and on contractual modification of remedy (Sections 2—718 and 2—719).

§ 2—317. Cumulation and Conflict of Warranties Express or Implied

Warranties whether express or implied shall be construed as consistent with each other and as cumulative, but if such construction is unreasonable the intention of the parties shall determine which warranty is dominant. In ascertaining that intention the following rules apply:

(a) Exact or technical specifications displace an inconsistent sample or model or general language of description.

(b) A sample from an existing bulk displaces inconsistent general language of description.

(c) Express warranties displace inconsistent implied warranties other than an implied warranty of fitness for a particular purpose.

§ 2—318. Third Party Beneficiaries of Warranties Express or Implied

Note: *If this Act is introduced in the Congress of the United States this section should be omitted. (States to select one alternative.)*

Alternative A

A seller's warranty whether express or implied extends to any natural person who is in the family or household of his buyer or who is a guest in his home if it is reasonable to expect that such person may use, consume or be affected by the goods and who is injured in person by breach of the warranty. A seller may not exclude or limit the operation of this section.

Alternative B

A seller's warranty whether express or implied extends to any natural person who may reasonably be expected to use, consume or be affected by the goods and who is injured in person by breach of the warranty. A seller may not exclude or limit the operation of this section.

Alternative C

A seller's warranty whether express or implied extends to any person who may reasonably be expected to use, consume or be affected by the goods and who is injured by breach of the warranty. A seller may not exclude or limit the operation of this section with respect to injury to the person of an individual to whom the warranty extends. As amended 1966.

§ 2—319. F.O.B. and F.A.S. Terms

(1) Unless otherwise agreed the term F.O.B. (which means "free on board") at a named place, even though used only in connection with the stated price, is a delivery term under which

(a) when the term is F.O.B. the place of shipment, the seller must at that place ship the goods in the manner provided in this Article (Section 2—504) and bear the expense and risk of putting them into the possession of the carrier; or

(b) when the term is F.O.B. the place of destination, the seller must at his own expense and risk transport the goods to that place and there tender delivery of them in the manner provided in this Article (Section 2—503);

    (c) when under either (a) or (b) the term is also F.O.B. vessel, car or other vehicle, the seller must in addition at his own expense and risk load the goods on board. If the term F.O.B. vessel the buyer must name the vessel and in an appropriate case the seller must comply with the provisions of this Article on the form of bill of lading (Section 2—323).

  (2) Unless otherwise agreed the term F.A.S. vessel (which means "free alongside") at a named port, even though used only in connection with the stated price, is a delivery term under which the seller must

    (a) at his own expense and risk deliver the goods alongside the vessel in the manner usual in that port or on a dock designated and provided by the buyer; and

    (b) obtain and tender a receipt for the goods in exchange for which the carrier is under a duty to issue a bill of lading.

  (3) Unless otherwise agreed in any case falling within subsection (1) (a) or (c) or subsection (2) the buyer must seasonably give any needed instructions for making delivery, including when the term is F.A.S. or F.O.B. the loading berth of the vessel and in an appropriate case its name and sailing date. The seller may treat the failure of needed instructions as a failure of cooperation under this Article (Section 2—311). He may also at his option move the goods in any reasonable manner preparatory to delivery or shipment.

  (4) Under the term F.O.B. vessel or F.A.S. unless otherwise agreed the buyer must make payment against tender of the required documents and the seller may not tender nor the buyer demand delivery of the goods in substitution for the documents.

§ 2—320. C.I.F. and C. & F. Terms

  (1) The term C.I.F. means that the price includes in a lump sum the cost of the goods and the insurance and freight to the named destination. The term C. & F. or C.F. means that the price so includes cost and freight to the named destination.

  (2) Unless otherwise agreed and even though used only in connection with the stated price and destination, the term C.I.F. destination or its equivalent requires the seller at his own expense and risk to

    (a) put the goods into the possession of a carrier at the port for shipment and obtain a negotiable bill or bills of lading covering the entire transportation to the named destination; and

    (b) load the goods and obtain a receipt from the carrier (which may be contained in the bill of lading) showing that the freight has been paid or provided for; and

    (c) obtain a policy or certificate of insurance, including any war risk insurance, of a kind and on terms then current at the port of shipment in the usual amount, in the currency of the contract, shown to cover the same goods covered by the bill of lading and providing for payment of loss to the order of the buyer or for the account of whom it may concern; but the seller may add to the price the amount of the premium for any such war risk insurance; and

    (d) prepare an invoice of the goods and procure any other documents required to effect shipment or to comply with the contract; and

    (e) forward and tender with commercial promptness all the documents in due form and with any indorsement necessary to perfect the buyer's rights.

(3) Unless otherwise agreed the term C. & F. or its equivalent has the same effect and imposes upon the seller the same obligations and risks as a C.I.F. term except the obligation as to insurance.

(4) Under the term C.I.F. or C. & F. unless otherwise agreed the buyer must make payment against tender of the required documents and the seller may not tender nor the buyer demand delivery of the goods in substitution for the documents.

§ 2—321.   C.I.F. or C. & F.: "New Landed Weights"; "Payment on Arrival"; Warranty of Condition on Arrival

Under a contract containing a term C.I.F. or C. & F.

(1) Where the price is based on or is to be adjusted according to "net landed weights", "delivered weights", "out turn" quantity or quality or the like, unless otherwise agreed the seller must reasonably estimate the price. The payment due on tender of the documents called for by the contract is the amount so estimated, but after final adjustment of the price a settlement must be made with commercial promptness.

(2) An agreement described in subsection (1) or any warranty of quality or condition of the goods on arrival places upon the seller the risk of ordinary deterioration, shrinkage and the like in transportation but has no effect on the place or time of identification to the contract for sale or delivery or on the passing of the risk of loss.

(3) Unless otherwise agreed where the contract provides for payment on or after arrival of the goods the seller must before payment allow such preliminary inspection as is feasible; but if the goods are lost delivery of the documents and payment are due when the goods should have arrived.

§ 2—322.   Delivery "Ex-Ship"

(1) Unless otherwise agreed a term for delivery of goods "ex-ship" (which means from the carrying vessel) or in equivalent language is not restricted to a particular ship and requires delivery from a ship which has reached a place at the named port of destination where goods of the kind are usually discharged.

(2) Under such a term unless otherwise agreed

(a) the seller must discharge all liens arising out of the carriage and furnish the buyer with a direction which puts the carrier under a duty to deliver the goods; and

(b) the risk of loss does not pass to the buyer until the goods leave the ship's tackle or are otherwise properly unloaded.

§ 2—323.   Form of Bill of Lading Required in Overseas Shipment; "Overseas"

(1) Where the contract contemplates overseas shipment and contains a term C.I.F. or C. & F. or F.O.B. vessel, the seller unless otherwise agreed must obtain a negotiable, bill of lading stating that the goods have been loaded on board or, in the case of a term C.I.F. or C. & F., received for shipment.

(2) Where in a case within subsection (1) a bill of lading has been issued in a set of parts, unless otherwise agreed if the documents are not to be sent from abroad the buyer may demand tender of the full set; otherwise only one part of the bill of lading

need be tendered. Even if the agreement expressly requires a full set

    (a) due tender of a single part is acceptable within the provisions of this Article on cure of improper delivery (subsection (1) of Section 2—508); and

    (b) even though the full set is demanded, if the documents are sent from abroad the person tendering an incomplete set may nevertheless require payment upon furnishing an indemnity which the buyer in good faith deems adequate.

(3) A shipment by water or by air or a contract contemplating such shipment is "overseas" insofar as by usage of trade or agreement it is subject to the commercial, financing or shipping practices characteristic of international deep water commerce.

§ 2—324. "No Arrival, No Sale" Term

Under a term "no arrival, no sale" or terms of like meaning, unless otherwise agreed,

    (a) the seller must properly ship conforming goods and if they arrive by any means he must tender them on arrival but he assumes no obligation that the goods will arrive unless he has caused the non-arrival; and

    (b) where without fault of the seller the goods are in part lost or have so deteriorated as no longer to conform to the contract or arrive after the contract time, the buyer may proceed as if there had been casualty to identified goods (Section 2—613).

§ 2—325. "Letter of Credit" Term; "Confirmed Credit"

(1) Failure of the buyer seasonably to furnish an agreed letter of credit is a breach of the contract for sale.

(2) The delivery to seller of a proper letter of credit suspends the buyer's obligation to pay. If the letter of credit is dishonored, the seller may on seasonable notification to the buyer require payment directly from him.

(3) Unless otherwise agreed the term "letter of credit" or "banker's credit" in a contract for sale means an irrevocable credit issued by a financing agency of good repute and, where the shipment is overseas, of good international repute. The term "confirmed credit" means that the credit must also carry the direct obligation of such an agency which does business in the seller's financial market.

§ 2—326. Sale on Approval and Sale or Return; Consignment Sales and Rights of Creditors

(1) Unless otherwise agreed, if delivered goods may be returned by the buyer even though they conform to the contract, the transaction is

    (a) a "sale on approval" if the goods are delivered primarily for use, and

    (b) a "sale or return" if the goods are delivered primarily for resale.

(2) Except as provided in subsection (3), goods held on approval are not subject to the claims of the buyer's creditors until acceptance; goods held on sale or return are subject to such claims while in the buyer's possession.

(3) Where goods are delivered to a person for sale and such person maintains a place of business at which he deals in goods of the kind involved, under a name other than the name of the person making delivery, then with respect to claims of creditors of the person conducting the business the goods are deemed to be on sale or return. The provisions of this subsection are applicable even though an

agreement purports to reserve title to the person making delivery until payment or resale or uses such words as "on consignment" or "on memorandum". However, this subsection is not applicable if the person making delivery

   (a) complies with an applicable law providing for a consignor's interest or the like to be evidenced by a sign, or

   (b) establishes that the person conducting the business is generally known by his creditors to be substantially engaged in selling the goods of others, or

   (c) complies with the filing provisions of the Article on Secured Transactions (Article 9).

(4) Any "or return" term of a contract for sale is to be treated as a separate contract for sale within the statute of frauds section of this Article (Section 2—201) and as contradicting the sale aspect of the contract within the provisions of this Article on parol or extrinsic evidence (Section 2—202).

§ 2—327. Special Incidents of Sale on Approval and Sale or Return

(1) Under a sale on approval unless otherwise agreed

   (a) although the goods are identified to the contract the risk of loss and the title do not pass to the buyer until acceptance; and

   (b) use of the goods consistent with the purpose of trial is not acceptance but failure seasonably to notify the seller of election to return the goods is acceptance, and if the goods conform to the contract acceptance of any part is acceptance of the whole; and

   (c) after due notification of election to return, the return is at the seller's risk and expense but a merchant buyer must follow any reasonable instructions.

(2) Under a sale or return unless otherwise agreed

   (a) the option to return extends to the whole or any commercial unit of the goods while in substantially their original condition, but must be exercised seasonably; and

   (b) the return is at the buyer's risk and expense.

§ 2—328. Sale by Auction

(1) In a sale by auction if goods are put up in lots each lot is the subject of a separate sale.

(2) A sale by auction is complete when the auctioneer so announces by the fall of the hammer or in other customary manner. Where a bid is made while the hammer is falling in acceptance of a prior bid the auctioneer may in his discretion reopen the bidding or declare the goods sold under the bid on which the hammer was falling.

(3) Such a sale is with reserve unless the goods are in explicit terms put up without reserve. In an auction with reserve the auctioneer may withdraw the goods at any time until he announces completion of the sale. In an auction without reserve, after the auctioneer calls for bids on an article or lot, that article or lot cannot be withdrawn unless no bid is made within a reasonable time. In either case a bidder may retract his bid until the auctioneer's announcement of completion of the sale, but a bidder's retraction does not revive any previous bid.

(4) If the auctioneer knowingly receives a bid on the seller's behalf or the seller

makes or procures such a bid, and notice has not been given that liberty for such bidding is reserved, the buyer may at his option avoid the sale or take the goods at the price of the last good faith bid prior to the completion of the sale. This subsection shall not apply to any bid at a forced sale.

PART 4

TITLE, CREDITORS AND GOOD FAITH PURCHASERS

§ 2—401. Passing of Title; Reservation for Security; Limited Application of This Section

Each provision of this Article with regard to the rights, obligations and remedies of the seller, the buyer, purchasers or other third parties applies irrespective of title to the goods except where the provision refers to such title. Insofar as situations are not covered by the other provisions of this Article and matters concerning title become material the following rules apply:

(1) Title to goods cannot pass under a contract for sale prior to their identification to the contract (Section 2—501), and unless otherwise explicitly agreed the buyer acquires by their identification a special property as limited by this Act. Any retention or reservation by the seller of the title (property) in goods shipped or delivered to the buyer is limited in effect to a reservation of a security interest. Subject to these provisions and to the provisions of the Article on Secured Transactions (Article 9), title to goods passes from the seller to the buyer in any manner and on any conditions explicitly agreed on by the parties.

(2) Unless otherwise explicitly agreed title passes to the buyer at the time and place at which the seller completes his performance with reference to the physical delivery of the goods, despite any reservation of a security interest and even though a document of title is to be delivered at a different time or place; and in particular and despite any reservation of a security interest by the bill of lading

> (a) if the contract requires or authorizes the seller to send the goods to the buyer but does not require him to deliver them at destination, title passes to the buyer at the time and place of shipment; but
>
> (b) if the contract requires delivery at destination, title passes on tender there.

(3) Unless otherwise explicitly agreed where delivery is to be made without moving the goods,

> (a) if the seller is to deliver a document of title, title passes at the time when and the place where he delivers such documents; or
>
> (b) if the goods are at the time of contracting already identified and no documents are to be delivered, title passes at the time and place of contracting.

(4) A rejection or other refusal by the buyer to receive or retain the goods, whether or not justified, or a justified revocation of acceptance revests title to the goods in the seller. Such revesting occurs by operation of law and is not a "sale".

§ 2—402. Rights of Seller's Creditors Against Sold Goods

(1) Except as provided in subsections (2) and (3), rights of unsecured creditors of

the seller with respect to goods which have been identified to a contract for sale are subject to the buyer's rights to recover the goods under this Article (Sections 2—502 and 2—716).

(2) A creditor of the seller may treat a sale or an identification of goods to a contract for sale as void if as against him a retention of possession by the seller is fraudulent under any rule of law of the state where the goods are situated, except that retention of possession in good faith and current course of trade by a merchant-seller for a commercially reasonable time after a sale or identification is not fraudulent.

(3) Nothing in this Article shall be deemed to impair the rights of creditors of the seller

(a) under the provisions of the Article on Secured Transactions (Article 9); or

(b) where identification to the contract or delivery is made not in current course of trade but in satisfaction of or

§ 2—403. Power to Transfer; Good Faith Purchase of Goods; "Entrusting"

(1) A purchaser of goods acquires all title which his transfer had or had power to transfer except that a purchaser of a limited interest acquires rights only to the extent of the interest purchased. A person with voidable title has power to transfer a good title to a good faith purchaser for value. When goods have been delivered under a transaction of purchase the purchaser has such power even though.

(a) the transferor was deceived as to the identity of the purchaser, or

(b) the delivery was in exchange for a check which is later dishonored, or

(c) it was agreed that the transaction was to be a "cash sale", or

(d) the delivery was procured through fraud punishable as larcenous under the criminal law.

(2) Any entrusting of possession of goods to a merchant who deals in goods of that kind gives him power to transfer all rights of the entruster to a buyer in ordinary course of business.

(3) "Entrusting" includes any delivery and any acquiescence in retention of possession regardless of any condition expressed between the parties to the delivery or acquiescence and regardless of whether the procurement of the entrusting or the possessor's disposition of the goods have been such as to be larcenous under the criminal law.

(4) The rights of other purchasers of goods and of lien creditors are governed by the Articles on Secured Transactions (Article 9), Bulk Transfers (Article 6) and Documents of Title (Article 7).

PART 5

PERFORMANCE

§ 2—501. Insurable Interest in Goods; Manner of Identification of Goods

(1) The buyer obtains a special property and an insurable interest in goods by identification of existing goods as goods to which the contract refers even though the goods

so identified are non-conforming and he has an option to return or reject them. Such identification can be made at any time and in any manner explicitly agreed to by the parties. In the absence of explicit agreement identification occurs

 (a) when the contract is made if it is for the sale of goods already existing and identified;
 (b) if the contract is for the sale of future goods other than those described in paragraph (c), when goods are shipped, marked or otherwise designated by the seller as goods to which the contract refers;
 (c) when the crops are planted or otherwise become growing crops or the young are conceived if the contract is for the sale of unborn young to be born within twelve months after contracting or for the sale of crops to be harvested within twelve months or the next normal harvest season after contracting whichever is longer.

 (2) The seller retains an insurable interest in goods so long as title to or any security interest in the goods remains in him and where the identification is by the seller alone he may until default or insolvency or notification to the buyer that the identification is final substitute other goods for those identified.

 (3) Nothing in this section impairs any insurable interest recognized under any other statute or rule of law.

§ 2—502. Buyer's Right to Goods on Seller's Insolvency

 (1) Subject to subsection (2) and even though the goods have not been shipped a buyer who has paid a part or all of the price of goods in which he has a special property under the provisions of the immediately preceding section may on making and keeping good a tender of any unpaid portion of their price recover them from the seller if the seller becomes insolvent within ten days after receipt of the first installment on their price.

 (2) If the identification creating his special property has been made by the buyer he acquires the right to recover the goods only if they conform to the contract for sale.

§ 2—503. Manner of Seller's Tender of Delivery

 (1) Tender of delivery requires that the seller put and hold conforming goods at the buyer's disposition and give the buyer any notification reasonably necessary to enable him to take delivery. The manner, time and place for tender are determined by the agreement and this Article, and in particular

 (a) tender must be at a reasonable hour, and if it is of goods they must be kept available for the period reasonably necessary to enable the buyer to take possession; but
 (b) unless otherwise agreed the buyer must furnish facilities reasonably suited to the receipt of the goods.

 (2) Where the case is within the next section respecting shipment tender requires that the seller comply with its provisions.

 (3) Where the seller is required to deliver at a particular destination tender requires that he comply with subsection (1) and also in any appropriate case tender documents as described in subsections (4) and (5) of this section.

(4) Where goods are in the possession of a bailee and are to be delivered without being moved
- (a) tender requires that the seller either tender a negotiable document of title covering such goods or procure acknowledgment by the bailee of the buyer's right to possession of the goods; but
- (b) tender to the buyer of a non-negotiable document of title or of a written direction to the bailee to deliver is sufficient tender unless the buyer seasonably objects, and receipt by the bailee of notification of the buyer's rights fixes those rights as against the bailee and all third persons; but risk of loss of the goods and of any failure by the bailee to honor the non-negotiable document of title or to obey the direction remains on the seller until the buyer has had a reasonable time to present the document or direction, and a refusal by the bailee to honor the document or to obey the direction defeats the tender.

(5) Where the contract requires the seller to deliver documents
- (a) he must tender all such documents in correct form, except as provided in this Article with respect to bills of lading in a set (subsection (2) of Section 2-323); and
- (b) tender through customary banking channels is sufficient and dishonor of a draft accompanying the documents constitutes non-acceptance or rejection.

§ 2—504. Shipment by Seller

Where the seller is required or authorized to send the goods to the buyer and the contract does not require him to deliver them at a particular destination, then unless otherwise agreed he must
- (a) put the goods in the possession of such a carrier and make such a contract for their transportation as may be reasonable having regard to the nature of the goods and other circumstances of the case; and
- (b) obtain and promptly deliver or tender in due form any document necessary to enable the buyer to obtain possession of the goods or otherwise required by the agreement or by usage of trade; and
- (c) promptly notify the buyer of the shipment.

Failure to notify the buyer under paragraph (c) or to make a proper contract under paragraph (a) is a ground for rejection only if material delay or loss ensues.

§ 2—505. Seller's Shipment Under Reservation

(1) Where the seller has identified goods to the contract by or before shipment:
- (a) his procurement of a negotiable bill of lading to his own order or otherwise reserves in him a security interest in the goods. His procurement of the bill to the order of a financing agency or of the buyer indicates in addition only the seller's expectation of transferring that interest to the person named.
- (b) a non-negotiable bill of lading to himself or his nominee reserves possession of the goods as security but except in a case of conditional delivery (subsection (2) of Section 2—507) a non-negotiable bill of lading naming the buyer as consignee reserves no security interest even though the seller retains possession of the bill of lading.

(2) When shipment by the seller with reservation of a security interest is in viola-

tion of the contract for sale it constitutes an improper contract for transportation within the preceding section but impairs neither the rights given to the buyer by shipment and identification of the goods to the contract nor the seller's powers as a holder of a negotiable document.

§ 2—506.   Rights of Financing Agency

(1) A financing agency by paying or purchasing for value a draft which relates to a shipment of goods acquires to the extent of the payment or purchase and in addition to its own rights under the draft and any document of title securing it any rights of the shipper in the goods including the right to stop delivery and the shipper's right to have the draft honored by the buyer.

(2) The right to reimbursement of a financing agency which has in good faith honored or purchased the draft under commitment to or authority from the buyer is not impaired by subsequent discovery of defects with reference to any relevant document which was apparently regular on its face.

§ 2—507.   Effect of Seller's Tender; Delivery on Condition

(1) Tender of delivery is a condition to the buyer's duty to accept the goods and, unless otherwise agreed, to his duty to pay for them. Tender entitles the seller to acceptance of the goods and to payment according to the contract.

(2) Where payment is due and demanded on the delivery to the buyer of goods or documents of title, his right as against the seller to retain or dispose of them is conditional upon his making the payment due.

§ 2—508.   Cure by Seller of Improper Tender or Delivery; Replacement

(1) Where any tender or delivery by the seller is rejected because non-conforming and the time for performance has not yet expired, the seller may seasonably notify the buyer of his intention to cure and may then within the contract time make a conforming delivery.

(2) Where the buyer rejects a non-conforming tender which the seller had reasonable grounds to believe would be acceptable with or without money allowance the seller may if he seasonably notifies the buyer have a further reasonable time to substitute a conforming tender.

§ 2—509.   Risk of Loss in the Absence of Breach

(1) Where the contract requires or authorizes the seller to ship the goods by carrier

  (a) if it does not require him to deliver them at a particular destination, the risk of loss passes to the buyer when the goods are duly delivered to the carrier even though the shipment is under reservation (Section 2—505); but

  (b) if it does require him to deliver them at a particular destination and the goods are there duly tendered while in the possession of the carrier, the risk of loss passes to the buyer when the goods are there duly so tendered as to enable the buyer to take delivery.

(2) Where the goods are held by a bailee to be delivered without being moved, the risk of loss passes to the buyer

(a) on his receipt of a negotiable document of title covering the goods; or

(b) on acknowledgment by the bailee of the buyer's right to possession of the goods; or

(c) after his receipt of a non-negotiable document of title or other written direction to delivery, as provided in subsection (4) (b) of Section 2—503.

(3) In any case not within subsection (1) or (2), the risk of loss passes to the buyer on his receipt of the goods if the seller is a merchant; otherwise the risk passes to the buyer on tender of delivery.

(4) The provisions of this section are subject to contrary agreement of the parties and to the provisions of this Article on sale on approval (Section 2—327) and on effect of breach on risk of loss (Section 2—510).

§ 2—510. Effect of Breach on Risk of Loss

(1) Where a tender or delivery of goods so fails to conform to the contract as to give a right of rejection the risk of their loss remains on the seller until cure or acceptance.

(2) Where the buyer rightfully revokes acceptance he may to the extent of any deficiency in his effective insurance coverage treat the risk of loss as having rested on the seller from the beginning.

(3) Where the buyer as to conforming goods already identified to the contract for sale repudiates or is otherwise in breach before risk of their loss has passed to him, the seller may to the extent of any deficiency in his effective insurance coverage treat the risk of loss as resting on the buyer for a commercially reasonable time.

§ 2—511. Tender of Payment by Buyer; Payment by Check

(1) Unless otherwise agreed tender of payment is a condition to the seller's duty to tender and complete any delivery.

(2) Tender of payment is sufficient when made by any means or in any manner current in the ordinary course of business unless the seller demands payment in legal tender and gives any extension of time reasonably necessary to procure it.

(3) Subject to the provisions of this Act on the effect of an instrument on an obligation (Section 3—802), payment by check is conditional and is defeated as between the parties by dishonor of the check on due presentment.

§ 2—512. Payment by Buyer Before Inspection

(1) Where the contract requires payment before inspection non-conformity of the goods does not excuse the buyer from so making payment unless

(a) the non-conformity appears without inspection; or

(b) despite tender of the required documents the circumstances would justify injunction against honor under the provisions of this Act (Section 5—114).

(2) Payment pursuant to subsection (1) does not constitute an acceptance of goods or impair the buyer's right to inspect or any of his remedies.

§ 2—513. Buyer's Right to Inspection of Goods

(1) Unless otherwise agreed and subject to subsection (3), where goods are tendered

or delivered or identified to the contract for sale, the buyer has a right before payment or acceptance to inspect them at any reasonable place and time and in any reasonable manner. When the seller is required or authorized to send the goods to the buyer, the inspection may be after their arrival.

(2) Expenses of inspection must be borne by the buyer but may be recovered from the seller if the goods do not conform and are rejected.

(3) Unless otherwise agreed and subject to the provisions of this Article on C.I.F. contracts (subsection (3) of Section 2—321), the buyer is not entitled to inspect the goods before payment of the price when the contract provides

    (a) for delivery "C.O.D." or on other like terms; or

    (b) for payment against documents of title, except where such payment is due only after the goods are to become available for inspection.

(4) A place or method of inspection fixed by the parties is presumed to be exclusive but unless otherwise expressly agreed it does not postpone identification or shift the place for delivery or for passing the risk of loss. If compliance becomes impossible, inspection shall be as provided in this section unless the place or method fixed was clearly intended as an indispensable condition failure of which avoids the contract.

§ 2—514. When Documents Deliverable on Acceptance; When on Payment

Unless otherwise agreed documents against which a draft is drawn are to be delivered to the drawee on acceptance of the draft if it is payable more than three days after presentment; otherwise, only on payment.

§ 2—515. Preserving Evidence of Goods in Dispute

In furtherance of the adjustment of any claim or dispute

    (a) either party on reasonable notification to the other and for the purpose of ascertaining the facts and preserving evidence has the right to inspect, test and sample the goods including such of them as may be in the possession or control of the other; and

    (b) the parties may agree to a third party inspection or survey to determine the conformity or condition of the goods and may agree that the findings shall be binding upon them in any subsequent litigation or adjustment.

PART 6

BREACH, REPUDIATION AND EXCUSE

§ 2—601. Buyer's Rights on Improper Delivery

Subject to the provisions of this Article on breach in installment contracts (Section 2—612) and unless otherwise agreed under the sections on contractual limitations of remedy (Sections 2—718 and 2—719), if the goods or the tender of delivery fail in any respect to conform to the contract, the buyer may

    (a) reject the whole; or

(b) accept the whole; or

(c) accept any commercial unit or units and reject the rest.

§ 2—602. Manner and Effect of Rightful Rejection

(1) Rejection of goods must be within a reasonable time after their delivery or tender. It is ineffective unless the buyer seasonably notifies the seller.

(2) Subject to the provisions of the two following sections on rejected goods (Sections 2—603 and 2—604),

(a) after rejection any exercise of ownership by the buyer with respect to any commercial unit is wrongful as against the seller; and

(b) if the buyer has before rejection taken physical possession of goods in which he does not have a security interest under the provisions of this Article (subsection (3) of Section 2—711), he is under a duty after rejection to hold them with reasonable care at the seller's disposition for a time sufficient to permit the seller to remove them; but

(c) the buyer has no further obligations with regard to goods rightfully rejected.

(3) The seller's rights with respect to goods wrongfully rejected are governed by the provisions of this Article on Seller's remedies in general (Section 2—703).

§ 2—603. Merchant Buyer's Duties as to Rightfully Rejected Goods

(1) Subject to any security interest in the buyer (subsection (3) of Section 2—711), when the seller has no agent or place of business at the market of rejection a merchant buyer is under a duty after rejection of goods in his possession or control to follow any reasonable instructions received from the seller with respect to the goods and in the absence of such instructions to make reasonable efforts to sell them for the seller's account if they are perishable or threaten to decline in value speedily. Instructions are not reasonable if on demand indemnity for expenses is not forthcoming.

(2) When the buyer sells goods under subsection (1), he is entitled to reimbursement from the seller or out of the proceeds for reasonable expenses of caring for and selling them, and if the expenses include no selling commission then to such commission as is usual in the trade or if there is none to a reasonable sum not exceeding ten percent on the gross proceeds.

(3) In complying with this section the buyer is held only to good faith and good faith conduct hereunder is neither acceptance nor conversion nor the basis of an action for damages.

§ 2—604. Buyer's Options as to Salvage of Rightfully Rejected Goods

Subject to the provisions of the immediately preceding section on perishables if the seller gives no instructions within a reasonable time after notification of rejection the buyer may store the rejected goods for the seller's account or reship them to him or resell them for the seller's account with reimbursement as provided in the preceding section. Such action is not acceptance or conversion.

§ 2—605. Waiver of Buyer's Objections by Failure to Particularize

(1) The buyer's failure to state in connection with rejection a particular defect which is ascertainable by reasonable inspection precludes him from relying on the unstated defect to justify rejection or to establish breach

    (a) where the seller could have cured it if stated seasonably; or

    (b) between merchants when the seller has after rejection made a request in writing for a full and final written statement of all defects on which the buyer proposes to rely.

(2) Payment against documents made without reservation of rights precludes recovery of the payment for defects apparent on the face of the documents.

§ 2—606. What Constitutes Acceptance of Goods

(1) Acceptance of goods occurs when the buyer

    (a) after a reasonable opportunity to inspect the goods signifies to the seller that the goods are conforming or that he will take or retain them in spite of their nonconformity; or

    (b) fails to make an effective rejection (subsection (1) of Section 2—602), but such acceptance does not occur until the buyer has had a reasonable opportunity to inspect them; or

    (c) does any act inconsistent with the seller's ownership; but if such act is wrongful as against the seller it is an acceptance only if ratified by him.

(2) Acceptance of a part of any commercial unit is acceptance of that entire unit.

§ 2—607. Effect of Acceptance; Notice of Breach; Burden of Establishing Breach After Acceptance; Notice of Claim or Litigation to Person Answerable Over

(1) The buyer must pay at the contract rate for any goods accepted.

(2) Acceptance of goods by the buyer precludes rejection of the goods accepted and if made with knowledge of a non-conformity cannot be revoked because of it unless the acceptance was on the reasonable assumption that the non-conformity would be seasonably cured but acceptance does not of itself impair any other remedy provided by this Article for non-conformity.

(3) Where a tender has been accepted

    (a) the buyer must within a reasonable time after he discovers or should have discovered any breach notify the seller of breach or be barred from any remedy; and

    (b) if the claim is one for infringement or the like (subsection (3) of Section 2—312) and the buyer is sued as a result of such a breach he must so notify the seller within a reasonable time after he receives notice of the litigation or be barred from any remedy over for liability established by the litigation.

(4) The burden is on the buyer to establish any breach with respect to the goods accepted.

(5) Where the buyer is sued for breach of a warranty or other obligation for which his seller is answerable over

    (a) he may give his seller written notice of the litigation. If the notice states that the seller may come in and defend and that if the seller does not do so he will be bound in any action against him by his buyer by any determination of fact common to the two litigations, then unless the seller after seasonable receipt of the notice does come in and defend he is so bound.

(b) if the claim is one for infringement or the like (subsection (3) of Section 2—312) the original seller may demand in writing that his buyer turn over to him control of the litigation including settlement or else be barred from any remedy over and if he also agrees to bear all expense and to satisfy any adverse judgement, then unless the buyer after seasonable receipt of the demand does turn over control the buyer is so barred.

(6) The provisions of subsections (3), (4) and (5) apply to any obligation of a buyer to hold the seller harmless against infringement or the like (subsection (3) of Section 2—312).

§ 2—608. Revocation of Acceptance in Whole or in Part

(1) The buyer may revoke his acceptance of a lot or commercial unit whose non-conformity substantially impairs its value to him if he has accepted it
(a) on the reasonable assumption that its non-conformity would be cured and it has not been seasonably cured; or
(b) without discovery of such non-conformity if his acceptance was reasonably induced either by the difficulty of discovery before acceptance or by the seller's assurances.

(2) Revocation of acceptance must occur within a reasonable time after the buyer discovers or should have discovered the ground for it and before any substantial change in condition of the goods which is not caused by their own defects. It is not effective until the buyer notifies the seller of it

(3) A buyer who so revokes has the same rights and duties with regard to the goods involved as if he had rejected them.

§ 2—609. Right to Adequate Assurance of Performance

(1) A contract for sale imposes an obligation on each party that the other's expectation of receiving due performance will not be impaired. When reasonable grounds for insecurity arise with respect to the performance of either party the other may in writing demand adequate assurance of due performance and until he receives such assurance may if commercially reasonable suspend any performance for which he has not already received the agreed return.

(2) Between merchants the reasonableness of grounds for insecurity and the adequacy of any assurance offered shall be determined according to commercial standards.

(3) Acceptance of any improper delivery or payment does not prejudice the aggrieved party's right to demand adequate assurance of future performance.

(4) After receipt of a justified demand failure to provide within a reasonable time not exceeding thirty days such assurance of due performance as is adequate under the circumstances of the particular case is a repudiation of the contract.

§ 2—610. Anticipatory Repudiation

When either party repudiates the contract with respect to a performance not yet due the loss of which will substantially impair the value of the contract to the other, the aggrieved party may

    (a) for a commercially reasonable time await performance by the repudiating party; or

    (b) resort to any remedy for breach (Section 2—703 or Section 2—711), even though he has notified the repudiating party that he would await the latter's performance and has urged retraction; and

    (c) in either case suspend his own performance or proceed in accordance with the provisions of this Article on the seller's right to identify goods to the contract notwithstanding breach or to salvage unfinished goods (Section 2—704).

§ 2—611. Retraction of Anticipatory Repudiation

(1) Until the repudiating party's next performance is due he can retract his repudiation unless the aggrieved party has since the repudiation cancelled or materially changed his position or otherwise indicated that he considers the repudiation final.

(2) Retraction may be by any method which clearly indicates to the aggrieved party that the repudiating party intends to perform, but must include any assurance justifiably demanded under the provisions of this Article (Section 2—609).

(3) Retraction reinstates the repudiating party's rights under the contract with due excuse and allowance to the aggrieved party for any delay occasioned by the repudiation.

§ 2—612. "Installment Contract"; Breach

(1) An "installment contract" is one which requires or authorizes the delivery of goods in separate lots to be separately accepted, even though the contract contains a clause "each delivery is a separate contract" or its equivalent.

(2) The buyer may reject any installment which is non-conforming if the non-conformity substantially impairs the value of that installment and cannot be cured or if the non-conformity is a defect in the required documents; but if the non-conformity does not fall within subsection (3) and the seller gives adequate assurance of its cure the buyer must accept that installment.

(3) Whenever non-conformity or default with respect to one or more installments substantially impairs the value of the whole contract there is a breach of the whole. But the aggrieved party reinstates the contract if he accepts a non-conforming installment without seasonably notifying of cancellation or if he brings an action with respect only to past installments or demands performance as to future installments.

§ 2—613. Casualty to Identified Goods

Where the contract requires for its performance goods identified when the contract is made, and the goods suffer casualty without fault of either party before the risk of loss passes to the buyer, or in a proper case under a "no arrival, no sale" term (Section 2-324) then

    (a) if the loss is total the contract is avoided; and

    (b) if the loss is partial or the goods have so deteriorated as no longer to conform to the contract the buyer may nevertheless demand inspection and at his option either treat the contract as avoided or accept the goods with due allowance from the contract price for the deterioration or the deficiency in quantity but without further right against the seller.

§ 2—614. Substituted Performance

(1) Where without fault of either party the agreed berthing, loading, or unloading facilities fail or an agreed type of carrier becomes unavailable or the agreed manner of delivery otherwise becomes commercially impracticable but a commercially reasonable substitute is available, such substitute performance must be tendered and accepted.

(2) If the agreed means or manner of payment fails because of domestic or foreign governmental regulation, the seller may withhold or stop delivery unless the buyer provides a means or manner of payment which is commercially a substantial equivalent. If delivery has already been taken, payment by the means or in the manner provided by the regulation discharges the buyer's obligation unless the regulation is discriminatory, oppressive or predatory.

§ 2—615. Excuse by Failure of Presupposed Conditions

Except so far as a seller may have assumed a greater obligation and subject to the preceding section on substituted performance:

    (a) Delay in delivery or non-delivery in whole or in part by a seller who complies with paragraphs (b) and (c) is not a breach of his duty under a contract for sale if performance as agreed has been made impracticable by the occurrence of a contingency the non-occurrence of which was a basic assumption on which the contract was made or by compliance in good faith with any applicable foreign or domestic governmental regulation or order whether or not it later proves to be invalid.

    (b) Where the causes mentioned in paragraph (a) affect only a part of the seller's capacity to perform, he must allocate production and deliveries among his customers but may at his option include regular customers not then under contract as well as his own requirements for further manufacture. He may so allocate in any manner which is fair and reasonable.

    (c) The seller must notify the buyer seasonably that there will be delay or non-delivery and, when allocation is required under paragraph (b), of the estimated quota thus made available for the buyer.

§ 2—616. Procedure on Notice Claiming Excuse

(1) Where the buyer receives notification of a material or indefinite delay or an allocation justified under the preceding section he may by written notification to the seller as to any delivery concerned, and where the prospective deficiency substantially impairs the value of the whole contract under the provisions of this Article relating to breach of installment contracts (Section 2—612), then also as to the whole,

    (a) terminate and thereby discharge any unexecuted portion of the contract; or

    (b) modify the contract by agreeing to take his available quota in substitution.

(2) If after receipt of such notification from the seller the buyer fails so to modify the contract within a reasonable time not exceeding thirty days the contract lapses with respect to any deliveries affected.

(3) The provisions of this section may not be negated by agreement except in so far as the seller has assumed a greater obligation under the preceding section.

PART 7

REMEDIES

§ 2—701. Remedies for Breach of Collateral Contracts Not Impaired

Remedies for breach of any obligation or promise collateral or ancillary to a contract for sale are not impaired by the provisions of this Article.

§ 2—702. Seller's Remedies on Discovery of Buyer's Insolvency

(1) Where the seller discovers the buyer to be insolvent he may refuse delivery except for cash including payment for all goods theretofore delivered under the contract, and stop delivery under this Article (Section 2—705).

(2) Where the seller discovers that the buyer has received goods on credit while insolvent he may reclaim the goods upon demand made within ten days after the receipt, but if misrepresentation of solvency has been made to the particular seller in writing within three months before delivery the ten day limitation does not apply. Except as provided in this subsection the seller may not base a right to reclaim goods on the buyer's fraudulent or innocent misrepresentation of solvency or of intent to pay.

(3) The seller's right to reclaim under subsection (2) is subject to the rights of a buyer in ordinary course or other good faith purchaser under this Article (Section 2—403). Successful reclamation of goods excludes all other remedies with respect to them. As amended 1966.

§ 2—703. Seller's Remedies in General

Where the buyer wrongfully rejects or revokes acceptance of goods or fails to make a payment due on or before delivery or repudiates with respect to a part or the whole, then with respect to any goods directly affected and, if the breach is of the whole contract (Section 2—612), then also with respect to the whole undelivered balance, the aggrieved seller may

    (a) withhold delivery of such goods;

    (b) stop delivery by any bailee as hereafter provided (Section 2—705);

    (c) proceed under the next section respecting goods still unidentified to the contract;

    (d) resell and recover damages as hereafter provided (Section 2—706);

    (e) recover damages for non-acceptance (Section 2—708) or in a proper case the price (Section 2—709);

    (f) cancel.

§ 2—704. Seller's Right to Identify Goods to the Contract Notwithstanding Breach or to Salvage Unfinished Goods

(1) An aggrieved seller under the preceding section may

(a) identify to the contract conforming goods not already identified if at the time he learned of the breach they are in his possession or control;

(b) treat as the subject of resale goods which have demonstrably been intended for the particular contract even though those goods are unfinished.

(2) Where the goods are unfinished an aggrieved seller may in the exercise of reasonable commercial judgment for the purposes of avoiding loss and of effective realization either complete the manufacture and wholly identify the goods to the contract or cease manufacture and resell for scrap or salvage value or proceed in any other reasonable manner.

§ 2—705. Seller's Stoppage of Delivery in Transit or Otherwise

(1) The seller may stop delivery of goods in the possession of a carrier or other bailee when he discovers the buyer to be insolvent (Section 2—702) and may stop delivery of carload, truckload, planeload or larger shipments of express or freight when the buyer repudiates or fails to make a payment due before delivery or if for any other reason the seller has a right to withhold or reclaim the goods.

(2) As against such buyer the seller may stop delivery until

(a) receipt of the goods by the buyer; or

(b) acknowledgment to the buyer by any bailee of the goods except a carrier that the bailee holds the goods for the buyer; or

(c) such acknowledgment to the buyer by a carrier by reshipment or as warehouseman; or

(d) negotiation to the buyer of any negotiable document of title covering the goods.

(3) (a) To stop delivery the seller must so notify as to enable the bailee by reasonable diligence to prevent delivery of the goods.

(b) After such notification the bailee must hold and deliver the goods according to the directions of the seller but the seller is liable to the bailee for any ensuing charges or damages.

(c) If a negotiable document of title has been issued for goods the bailee is not obliged to obey a notification to stop until surrender of the document.

(d) A carrier who has issued a non-negotiable bill of lading is not obliged to obey a notification to stop received from a person other than the consignor.

§ 2—706. Seller's Resale Including Contract for Resale

(1) Under the conditions stated in Section 2—703 on seller's remedies, the seller may resell the goods concerned or the undelivered balance thereof. Where the resale is made in good faith and in a commercially reasonable manner the seller may recover the difference between the resale price and the contract price together with any incidental damages allowed under the provisions of this Article (Section 2—710), but less expenses saved in consequence of the buyer's breach.

(2) Except as otherwise provided in subsection (3) or unless otherwise agreed resale may be at public or private sale including sale by way of one or more contracts to sell or of identification to an existing contract of the seller. Sale may be as a unit or in parcels and at any time and place and on any terms but every aspect of the sale including the method, manner, time, place and terms must be commercially reasonable. The resale must be reasonably identified as referring to the broken contract, but it is not necessary

that the goods be in existence or that any or all of them have been identified to the contract before the breach.

(3) Where the resale is at private sale the seller must give the buyer reasonable notification of his intention to resell.

(4) Where the resale is at public sale

(a) only identified goods can be sold except where there is a recognized market for a public sale of futures in goods of the kind; and

(b) it must be made at a usual place or market for public sale if one is reasonably available and except in the case of goods which are perishable or threaten to decline in value speedily the seller must give the buyer reasonable notice of the time and place of the resale; and

(c) if the goods are not to be within the view of those attending the sale the notification of sale must state the place where the goods are located and provide for their reasonable inspection by prospective bidders; and

(d) the seller may buy.

(5) A purchaser who buys in good faith at a resale takes the goods free of any rights of the original buyer even though the seller fails to comply with one or more of the requirements of this section.

(6) The seller is not accountable to the buyer for any profit made on any resale. A person in the position of a seller (Section 2—707) or a buyer who has rightfully rejected or justifiably revoked acceptance must account for any excess over the amount of his security interest, as hereinafter defined (subsection (3) of Section 2—711).

§ 2—707. "Person in the Position of a Seller"

(1) A "person in the position of a seller" includes as against a principal an agent who has paid or become responsible for the price of goods on behalf of his principal or anyone who otherwise holds a security interest or other right in goods similar to that of a seller.

(2) A person in the position of a seller may as provided in this Article withhold or stop delivery (Section 2—705) and resell (Section 2—706) and recover incidental damages (Section 2—710).

§ 2—708. Seller's Damages for Non-acceptance or Repudiation

(1) Subject to subsection (2) and to the provisions of this Article with respect to proof of market price (Section 2—723), the measure of damages for non-acceptance or repudiation by the buyer is the difference between the market price at the time and place for tender and the unpaid contract price together with any incidental damages provided in this Article (Section 2—710), but less expenses saved in consequence of the buyer's breach.

(2) If the measure of damages provided in subsection (1) in inadequate to put the seller in as good a position as performance would have done then the measure of damages is the profit (including reasonable overhead) which the seller would have made from full performance by the buyer, together with any incidental damages provided in this Article (Section 2—710), due allowance for costs reasonably incurred and due credit for payments or proceeds of resale.

§ 2—709. Action for the Price

(1) When the buyer fails to pay the price as it becomes due the seller may recover, together with any incidental damages under the next section, the price

    (a) of goods accepted or of conforming goods lost or damaged within a commercially reasonable time after risk of their loss has passed to the buyer; and

    (b) of goods identified to the contract if the seller is unable after reasonable effort to resell them at a reasonable price or the circumstances reasonably indicate that such effort will be unavailing.

(2) Where the seller sues for the price he must hold for the buyer any goods which have been identified to the contract and are still in his control except that if resale becomes possible he may resell them at any time prior to the collection of the judgment. The net proceeds of any such resale must be credited to the buyer and payment of the judgment entitles him to any goods not resold.

(3) After the buyer has wrongfully rejected or revoked acceptance of the goods or has failed to make a payment due or has repudiated (Section 2—610), a seller who is held not entitled to the price under this section shall nevertheless be awarded damages for non-acceptance under the preceding section.

§ 2—710. Seller's Incidental Damages

Incidental damages to an aggrieved seller include any commercially reasonable charges, expenses or commissions incurred in stopping delivery, in the transportation, care and custody of goods after the buyer's breach, in connection with return or resale of the goods or otherwise resulting from the breach.

§ 2—711. Buyer's Remedies in General; Buyer's Security Interest in Rejected Goods

(1) Where the seller fails to make delivery or repudiates or the buyer rightfully rejects or justifiably revokes acceptance then with respect to any goods involved, and with respect to the whole if the breach goes to the whole contract (Section 2—612), the buyer may cancel and whether or not he has done so may in addition to recovering so much of the price as has been paid

    (a) "cover" and have damages under the next section as to all the goods affected whether or not they have been identified to the contract; or

    (b) recover damages for non-delivery as provided in this Article (Section 2—713).

(2) Where the seller fails to deliver or repudiates the buyer may also

    (a) if the goods have been identified recover them as provided in this Article (Section 2—502); or

    (b) in a proper case obtain specific performance or replevy the goods as provided in this Article (Section 2—716).

(3) On rightful rejection or justifiable revocation of acceptance a buyer has a security interest in goods in his possession or control for any payments made on their price and any expenses reasonably incurred in their inspection, receipt, transportation, care and custody and may hold such goods and resell them in like manner as an aggrieved seller (Section 2—706).

§ 2—712. "Cover"; Buyer's Procurement of Substitute Goods

(1) After a breach within the preceding section the buyer may "cover" by making in good faith and without unreasonable delay any reasonable purchase of or contract to purchase goods in substitution for those due from the seller.

(2) The buyer may recover from the seller as damages the difference between the cost of cover and the contract price together with any incidental or consequential damages as hereinafter defined (Section 2—715), but less expenses saved in consequence of the seller's breach.

(3) Failure of the buyer to effect cover within this section does not bar him from any other remedy.

§ 2—713. Buyer's Damages for Non-Delivery or Repudiation

(1) Subject to the provisions of this Article with respect to proof of market price (Section 2—723), the measure of damages for non-delivery or repudiation by the seller is the difference between the market price at the time when the buyer learned of the breach and the contract price together with any incidental and consequential damages provided in this Article (Section 2—715), but less expenses saved in consequence of the seller's breach.

(2) Market price is to be determined as of the place for tender or, in cases of rejection after arrival or revocation of acceptance, as of the place of arrival.

§ 2—714. Buyer's Damages for Breach in Regard to Accepted Goods

(1) Where the buyer has accepted goods and given notification (subsection (3) of Section 2—607) he may recover as damages for any non-conformity of tender the loss resulting in the ordinary course of events from the seller's breach as determined in any manner which is reasonable.

(2) The measure of damages for breach of warranty is the difference at the time and place of acceptance between the value of the goods accepted and the value they would have had if they had been as warranted, unless special circumstances show proximate damages of a different amount.

(3) In a proper case any incidental and consequential damages under the next section may also be recovered.

§ 2—715. Buyer's Incidental and Consequential Damages

(1) Incidental damages resulting from the seller's breach include expenses reasonably incurred in inspection, receipt, transportation and care and custody of goods rightfully rejected, any commercially reasonable charges, expenses or commissions in connection with effecting cover and any other reasonable expense incident to the delay or other breach.

(2) Consequential damages resulting from the seller's breach include
   (a) any loss resulting from general or particular requirements and needs of which the seller at the time of contracting has reason to know and which could not reasonably be prevented by cover or otherwise; and
   (b) injury to person or property proximately resulting from any breach of warranty.

§ 2—716. Buyer's Right to Specific Performance or Replevin

(1) Specific performance may be decreed where the goods are unique or in other proper circumstances.

(2) The decree for specific performance may include such terms and conditions as to payment of the price, damages, or other relief as the court may deem just.

(3) The buyer has a right of replevin for goods identified to the contract if after reasonable effort he is unable to effect cover for such goods or the circumstances reasonably indicate that such effort will be unavailing or if the goods have been shipped under reservation and satisfaction of the security interest in them has been made or tendered.

§ 2—717. Deduction of Damages From the Price

The buyer on notifying the seller of his intention to do so may deduct all or any part of the damages resulting from any breach of the contract from any part of the price due under the same contract.

§ 2—718. Liquidation or Limitation of Damages; Deposits

(1) Damages for breach by either party may be liquidated in the agreement but only at an amount which is reasonable in the light of the anticipated or actual harm caused by the breach, the difficulties of proof of loss, and the inconvenience or nonfeasibility of otherwise obtaining an adequate remedy. A term fixing unreasonably large liquidated damages is void as a penalty.

(2) Where the seller justifiably withholds delivery of goods because of the buyer's breach, the buyer is entitled to restitution of any amount by which the sum of his payments exceeds

    (a) the amount to which the seller is entitled by virtue of terms liquidating the seller's damages in accordance with subsection (1), or

    (b) in the absence of such terms, twenty percent of the value of the total performance for which the buyer is obligated under the contract or $500, whichever is smaller.

(3) The buyer's right to restitution under subsection (2) is subject to offset to the extent that the seller establishes

    (a) a right to recover damages under the provisions of this Article other than subsection (1), and

    (b) the amount of value of any benefits received by the buyer directly or indirectly by reason of the contract.

(4) Where a seller has received payment in goods their reasonable value or the proceeds of their resale shall be treated as payments for the purposes of subsection (2); but if the seller has notice of the buyer's breach before reselling goods received in part performance, his resale is subject to the conditions laid down in this Article on resale by an aggrieved seller (Section 2—706).

§ 2—719. Contractual Modification or Limitation of Remedy

(1) Subject to the provisions of subsections (2) and (3) of this section and of the preceding section on liquidation and limitation of damages,

(a) the agreement may provide for remedies in addition to or in substitution for those provided in this Article and may limit or alter the measure of damages recoverable under this Article, as by limiting the buyer's remedies to return of the goods and repayment of the price or to repair and replacement of non-conforming goods or parts; and

(b) resort to a remedy as provided is optional unless the remedy is expressly agreed to be exclusive, in which case it is the sole remedy.

(2) Where circumstances cause an exclusive or limited remedy to fail of its essential purpose, remedy may be had as provided in this Act.

(3) Consequential damages may be limited or excluded unless the limitation or exclusion is unconscionable. Limitation of consequential damages for injury to the person in the case of consumer goods is prima facie unconscionable but limitation of damages where the loss is commercial is not.

§ 2—720. Effect of "Cancellation" or "Rescission" on Claims for Antecedent Breach

Unless the contrary intention clearly appears, expressions of "cancellation" or "rescission" of the contract or the like shall not be construed as a renunciation or discharge of any claim in damages for an antecedent breach.

§ 2—721. Remedies for Fraud

Remedies for material misrepresentation or fraud include all remedies available under this Article for non-fraudulent breach. Neither rescission or a claim for rescission of the contract for sale nor rejection or return of the goods shall bar or be deemed inconsistent with a claim for damages or other remedy.

§ 2—722. Who Can Sue Third Parties for Injury to Goods

Where a third party so deals with goods which have been identified to a contract for sale as to cause actionable injury to a party to that contract

(a) a right of action against the third party is in either party to the contract for sale who has title to or a security interest or a special property or an insurable interest in the goods; and if the goods have been destroyed or converted a right of action is also in the party who either bore the risk of loss under the contract for sale or has since the injury assumed that risk as against the other;

(b) if at the time of the injury the party plaintiff did not bear the risk of loss as against the other party to the contract for sale and there is no arrangement between them for disposition of the recovery, his suit or settlement is, subject to his own interest, as a fiduciary for the other party to the contract;

(c) either party may with the consent of the other sue for the benefit of whom it may concern.

§ 2—723. Proof of Market Price: Time and Place

(1) If an action based on anticipatory repudiation comes to trial before the time for performance with respect to some or all of the goods, any damages based on market price (Section 2—708 or Section 2—713) shall be determined according to the price of such goods prevailing at the time when the aggrieved party learned of the repudiation.

(2) If evidence of a price prevailing at the times or places described in this Article is not readily available the price prevailing within any reasonable time before or after the time described or at any other place which in commercial judgment or under usage of trade would serve as a reasonable substitute for the one described may be used, making any proper allowance for the cost of transporting the goods to or from such other place.

(3) Evidence of a relevant price prevailing at a time or place other than the one described in this Article offered by one party is not admissible unless and until he has given the other party such notice as the court finds sufficient to prevent unfair surprise.

§ 2—724. Admissibility of Market Quotations

Whenever the prevailing price or value of any goods regularly bought and sold in any established commodity market is in issue, reports in official publications or trade journals or in newspapers or periodicals of general circulation published as the reports of such market shall be admissible in evidence. The circumstances of the preparation of such a report may be shown to affect its weight but not its admissibility.

§ 2—725. Statute of Limitations in Contracts for Sale

(1) An action for breach of any contract for sale must be commenced within four years after the cause of action has accrued. By the original agreement the parties may reduce the period of limitation to not less than one year but may not extend it.

(2) A cause of action accrues when the breach occurs, regardless of the aggrieved party's lack of knowledge of the breach. A breach of warranty occurs when tender of delivery is made, except that where a warranty explicitly extends to future performance of the goods and discovery of the breach must await the time of such performance the cause of action accrues when the breach is or should have been discovered.

(3) Where an action commenced within the time limited by subsection (1) is so terminated as to leave available a remedy by another action for the same breach such other action may be commenced after the expiration of the time limited and within six months after the termination of the first action unless the termination resulted from voluntary discontinuance or from dismissal for failure or neglect to prosecute.

(4) This section does not alter the law on tolling of the statute of limitations nor does it apply to causes of action which have accrued before this Act becomes effective.

Index

registration
 cancellation of state, 41
revolving credit accounts, 9

S

sale
 gross receipts of, 32
sales, 112
 auction, 36
 execution, 76
sales tax permit
 application for, 32
sales tax permits, 29
sales taxes
 exemptions from, 34
security deposits, 97
self-incorporation, 25
service marks, 38
Small Business Administration, 8, 113
Small Business Institute, 115

small claims court, 69
small claims courts' rules
 summary of, 158
state court systems, 5

T

tax
 retailer's absorption of, 34
taxes
 use, 34
title
 implied warranty of, 52
trade names, 38, 39
trademark research
 federal, 43
trademarks, 38
transactions
 secured, 112

U

Uniform Commercial Code, 184

uniform fraudulent conveyance act, 125
Uniform Limited Partnership Act, 148
Uniform Partnership Act, 132
uniform vendor and purchaser risk act, 54

V

venue, 69

W

warranties
 conflicting, 53
 limited, 53
 product, 51
warranty of fitness
 implied, 52
warranty of title
 implied, 52
words and designs
 descriptive, 40

Other Bestsellers From TAB

☐ **BECOMING SELF-EMPLOYED: HOW TO CREATE AN INDEPENDENT LIVELIHOOD—Susan Elliott**

If you've ever left the urge to leave the corporate world to become your own boss, you'll want this book. It reveals what it's like to go out on your own, what it takes to become successful, and what mistakes to avoid. Includes the stories of twenty successful entrepreneur—what they did right, what they did wrong, and they plan for the future and why.

Paper $7.95   **Book No. 30149**

☐ **THE PERSONAL TAX ADVISOR: UNDERSTANDING THE NEW TAX LAW—Cliff Roberson, LLM. Ph.D.**

How will the new tax law affect your tax return this filing season? Any reform is certain to mean a change in the way your taxes are prepared. But you don't have to be an accountant or a lawyer to understand the new tax laws . . . use this easy-to-read guide, and learn how to reduce your income taxes under the new federal rules!

Paper $12.95   **Book No. 30134**

☐ **THE SMALL BUSINESS TAX ADVISOR: UNDERSTANDING THE NEW TAX LAW—Cliff Roberson, LLM., Ph.D**

The most extensive changes ever in the history of American tax laws were made in 1986. And to help you better understand these changes. Cliff Roberson has compiled the information every small business operator, corporate officer, director, or stockholder needs to know into a manageable and readily understandable new sourcebook.

Paper $12.95   **Book No. 30024**

☐ **LIVING IN SPACE—A MANUAL FOR SPACE TRAVELERS—Peter Smolders**

" . . . thought-provoking and fun."—*West Coast Book Review*. Features full-color photographs and drawings from NASA, the Soviet Space Agency, and the European space programs . . . guaranteed to provide hours of fascinating reading for anyone interested in space travel. 160 pp., 200 color photos., 8 1/2″ × 10 3/4″.

Paper $14.95   **Book No. 24180**

☐ **DREAM HOMES: 66 PLANS TO MAKE YOUR DREAMS COME TRUE—by Jerold L. Axelrod**

Compiled by a well-known architect whose home designs have been featured regularly in the syndicated "House of the Week" and *Home* magazine, this beautifully bound volume presents one of the finest collections of luxury home designs ever assembled in a single volume! 88 pp., 201 illus., 20 pp., in full-color 8 1/2″ × 11″.

Paper $16.95   **Hard $29.95**
Book No. 2829

☐ **FORMING CORPORATIONS AND PARTNERSHIPS—John C. Howell**

If you're considering offering a service out of your home, buying a franchise, incorporating your present business, or starting a business venture of any type you need this time- and money-saving guide. It explains the process of creating a corporation, gives information on franchising, the laws of partnership, and more. 192 pp., 5 1/2″ × 8″.

Paper $9.95   **Book No. 30143**

☐ **HOW TO WRITE YOUR OWN WILL—John C. Howell**

Written by a nationally-respected trial lawyer and corporate attorney with over 25 years experience, this invaluable book defines all the necessary terms, offers precise explanations for each type of will, and even relates the circumstances under which consultation with a lawyer is advisable. The necessary forms are clearly illustrated and easy to follow. Also presented are the methods of completely avoiding or minimizing the effect of prohalic. The instructions and documents discussed are in accordance with the statutes of all 50 states.

Paper $9.95   **Book No. 30137**

☐ **THE ENTREPRENEUR'S GUIDE TO STARTING A SUCCESSFUL BUSINESS—James W. Halloran**

Here's a realistic approach to what it takes to start a small business, written by a successful entrepreneur and business owner. You'll learn step-by-step every phase of a business start-up from getting the initial idea to realizing a profit. Included is advice on designing a store layout, pricing formulas and strategies, advertising and promotion, small business organization charts, an analysis of future small business opportunities, and more.

Paper $15.95   **Book No. 30049**

☐ **THE ILLUSTRATED HANDBOOK OF DESKTOP PUBLISHING AND TYPESETTING—Michael L. Kleper**

Desktop publishing is not only the newest and hottest topic in computers, it is a dazzling and useful tool that allows you to easily perform printing tasks previously possible only with traditional printing methods! Now, one of the nation's top authorities in this emerging field has written the first comprehensive analysis of desktop publishing—a book that all those who have seen believe will be *the definitive sourcebook* on the subject! 784 pp., 615 illus., Extra Large Format 8 1/2″ × 11″

Paper $29.95   **Hard $49.95**
Book No. 2700

Other Bestsellers From TAB

☐ **SUNSPACES—HOME ADDITIONS FOR YEAR-ROUND NATURAL LIVING—John Mauldin, Photography by John H. Mauldin and Juan L. Espinosa**

Have you been thinking of Juan L. Espinosa to increase your living space? A sunporch provides bright, imaginative room for work, play, or relaxation. Want to add a family room, but want the best use of the space for the money? Solar energy provides "free" heat and light from the sun. Do you simply want more information on solar energy and some ideas on how you can make it work in the home for you? If "yes" is your answer to any of these questions, you'll want to own this fascinating guide! 256 pp., 179 illus.
Paper $14.95   **Hard $21.95**
Book No. 2816

☐ **STARTING AND RUNNING A MONEY-MAKING BAR—Bruce Fier**

Everything you need to start and successfully operate a bar business is here: obtaining financing, keeping records, legal responsibilities, personnel and management, food service, and advertising. You'll learn about liquor selection, pricing, merchandising, purchasing, inventory, even the latest trends in bar attractions. 240 pp., 192 illus.
Paper $14.95   **Book No. 2661**

☐ **THE BUSINESSPERSON'S LEGAL ADVISOR—Cliff Roberson**

Avoid legal problems and get the best legal advice when needed at the least possible cost! This invaluable business guide covers how and where to obtain licenses and permits, collecting accounts receivable, business insurance, product warranties, and disclaimers, hiring and dealing with attorneys, actions to take if your business is failing and more.
Paper $14.95   **Book No. 2624**

☐ **TIME GATE: HURTLING BACKWARD THROUGH HISTORY—Charles R. Pellegrino**

"The author presents much scientific information and does it lucidity for the nonscientific reader."—*Atlantic Monthly*. This fascinating history of life on Earth transports you backward from today's modern world through the very beginnings of man's existence. Exceptional drawings and photographs. 275 pp., 135 illus.
Paper $16.95   **Book No. 1863**

*Prices subject to change without notice.

Look for these and other TAB books at your local bookstore.

TAB BOOKS Inc.
Blue Ridge Summit, PA 17294

Send for FREE TAB Catalog describing over 1200 current titles in print.
OR CALL TOLL-FREE TODAY: **1-800-233-1128**
IN PENNSYLVANIA AND ALASKA, CALL: **717-794-2191**